Women Status and Empowerment in India

Women Status and Empowerment in India

By

Shyam Kartik Mishra
Associate Professor of Economics,
Post-graduate College, Sakaldiha,
Chandauli (Varanasi), Uttar Pradesh

and

Pradeep Kumar Pandey
Professor of Economics,
M.G. Kashi Vidyapeeth, Varanasi, Uttar Pradesh

New Century Publications
New Delhi, India

NEW CENTURY PUBLICATIONS
4800/24, Bharat Ram Road,
Ansari Road, Daryaganj,
New Delhi – 110 002 (India)

Tel.: 011-2324 7798, 4358 7398, 6539 6605
Fax: 011-4101 7798
E-mail: indiatax@vsnl.com • info@newcenturypublications.com
www.newcenturypublications.com

Editorial office:
LG–7, Aakarshan Bhawan
4754-57/23, Ansari Road, Daryaganj,
New Delhi – 110 002

Tel.: 011-4356 0919

First Published: **July 2012**

ISBN: **978-81-7708-313-2**

Published by New Century Publications and printed at Salasar Imaging Systems, New Delhi

Designs: Patch Creative Unit, New Delhi

PRINTED IN INDIA

About the Book

According to Census 2011, population of India increased from 103 crore in 2001 to 121 crore in 2011, an increase of 18 crore or 17.6 percent. Out of 121 crore, 62.4 crore (51.6 percent) were males and 58.6 crore (48.4) females. Unfortunately, Census 2011 data shows that the sex ratio for children below 6 years (i.e. number of girls for every 1,000 boys) dropped from 927 in 2001 to a dismal 914 in 2011. This decline is unabated since 1961 Census. This gender bias draws attention to a lingering societal flaw which economic growth is not being able to correct.

Gender equality is a constituent of development as well as an instrument of development. No country can be deemed developed if half of its population is severely disadvantaged in terms of basic needs, livelihood options, access to knowledge, and political voice.

Discrimination on the lines of gender is not always overt. It appears in very subtle forms such as in the nature of work performed, skills required to perform the work and the valuation of these skills and the technology used by men and women. One problem more specific to women is that they are subject to various forms of harassment at the workplace. Verbal and physical violence against women has been an age-old method of subjugating them.

Advancement and empowerment of women has been a leading objective of state policy ever since the attainment of Independence in 1947. Institutions of different types—Central, State and Local Governments, non-governmental organisations (NGOs), civil society and other bodies—are active to ensure gender equality as laid down in the Constitution of India.

Eleventh Five Year Plan (2007-12) of India recognized women, for the first time, not just as equal citizens but as agents of economic and social growth. Women's lack of economic empowerment not only impedes growth and poverty reduction, but also has a host of other negative impacts including less favourable education and health outcomes for children. Thus, it is extremely important to ensure that women are economically, socially and politically empowered.

This book provides a vivid account of the problems faced by Indian women, particularly those belonging to vulnerable and disadvantaged groups. It explains comprehensively the various policies, programmes and schemes initiated by the Government of India in co-operation with other agencies for the welfare, development and empowerment of women in India.

The book will be of interest to those involved/interested in the socio-economic empowerment of women, including researchers, academicians, industry associations, and policy formulators.

About the Authors

Dr. Shyam Kartik Mishra is Associate Professor of Economics at Post-graduate College, Sakaldiha, Chandauli (Varanasi), Uttar Pradesh. He holds M.A. (Economics) and Ph.D. degrees and a certificate in population studies from International Institute for Population Sciences, Mumbai. He has taught at S.N.D.T. University, Mumbai. Dr. Mishra has published a number of research papers in reputed journals, edited books and conference volumes. He has 4 books to his credit published from New Delhi, Kanpur and Varanasi.

Dr. Mishra has completed 5 research projects sponsored by University Grants Commission (UGC), New Delhi and Indian Council of Social Science Research (ICSSR), New Delhi. He is founder General Secretary of Uttar Pradesh-Uttarakhand Economic Association (UPUEA). He specializes in demography and gender economics.

Dr. Pradeep Kumar Pandey is Professor of Economics at M.G. Kashi Vidyapeeth, Varanasi, Uttar Pradesh. He got accolade for his widely circulated book, *Gandhi Ka Arthik Evam Samajik Chintan,* published by University of Delhi. *Banking Reforms and Globalisation* and *Demographic Impact of Women's Age at Marriage in India* are the other two books authored by him. Dr. Pandey has successfully completed several major and minor research projects sponsored by ICSSR and UGC. He has published a number of research papers in journals of repute and edited volumes. His areas of specialization include Gandhian economics and gender issues.

Contents

Preface

According to Census 2011, population of India increased from 103 crore in 2001 to 121 crore in 2011, an increase of 18 crore or 17.6 percent. Out of 121 crore, 62.4 crore (51.6 percent) were males and 58.6 crore (48.4) were females.

Role of Women in Society

Women play a critical role in the family which is the basic unit of society. Family is a strong force for social cohesion and integration and as such should be strengthened. The inadequate support to women and insufficient protection to their respective families affect society as a whole and undermines efforts to achieve gender equality. In different cultural, political and social systems, various forms of family exist and the rights, capabilities and responsibilities of family members must be respected.

Women's social and economic contributions to the welfare of the family and the social significance of maternity and paternity continue to be inadequately addressed. Motherhood and fatherhood and the role of parents and legal guardians in the family and in the upbringing of children and the importance of all family members to the family's well-being is also acknowledged and must not be a basis for discrimination. Women also continue to bear a disproportionate share of the household responsibilities and the care of children, the sick and the elderly. In order to achieve full partnership, both in public and private spheres, both women and men must be enabled to reconcile and share equally work responsibilities and family responsibilities.

Declining Child Sex Ratio

Improved medical technology, education and improvement in quality of life during the first decade of the 21st century resulted in the overall gender ratio improving from 933 in 2001 to 940 in 2011. This is in line with general improvement in the overall sex ratio since 1991. Unfortunately, Census 2011 data show that the sex ratio for children below 6 years (i.e. number of girls for every 1,000 boys) dropped from 927 in 2001 to a dismal 914 in 2011. This decline is unabated since 1961 Census. This gender bias draws attention to a lingering societal flaw which economic growth is not being able to correct.

As a result of this declining sex ratio, millions of girls/women are missing in India. It is an alarming scenario and if this trend continues, violence against women would increase and there would be forced polyandry. The demographic balance would be permanently damaged.

One of the reasons for the declining sex ratios is the incidence of sex selection, and or sex determination followed by sex selective abortions. This constitutes a grave form of discrimination against women as women are affected as being part of a social class. This is not a pro-life or pro-choice issue. A woman's right to abortion has to be upheld on grounds of promoting women's rights to equality. The right to abortion is the right to abort any foetus. The abortion of a female foetus following a sex determination test is an act of discrimination. As this act of discrimination cannot be committed without the active intervention of medical professionals, it is essential to strictly enforce laws directed towards regulating the practice of medical professionals. However, keeping in mind the pressures that a woman is subjected to for bearing a male child, the implementation and enforcement of such laws should not lead to the further victimization of women.

The laws regulating sex determination and abortions are provided for in the Pre-conception and Pre-natal Diagnostic Techniques (Prohibition of Misuse) Act and the Medical Termination of Pregnancies Act 1971. In addition, penal provisions on "causing miscarriages" are also provided in Sections 312-316 of the Indian Penal Code.

Sex determination before birth is widely prevalent. Certain districts in Punjab and Haryana account for a substantial drop in the decennial child sex ratio. Richer districts tend to account for a larger decline in the child sex ratio. The incidence of the use of sex determination techniques tends to be more in the most modern and developed districts. This calls into question the argument that the market economy undermines patriarchal authoritarian and male-biased traditional attitudes and spreads egalitarian values. Policy has to address the concern that inculcation of the values of market economy seems to be only enhancing gender inequity as reflected in the female foeticide and infanticide indicators.

There are two important issues of policy associated with this decline in the child sex ratio. One is the obsession with population control, which assumes that all the failures in development can be mono-causally linked to population explosion.

The other more recent issue is the intrusion of the two-child norm into the Panchayati Raj Acts of many states, despite its absence from the Population Policy of 2000, leading to disqualification of many elected representatives. Most of the excluded belong to the SCs and STs. Some experts have suggested a link between the imposition of the two-child norm and sex selective abortions. Imposition of the two-child norm, then, cannot be the route to population stabilisation, for it may lead to a disturbingly unbalanced population.

Problems of Women

With the growing globalization and liberalization of the economy as well as increased privatization of services, women as a whole have been left behind and not been able to partake in the fruits of success. Mainstreaming of women into the new and emerging areas of growth is imperative. This will require training and skill upgradation in emerging trades and encouraging more women to take up vocational training and employment in the booming sectors. This will also require women to migrate to cities and metros for work. Provision of safe housing, and other gender friendly facilities at work needs an improvement.

The problems of women workers in general—and in the unorganised sector in particular—deserve special attention and focus in view of their marginalised position within the class of workers. The position of women workers in rural India is considerably lower than that of women in general. The bottom layer is constituted by women belonging to the lowest social status groups. A number of national and international studies have documented the sex-typing of jobs and occupations by women. Occupational segregation represents a form of discrimination.

Female and child domestic workers constitute a large portion of migrant worker population. Working in the unregulated domain of a private home, mostly without the protection of national labour legislations, allows for female domestic workers to be maltreated by their employers with impunity.

It is quite clear that the position of women workers in rural India is considerably lower than that of women in general. But the bottom layer is constituted by women belonging to the lowest social status groups. Urban women workers in general are better off than even rural men workers. But this advantage is somewhat dented when we look at the status of urban women belonging to Scheduled Castes (SCs) and Scheduled Tribes (STs). However, rural women workers in general seem to be more disadvantaged than even the urban SCs/STs women workers.

A number of national and international studies have documented the sex-typing of jobs and occupations by women. Occupational segregation represents a form of discrimination when large segments of the labour force are in essence restricted from entering many occupations. Sexual division of labour has implications for the wages earned, permanency in the job and the possibilities for upward mobility in the industry.

Female and child domestic workers constitute a large portion of today's migrant worker population. Sadly, they also join the category of migrant workers, most being at the risk of exploitation and human rights abuse. Working in the unregulated domain of a private home, mostly without the protection of national labour legislation, allows for female domestic workers to be maltreated by their employers with impunity. Women are often subjected to long working hours and excessively arduous tasks. They may be strictly confined to their places of work. They are frequently the victims of sexual harassment and, in the very worst cases, rape and torture. Thus, women as well as children working as domestic servants are often forced to work in sub-human conditions with no job security, no benefits and no dignity. The increasing demand for domestic workers in all big cities and towns of the country played a major role in the migration of women from rural or tribal areas. Most of them are from poor families and are illiterate. Due to the lack of education and skill they become easy victims of exploitation.

Discrimination on the lines of gender is not always overt. It appears in very subtle forms such as in the nature of work performed, skills required to perform the work and the valuation of these skills and the technology used by men and women.

One problem more specific to women is that they are subject to various forms of harassment in the workplace. Verbal and physical violence against women has been an age-old method of subjugating women. This is used in the workplace to further strengthen the sexual division of labour and keep women at the bottom of the work hierarchy. Such harassment leads to stress and reduces the productivity of the workers. It can also be used to curb upward mobility and inhibit growth of women-operated enterprises.

The overall picture that emerges is one of greater disadvantage for women workers in general and those belonging to rural as well as SCs/STs in particular. Apart from such inherited disadvantages as lower social position, a number of other factors also contribute to such a picture. These are their limited asset position, access to resources, and low level of education and skill. Education, and consequently some ability to acquire formal skills, could be a moderating force but this aspect presents a dismal picture.

Girls and women of all ages with any form of disability are generally among the more vulnerable and marginalized of society. There is therefore need to take into account and to address their concerns in all policy making and programming. Special measures are needed at all levels to integrate them into the mainstream of development.

Need for Gender Equality

Gender equality is a constituent of development as well as an instrument of development. No country can be deemed developed if half of its population is severely disadvantaged in terms of basic needs, livelihood options, access to knowledge, and political voice. It is an instrument of development because without gender equality other goals of development will also be difficult to achieve, namely the goals of poverty alleviation, economic growth, environmental sustainability etc. A natural corollary of ensuring gender equality is the elimination of gender discrimination. Inequalities between girls and boys in access to schooling or adequate health care prove a very serious disadvantage to women and girls and limit their capacity to participate in the benefits of development.

The socio-economic development of a country cannot be fully realized so long as its women are confined to subordinate position and their talents remain unexplored. Women entrepreneurship is becoming a reality now-a-days due to pull and push factors. Between the pull and push factors, the women take it as a real challenge with an urge to do something new and take up an independent occupation. In order to achieve the objective of social justice, it is necessary to harness the latent skills and potential of women, especially the rural women. They play a key role in the rapid and sustained economic development in rural areas and the ultimate prosperity and development of the nation.

Advancement and empowerment of women has been a leading objective of state policy ever since the attainment of Independence in 1947. Institutions of different types—Central, State and Local Governments, non-governmental organisations (NGOs), civil society and other bodies—are active to ensure gender equality as laid down in the Constitution of India.

Eleventh Five Year Plan (2007-12) of India recognized women, for the first time, not just as equal citizens but as agents of economic and social growth. The Plan's approach to gender equity was based on the recognition that interventions in favour of women must be multi-pronged and that they must be provided with basic entitlements.

Strategies for Women Empowerment

Women's lack of economic empowerment not only impedes growth and poverty reduction, but also has a host of other negative impacts including less favourable education and health outcomes for children. Thus, it is extremely important to ensure that women are economically, socially and politically empowered.

Empowerment of women through gainful employment is a constituent—as well as instrument—of development in any country. No country can be deemed developed if half of its population is severely disadvantaged in terms of basic needs, livelihood options, access to knowledge, and political voice. A natural corollary of ensuring gender equality is the elimination of gender discrimination.

Effective and coordinated plans and programmes for the full implementation of women-oriented policies require a clear research-based knowledge of ground realities of the socio-economic status of women, particularly rural women.

The realization of the goals of women empowerment needs to be supported by the allocation of necessary human and financial resources for specific and targeted activities to ensure gender equality at the local, regional, national, and international levels as well as by enhanced and increased international cooperation.

Strong national machineries for the advancement of women and promotion of gender equality require political commitment at the highest level. Reforms to meet the challenges of the changing world are essential to ensure women's equal access to institutions and organizations. Institutional and conceptual changes are a strategic and important aspect of creating an enabling environment for the implementation of policies and programmes for the advancement of women.

Programme support to enhance women's opportunities, potentials and activities need to have a dual focus: one the one hand, programmes aimed at meeting the basic as well as the specific needs of women for capacity building, organizational development and empowerment; and on the other, gender mainstreaming in all programme formulation and implementation activities. It is particularly important to expand into new areas of programming to advance gender equality in response to current challenges.

Effective and coordinated plans and programmes for the full implementation of women-oriented policies require a clear knowledge on the situation of women and girls, a clear research-based knowledge and data disaggregated by sex, short and long-term time-bound targets and measurable goals and follow-up mechanisms to assess progress. Efforts are needed to ensure capacity building for all the actors involved in the achievement of these goals. Efforts are also needed at the national level to increase transparency and accountability.

The explicit attention to these goals in budgetary processes at the national, regional and international level is essential. Recognizing the persistent and increasing burden of poverty on women in many countries, particularly in developing countries, it is essential to continue from a gender perspective to review, modify and implement integrated macro-economic and social policies and programmes to ensure universal and equitable access to social services, in particular to education, and affordable quality health care services and equal access to and control over economic resources.

Women entrepreneurship has emerged as an effective strategy for empowering them in terms of employment and income generation. It harnesses their latent energy. Thus, women must be conversant with modern technologies and management practices in the context of the global environment.

Small enterprises are the best vehicle for stimulating entrepreneurial talent and participation of women in the development process. Small enterprises provide livelihood, check rural-urban migration, generate export earnings and touch upon the lives of the marginalized, disadvantaged and vulnerable women, in both urban and rural areas.

The Constitution (112th Amendment) Bill 2009 to provide for 50 percent reservation of women in Urban Local Bodies (ULBs) was introduced in Lok Sabha on November 24, 2009. Through this Bill the Government of India seeks to increase the representation of women in ULBs from the present level of one-third to 50 percent which would also include enhancement of reservation for women up to 50 percent in seats reserved for Scheduled Castes (SCs), Scheduled Tribes (STs), and 50 percent reservations for women in the posts of Chairpersons. This would result in increased representation of women in ULBs and is likely to yield significant benefits in terms of higher priority to women's issues in critical areas of urban Governance and service delivery such as water supply, sanitation, solid waste management, education and health, etc. Presently the bill is under the consideration of the Parliamentary Standing Committee on Urban Development.

May 2012
Varanasi

Shyam Kartik Mishra
Pradeep Kumar Pandey

English Equivalents of Some Hindi Terms

Adhyapika Manch	Female teachers' forum
Anganwadi	Early childhood care and education centre for pre-school children
Balika Samriddhi Yojana	A programme for welfare of adolescent girls
Balika Shivir	Girls camp
Hukumnama	Diktat
Jan Shiksha Adhiniyam	People Education Act
Kishori Shakti Yojana	A programme for adolescent girls
Lok Adalat	Peoples' court
Lok Jumbish	An educational programme started in Rajasthan in 1992.
Mahila Mandal	Women's group
Mahila Samakhya	Programme for women's empowerment
Mahila Shiksha Kendra	Women Education Centre
Mohalla	Neighbourhood
Nari Adalat	Women's court
Parivarik Mahila Lok Adalat	Women's family court
Pradhan Mantri Gramoday Yojana	A scheme for all-round social and economic development of rural areas.
Pradhan Mantri Swasthya Suraksha Yojana	A Health Insurance Programme
Rashtriya Mahila Kosh	National Credit Fund for Women
Sahyogini	Animator
Sanjeevani	A federation of women's organisations in Madhya Pradesh
Sarpanch	Head of village level body (panchayat)
Shalishi	A traditional system of dispute resolution
Stree Adhar	Kendra An NGO
Swadhar	A scheme for holistic rehabilitation of women in difficult circumstances
Tarun Bharat Sangh	An NGO

Abbreviations/Acronyms

AAY	Antyodaya Anna Yojana
ADIP	Aids and Appliances for Disabled Persons
AFSPA	Armed Forces Special Powers Act
AIE	Alternative and Innovative Education
AIIMS	All India Institute of Medical Sciences
AIR	All India Radio
ANM	Auxiliary Nurse and Midwife
ARV	Anti Retroviral
AWW	Anganwadi Workers
BMC	Brihan Mumbai Municipal Corporation
BPL	Below Poverty Line
CEDAW	Convention on the Elimination of all Forms of Discrimination against Women
CHETNA	Centre for Health Education, Training and Nutrition
CRC	Convention on the Rights of the Child
CRSP	Central Rural Sanitation Programme
CSE	Centre for Science and Environment
DANIDA	Danish International Development Agency
DPEP	District Primary Education Programme
DWCD	Department of Women and Child Development
DWCUA	Development of Women and Children in Urban Areas
EGS	Education Guarantee Scheme
EFA	Education for All
EWR	Elected Women Representatives
FAO	Food and Agricultural Organisation
FDA	Forest Development Agencies
HDR	Human Development Report
HDRC	Human Development Resource Centre
HIV/AIDS	Human Immunodeficiency Virus/Acquired Immunodeficiency Syndrome
IAY	Indira Awas Yojana
ICDS	Integrated Child Development Services
ICPD	International Conference on Population and Development
ICT	Information and Communication Technology
ILO	International Labour Organisation

IMGS	Indira Mahila Gramabhivirdhi Samatha
IMR	Infant Mortality Rate
IMY	Indira Mahila Yojana
ITPA	Immoral Traffic (Prevention) Act
JFMC	Joint Forest Management Committee
JNVs	Jawahar Navodaya Vidyalayas
MDG	Millennium Development Goal
MFI	Micro Finance Institutions
MMR	Maternal Mortality Rate
MTP	Medical Termination of Pregnancy
NCW	National Commission for Women
NABARD	National Bank for Agriculture and Rural Development
NGO	Non-government Organisation
NHFDC	National Handicapped Fund for Disabled
NHHP	National Housing and Habitat Policy
NHRC	National Human Rights Commission
NIPCCD	National Institute of Public Co-operation and Child Development
NLM	National Literacy Mission
NMBS	National Maternity Benefit Scheme
NNM	National Nutrition Mission
NPEGEL	National Programme for Education of Girls at Elementary Level
NPEGEL	National Plan for Education at the Elementary Level
NSDP	National Slum Development Programme
NSS	National Sample Survey
PDS	Public Distribution System
PFA	Platform for Action
PHC	Public Health Centres
PMLA	Parivarik Mahila Lok Adalat
PRI	Panchayati Raj Institutions
RCH	Reproductive and Child Health
RMK	Rashtriya Mahila Kosh
RNTCP	Revised National Tuberculosis Control Programme
RRC	Regional Resource Centre
RTI	Reproductive Tract Infection
SATHI	Support for Advocacy and Training to Health Initiatives

SC/ST	Scheduled Caste / Scheduled Tribe
SCW	State Commission for Women
SEWA	Self Employed Women's Association
SGRY	Sampoorna Grameen Rozgar Yojana
SGSY	Swarnajayanti Gram Swarozgar Yojana
SHG	Self-help Group
SJSRY	Swarna Jayanti Shahari Swarozgar Yojana
SNA	State Nodal Agencies
SSA	Sarva Shiksha Abhiyan
SSSY	Swarnajayanthi Shahari Swarozgar Yojana
STEP	Support to Training and Employment Programme
STI	Sexually Transmitted Infection
TFR	Total Fertility Rate
TLC	Total Literacy Campaign
UGC	University Grants Commission
UNFPA	United Nations Population Fund
UNIFEM	United Nations Development Fund for Women
VAW	Violence Against Women
WCP	Women's Component Plan
WHO	World Health Organisation

Women and Society: An Introduction

1.1 Women and Family

Women play a critical role in the family which is the basic unit of society. Family is a strong force for social cohesion and integration and as such should be strengthened. The inadequate support to women and insufficient protection to their respective families affect society as a whole and undermines efforts to achieve gender equality. In different cultural, political and social systems, various forms of family exist and the rights, capabilities and responsibilities of family members must be respected. Women's social and economic contributions to the welfare of the family and the social significance of maternity and paternity continue to be inadequately addressed. Motherhood and fatherhood and the role of parents and legal guardians in the family and in the upbringing of children and the importance of all family members to the family's well-being is also acknowledged and must not be a basis for discrimination. Women also continue to bear a disproportionate share of the household responsibilities and the care of children, the sick and the elderly. In order to achieve full partnership, both in public and private spheres, both women and men must be enabled to reconcile and share equally work responsibilities and family responsibilities.

Strong national machineries for the advancement of women and promotion of gender equality require political commitment at the highest level. Reforms to meet the challenges of the changing world are essential to ensure women's equal access to institutions and organizations. Institutional and conceptual changes are a strategic and important aspect of creating an enabling environment for the implementation of policies and programmes for the advancement of women.

Programme support to enhance women's opportunities, potentials and activities need to have a dual focus: one the one hand, programmes aimed at meeting the basic as well as the specific needs of women for capacity building, organizational development and empowerment; and on the other, gender mainstreaming in all programme formulation and implementation activities. It is particularly important to expand into new areas of programming to advance gender equality in response to current challenges.

Girls and women of all ages with any form of disability are generally among the more vulnerable and marginalized of society. There is therefore need to take into account and to address their concerns in all policy making and programming.

Special measures are needed at all levels to integrate them into the mainstream of development.

Effective and coordinated plans and programmes for the full implementation of women-oriented policies require a clear knowledge on the situation of women and girls, a clear research-based knowledge and data disaggregated by sex, short and long-term time-bound targets and measurable goals and follow-up mechanisms to assess progress. Efforts are needed to ensure capacity building for all the actors involved in the achievement of these goals. Efforts are also needed at the national level to increase transparency and accountability.

The realization of the goals of gender equality needs to be supported by the allocation of necessary human and financial resources for specific and targeted activities to ensure gender equality at the local, national, regional and international level as well as by enhanced and increased international cooperation. The explicit attention to these goals in budgetary processes at the national, regional and international level is essential.

Recognizing the persistent and increasing burden of poverty on women in many countries, particularly in developing countries, it is essential to continue from a gender perspective to review, modify and implement integrated macro-economic and social policies and programmes to ensure universal and equitable access to social services, in particular to education, and affordable quality health care services and equal access to and control over economic resources.

1.2 Gender Equality and Development

Gender equality is a constituent of development as well as an instrument of development. No country can be deemed developed if half of its population is severely disadvantaged in terms of basic needs, livelihood options, access to knowledge, and political voice. It is an instrument of development because without gender equality other goals of development will also be difficult to achieve, namely the goals of poverty alleviation, economic growth, environmental sustainability etc. A natural corollary of ensuring gender equality is the elimination of gender discrimination. Inequalities between girls and boys in access to schooling or adequate health care prove a very serious disadvantage to women and girls and limit their capacity to participate in the benefits of development.

While the gender sensitization of policies, programmes and schemes go a long way in empowering women, it is human development indicators, which reflect the ultimate and true empowerment of women in a country. Unfortunately, the basic parameters of health (sex ratio, IMR, MMR, immunization levels, morbidity, mortality, anaemia etc.), nutrition (malnutrition, underweight, anaemia etc.), education, (illiteracy, poor enrolment, drop out etc.) employment and training (unorganised, unpaid sectors, discrimination in wages, poor skill development, drudgery areas of occupations such as agriculture and construction) reflect the continuing dismal status of women in various parts of the world.

1.3 Women and Armed Conflict

There is a wider recognition that armed conflict has different destructive impacts on women and men and that a gender sensitive approach to the application of international human rights law and international humanitarian law is important. Steps have been taken at the national and international levels to address abuses against women, including increased attention to ending impunity for crimes against women in situations of armed conflict. The work of the International Criminal Tribunal for the Former Yugoslavia and the International Criminal Tribunal for Rwanda has been an important contribution to address violence against women in the context of armed conflict. Also of historical significance is the adoption of the Rome Statute of the International Criminal Court which provides that rape, sexual slavery, enforced prostitution, forced pregnancy, enforced sterilization and other forms of sexual violence are war crimes when committed in the context of armed conflict and also under defined circumstances. Women's contribution in peace-building, peacemaking and conflict resolution is being increasingly recognized.

Gender-based persecution has been accepted as a basis for refugee status in some countries. There is recognition by governments, international community and organizations, in particular the United Nations, that women and men experience humanitarian emergencies differently. There is, thus, a need for a more holistic support for refugee and displaced women, including those who have suffered all forms of abuse, including gender-specific abuse to ensure equal access to appropriate and adequate food and nutrition, clean water, safe sanitation, shelter, education, social and health services, including reproductive health care and maternity care. There is greater recognition of the need to integrate a gender perspective in the planning, design and implementation of humanitarian assistance and to provide adequate resources. Humanitarian relief agencies and civil society, including non-governmental organizations have a special responsibility to address the needs of women and girls—including refugee and displaced women and girls—in humanitarian emergencies, and in conflict and post-conflict situations.

Peace is inextricably linked to equality between women and men and development. Armed and other types of conflicts, wars of aggression, foreign occupation, colonial or other alien domination, as well as terrorism, continue to cause serious obstacles to the advancement of women. The targeting of civilians, including women and children, the displacement of people,. and the recruitment of child soldiers in violation of national or international law, by state and/or non-state actors, which occur in armed conflicts, have had a particular adverse impact on gender equality and human rights of women.

The under-representation, at all levels, of women from decision-making positions in peace-keeping, peace-building, post-conflict reconciliation and reconstruction as well as lack of gender awareness in these areas presents serious obstacles. There has been a failure to provide sufficient resources and to adequately distribute those resources, to address the needs of increasing numbers of refugees, who are mostly women and children, particularly to developing countries hosting large numbers of refugees. International assistance has not kept pace with the increasing number of refugees. The growing number of internally displaced persons and the provision of their needs, in particular women and children, continue to represent a double burden to the affected countries and their financial resources. Inadequate training of personnel dealing with the needs of women in situations of armed conflict or as refugees such as a shortage of specific programmes that address healing of women from trauma and skills training, remains a problem.

Excessive military expenditures—including global military expenditures, trade in arms and investment for arms production taking into consideration national security requirements—direct the possible allocation of funds away from social and economic development, in particular for the advancement of women. In several countries, economic sanctions have had social and humanitarian impact on the civilian population in particular women and children.

In situations of armed conflict there are continued violations of human rights of women, which are violations of fundamental principles of international human rights law and international humanitarian law. There has been an increase of all forms of violence against women, including sexual slavery, rape, systematic rape, sexual abuse and forced pregnancies in the situations of armed conflict. Displacement compounded by loss of home and property, poverty, family disintegration and separation and other consequences of armed conflict is severely affecting population, especially women and children. Girls are also abducted or recruited, in violation of international law, into situations of armed conflict including, *inter alia,* as combatants, sexual slaves or providers of domestic services.

1.4 Globalization and Women

1.4.1 Adverse Effects of Globalization on Women: With the growing globalization and liberalization of the economy as well as increased privatization of services, women as a whole have been left behind and not been able to partake of the fruits of success. Mainstreaming of women into the new and emerging areas of growth is imperative. This will require training and skill upgradation in emerging trades, encouraging more women to take up vocational training and employment in the boom sectors. This will also require women to migrate to cities and metros for work. Provision of safe housing, and other gender friendly facilities at work will need to be provided.

Another facet of globalization is related to the fact that many persons especially women will be severely affected with the advent of setting up of industrial parks, national highways, special economic zones (SEZs) etc. as huge tracts of farm land are likely to be acquired for this purpose. This would require massive resettlement of the displaced persons and their families. It is therefore essential that a viable resettlement policy and strategy is formulated and put in place immediately which clearly reflects the needs of women impacted by globalization/displacement.

With the removal of all quantitative restrictions on the import of various products, the self-employed women's groups, especially in the informal sector, have started facing competition from the low-priced imported consumer goods which are invading the Indian market. Although this has the imminent danger of displacing a large number of employed/self-employed women, but at the same time, the process of globalization has also opened up opportunities for women entrepreneurs for exporting their products to the markets all over the world. Globalization has thus opened up new challenges for the realization of the goal of women's empowerment. Hence, strategies should be designed to enhance the capacity of women and empower them to cope with the negative economic and social impacts of the globalization process.

Several studies have indicated that adverse consequences of globalisation are disproportionately borne by women. Increased mechanization leading to displacement of female unskilled workers, increased migration of male workers in traditionally women-dominated areas, increase in female-headed household due to migration of males are some of the trends established in various studies.

Globalization has presented new challenges for the realization of the goal of women's equality, the gender impact of which has not been systematically evaluated fully. However, it is evident that there is a need for re-framing policies for access to employment and equality of employment. Benefits of the growing global economy have been unevenly distributed leading to wider economic disparities, the feminization of poverty, increased gender inequality through deteriorating working conditions and unsafe working environment especially in the informal economy and rural areas. Strategies need to be designed to enhance the capacity of women and empower them to meet the negative social and economic impacts, which may flow from the globalization process.

With upgradation of skills, opportunities for employment of women exist in several areas such as health services, food processing and crafts. Key areas of concern include women in small subsistence farming households, women workers in garment and textiles who will face increased competition after the phasing out of the Multi Fibre Agreement in 2005, and women displaced by new technologies in sectors such as construction, which have traditionally absorbed large numbers of women.

With the onset of trade liberalisation, women in India today are linked to the global economy to a very significant extent, as producers, entrepreneurs, service providers, consumers and citizens. There is a need to identify capacity constraints and entry barriers that prevent women from securing gains from trade. Trade-related awareness and capacity building of the women stakeholders need to be prioritised.

The globalization process has, in some countries, resulted in policy shifts in favour of more open trade and financial flows, privatization of state-owned enterprises and in many cases lower public spending particularly on social services. This change has transformed patterns of production and accelerated technological advances in information and communication and affected the lives of women, both as workers and consumers. In a large number of countries, particularly in developing and least developed countries, these changes have also adversely impacted on the lives of women and have increased inequality. The gender impact of these changes has not been systematically evaluated. Globalization has also affected cultural values, lifestyles and forms of communication.

In countries with economies in transition women are bearing most of the hardships induced by the economic restructuring and being the first to lose jobs in times of recession. They are being squeezed out from fast growth sectors. Loss of childcare facilities due to elimination or privatization of state work places, increased need for older care without the corresponding facilities, continuing inequality of access to training for finding re-employment and to productive assets for entering or expanding businesses are current challenges facing women in these countries.

1.4.2 Opportunities Offered by Globalization: Science and technology, as fundamental components of development, are transforming patterns of production, contributing to the creation of jobs and new job classifications, and ways of working, and contributing to the establishment of a knowledge-based society. Technological change can bring new opportunities for all women in all fields if they have equal access, and adequate training. Women should also be actively involved in the definition, design, development, implementation and gender impact evaluation of policies related to these changes. Many women world-wide are yet to effectively use these new communications technologies for networking, advocacy, exchange of information business, education, media consultation and e-commerce initiatives. For instance, millions of the world's poorest women and men still do not have access to and benefits from science and technologies and are currently excluded from this new field and the opportunities it presents.

The patterns of migratory flows of labour are changing. Women and girls are increasingly involved in internal, regional and international labour migration to pursue many occupations mainly in farm labour, domestic work and some forms of entertainment work. While this situation increases their earning opportunities and self-reliance, it also exposes them—particularly the poor, uneducated, unskilled and/or undocumented migrants—to inadequate working conditions, increased health risk, the risk of trafficking, economic and sexual exploitation, racism, racial discrimination and xenophobia, and other forms of abuse.

Further, globalization has dramatically changed the conditions under which the work for gender equality must be carried out, especially in high growth countries like India. While globalization has generated opportunities for local producers and entrepreneurs to reach international markets, it has at times intensified existing inequalities and insecurities for many poor women. Since the gains of globalization are often concentrated in the hands of those with higher education—those who own resources and have access to capital—poor women are usually the least able to seize the longer term opportunities offered.

This disadvantage has been exacerbated as in most of the countries, policies reflect a commitment to global norms of markets and social policy is increasingly determined by market dynamics. Market friendly policies generate high growth rates that fail to translate into improved standards of health, education and human security. Feminist scholars have highlighted the gendered impact of such policies, many of which increase women's job vulnerability, unpaid work burden, while reducing state level resources that might be used to provide a social safety net. Owing to dissent voiced by feminist scholars on the widespread assumption that gender inequality as a challenge can be overcome with effective and sustained advocacy as it is more about mindsets and less about policies, especially economic policies, there have been some attempts to integrate economic and social policies but gender concerns have not been accorded requisite attention. These disadvantages have led to a situation where gains in women's economic opportunities lag behind those in women's capabilities.

In short, in a semi-industrialised country like India, the working class in destined to be one of the weaker sections of society. Moreover, society being male-dominated, female labour receives very poor recognition or value. Not that there are no statutory provisions. In fact, the Constitution of India provides equal rights and opportunities to both the genders. In addition there are specific provisions for protection and welfare of working women in many of the labour laws. However, most of these statutes do not cover the units in small and informal sectors which are the predominant workplaces of women.

Even where they are covered by the statutes, the poor enforcement practically nullifies the provisions. Moreover, there is another tragic factor that has to be noted. The very laws which are meant for working women are paradoxically turned against their interests by unscrupulous employers. If the employers find it difficult to bypass these provisions, they get rid of the women workers and thus strike at the economic base of their livelihood. All these factors need to be studied in depth while drafting policy and legal provisions for the working women in order to plug all possible loopholes.

For the reasons mentioned above, as also for the benefit of working women, their union leaders—and for all those who are interested in the welfare of women workers—knowledge of existing provisions of labour laws is very essential. Women's emancipation is part of India's general developmental plans but government action can be neither effective nor adequate unless women themselves become more aware of their rights and the corresponding responsibilities. Every woman is a working woman, whether she works in the home or outside it. Many women work to earn money. Working women must know that they have some basic rights which are given by the law.

Though India has created protective legislations for women, the enactments have not been easy to implement. The very vastness of the country, the scattered nature of women workers, their lack of education and legal literacy, indifferent attitude of bureaucracy and the general status of women in society have added to vulnerability of women. This is true not only of rural unorganised women, but to an extent of the urban women workers also.

The overall picture that emerges is one of greater disadvantage for women workers in general and those belonging to rural as well as Scheduled Castes (SCs)/Scheduled Tribes (STs) in particular. Apart from such inherited disadvantages as lower social position, a number of other factors also contribute to such a picture. These are their limited asset position, access to resources, and low level of education and skill. Education, and consequently some ability to acquire formal skills, could be a moderating force but this aspect presents a dismal picture. The overall situation of women workers calls for interventions of a promotional nature from different entry points but with a strong emphasis on education.

1.5 Gender Budgeting

Government budgets are universally accepted as a powerful tool in achieving development objectives and act as an indicator of commitment to the stated policy of the Government. National budgets reflect how governments mobilize and allocate public resources, and how they aim to meet the social and economic needs of their people.

1.5.1 Meaning of Gender Budgeting: A budget, on the face of it, appears to be gender-neutral. Public expenditure and revenue are not intrinsically gendered. However, this apparent gender neutrality hides a deeper gender blindness, which tends to operate to the disadvantage of women. Budgetary policies can ignore gender-specific needs and have differential impacts on men and women because of the systemic differences between the sexes in relation to the economy.

Gender budgeting looks at government budget from a gender perspective to assess how it addresses the needs of women. In other words, gender budgeting is the application of gender mainstreaming in the budgetary process. It incorporates a gender perspective at all levels and stages of the budgetary process and paves the way for translating gender commitments to budgetary commitments and carrying out an assessment of the budget to establish its gender differential impact. It does not seek to create a separate budget but seeks to put in place affirmative action for meeting women-specific needs, thus bringing into effect gender responsive budgeting. The ultimate objective of gender budgeting is to transform traditional perceptions towards women and awaken a gender sensitive consciousness to come into the mainstream and give them their due recognition as equal citizens of the country.

1.5.2 Meaning of Gender Mainstreaming: The conventional approach to gender budgeting emphasizes isolating public expenditure—direct and indirect—for women. It is necessary to recognize that women are equal players in the economy whether they participate directly as workers or indirectly as members of the care economy. To that extent, every policy of the government—fiscal, monetary, agriculture, industry and trade—has a direct impact on the well-being of women. Thus, it is not adequate to analyze allocation of resources for a few sectors of the economy which are traditionally considered as women-related. The exercise has to cover a gender-sensitive analysis of monetary policies, covering impact of indicators like inflation, interest rates etc and fiscal policies covering both direct and indirect taxes. Hence, gender budgeting analysis has to go hand in hand with gender mainstreaming. This is a mammoth task when there is a lot of disaggregated data which has to be gender sensitized and analyzed. Micro studies will have to be conducted to study the impact of public and fiscal policy so that they may guide macro policies. Thus, gender mainstreaming is a broader term covering a wide gamut of governmental activities.

1.5.3 Objectives of Gender Budgeting: A gender-responsive budget aims at examining budgetary resource allocations through a gender lens. It is not a separate budget for women; rather it is an analysis of the government budget in order to establish its gender-specific impact and translate gender commitments into budgetary commitments. It also examines the gendered incidence of budgetary policies for effective targeting of public spending and to offset any undesirable gender-specific consequences of previous budgetary measures).

Gender budgeting lays stress on *reprioritisation* rather than an increase in overall public expenditure and, in particular, the *reorientation* of programmes within sectors rather than changes in the overall amounts allocated to particular sectors. Moreover, one of the key thrusts of a gender-sensitive budget is to ensure a greater visibility of the unpaid *care economy.* In other words, gender responsive budgeting applies a gender lens to budgetary resource allocation, providing more visibility to women's unpaid work.

Generally, budgeting involves the following four components: (a) budgetary allocation of resources to various heads, (b) actual government outlays on various heads, (c) an accounting of how resources are utilised for a particular purpose (e.g. on administrative overheads and wages and salaries, operation and maintenance etc.) and (d) an evaluation of the effectiveness of the resources utilised in delivering the intended results.

Gender budgeting involves looking at all the four components from the point of view of women as beneficiaries. Many public goods and services, like defence and infrastructure, are not amenable to gender partitioning. However, they can have differential impact on the two sexes. For example, outlays for augmenting the supply of safe drinking water can benefit women more than men by cutting down on the time spent in fetching water from the river or ponds. The existing practice of budgeting does not pay any special attention to the impact of budgets on empowerment of women and on gender equality.

In short, the objective of gender budgeting is to enable gender mainstreaming of all sectors at all levels and stages of policies, programmes/schemes and also at the level of the implementation stage and instituting gender-friendly delivery mechanisms. Only then it can pave the way for translating gender commitments into budgetary commitments.

1.5.4 Rationale of Gender Budgeting: The rationale of gender budgeting arises from recognition of the fact that national budgets impact various sections of the society differently through the pattern of resource allocation and priority accorded to competing sectors. The budgetary policy of the government has a major role to play in achieving objectives of gender equality and growth through content and direction of fiscal and monetary policies, measures for resource mobilization, affirmative action for under privileged sections. Women stand apart as one segment of the population that warrants special attention due to their vulnerability and lack of access to state resources.

Thus, gender responsive budgetary policies can contribute to achieving the objectives of gender equality, human development and economic efficiency. The purpose of gender budgeting exercise is to assess quantum and adequacy of allocation of resources for women and establish the extent to which gender commitments are translated in to budgetary commitments. This exercise facilitates increase in accountability, transparency and participation of the community. The macro policies of the Government can have a significant impact on gender gaps in various macro indicators related to health, education, income etc. When gender equality considerations are incorporated into policy making, the concerns and needs of both women and men become integral part of the design, implementation, monitoring and evaluation of policies and programmes in all sections of society.

1.5.5 Tools of Gender Budgeting: Policies of the Government form the genesis for programmes and schemes providing the direction and describing the components of inputs that go into them. They determine the quantum of flow of the funds to different schemes, its components and also spatial spread of the programme. Unless the policies are engendered, it cannot be hoped that the programmes and the schemes that emerge from this will be gender sensitive. Therefore, it is very essential that all policies of the Government from its very inception and formulation stage be thoroughly examined from a gender perspective. The fiscal and monetary policies will need to be analyzed from a gender perspective as both have tremendous potential to have benign influence on the lives of women.

A. Gender-sensitive Indirect Taxes: Indirect taxes (i.e. taxes on commodities) impinge heavily on women as the tax incidence, by and large, affects important items of sustenance which are generally price-inelastic and even a small price rise in such items can have a negative impact on women. Conversely, withdrawal of subsidies can adversely impinge on women. For example, withdrawal of subsidy on kerosene with no other alternative fuel options will result in the woman wasting valuable productive time in gathering firewood, twigs etc and in the process also face health hazards. Thus, the ramifications of indirect taxes are quite significant as far as women's well-being is considered.

B. Gender-sensitive Direct Taxes: The gender affirmative role of direct taxes (income tax, wealth tax etc.) can be enhanced through various incentives like reduction in stamp duties for women if assets are registered in their name, lowering of income tax slabs for women etc. For example, till recently, the basic exemption limit for women assesses was more as compared to general category of assesses under the Indian income tax system.

C. Gender-sensitive Monetary Policy: Monetary policy has to be viewed from a gender angle, especially in the case of credit and loan facilities and easy access of women to financial instruments and attractive saving options. In this context the spread of private micro credit lending instruments needs to be carefully regulated to ensure that women and SHGs are not exploited through high interest rates.

D. Gender-sensitive National Income Accounting: Informal farm work and non-farm work where women are increasingly employed are mostly non-monetized and therefore cannot be captured in the national accounting system. Despite the sizeable value addition to the national economy, on account of home-based and other non-farm and informal activities, the contribution of women's work continues to be invisible. Women also spend considerable time in collecting fuel, fodder, and water and on care-related activities, which is not recognized as an economic activity. The statistical invisibility of such unpaid work implies that the economic system is missing out on a substantial part of the income generated and value added. It should be ensured that the national income includes these activities in their accounting system so that it forms a part of the GDP.

1.5.6 Gender Budgeting in Select Countries: World-wide, there is a growing recognition of the need for a fundamental rethinking of the macro-policy framework from a gender perspective. The United Nations conferences of the 1990s affirmed a global consensus on the need for a new approach to macro policy in the sustainable human development paradigm, which is based on the cornerstones of gender equality, poverty eradication, environmental regeneration, sustainable livelihoods, employment creation and democratic governance.

The United Nations Fourth World Conference on Women 1995 (the Beijing Conference) and the subsequent Beijing Platform for Action contributed to the emergence of an international consensus in integrating a gender perspective in all policies and their budgetary dimensions.

A. Australia: Australia was the first country to develop a gender-sensitive budget. In 1984, the government introduced a comprehensive assessment of the gender differential impacts of its Federal Budget. Each government agency was required to provide a *gender audit* (i.e. achievements in relation to women and girls). The audit was a comprehensive gender analysis of mainstream public expenditure, and not merely those expenditures directly allotted to females. It was found that expenditures specifically targeted to women and girls made up less than 1 per cent of the total budget.

B. South Africa: Started in 1995, the gender budget initiative in South Africa was a joint effort of parliamentarians and non-governmental organisations (NGOs). This parliamentary-NGO initiative undertook a detailed gender-sensitive analysis of expenditure portfolios like education, health, welfare, housing, labour, trade and industry, land affairs, agriculture, safety and security, transport, energy, foreign affairs well as the cross-sectoral areas of public sector employment and taxation. Later, during 1997, the Department of Finance began a parallel exercise, as a pilot for the Commonwealth initiative to integrate gender perspectives into macroeconomic policy. In a major step forward, several sections of the 1998 *Budget Review* (document tabled along with the budget) discussed gender issues in the various departments.

C. Sri Lanka: The Commonwealth initiative to integrate gender into national budgetary processes was initiated on a test basis in some countries including Sri Lanka. Sri Lanka joined the Commonwealth countries' pilot project in 1997 and the initial gender-sensitive budget exercise was co-ordinated by the Department of National Planning. It focussed on the portfolios of health, education, public sector employment, agriculture, industry and social services. The first stage of the pilot project was completed with the establishment of a gender-conscious planning mechanism in the allocation of resources coupled with greater capacity for sex-segregated data collation.

An inter-ministerial committee, comprising of representatives of the ministries of education, health, social services, industries, agriculture, women affairs and the department of census and statistics, was set up to assess the progress and performance of the gender budgeting project in Sri Lanka. The survey-based report found that there was equality of access and usage in mainstream public expenditure: 48 percent of recurrent expenditure in the education sector, 56 percent in the health sector and 57 percent in the social services sector benefited females. The report stressed that there is no need for an increase in funding for women. What was needed, instead, was an evaluation and redesign of the existing programmes, and devising appropriate benefit impact monitoring systems that would be sensitive to gender imbalances.

D. Canada: In Canada, members of Centre for Policy Alternatives, a social justice research group, have developed a gender-sensitive budget as part of the

Centre's annual Alternative Federal Budget. Though there are no formal guidelines regarding gender budgeting, Human Resource Development Canada (HRDC), a government department, is committed to implementing a gender-based analysis as a part of the policy and programme development process in the country.

Following its international commitment to the Beijing Platform for Action initiative, the Government of Canada adopted the Federal Plan for Gender Equality (1995-2000). The plan was prepared through the collaboration of 24 departments and agencies, led by Status of Women Canada (SWC), another government department. The first of the Federal Plan's eight objectives made a commitment to government-wide implementation of gender-based analysis (GBA) in the development of policies, programmes and legislations GBA involves collecting reliable sex-disaggregated information about the policy area of concern, and understanding the gender trends in the economy that might have an impact on a proposed policy, programme or piece of legislation.

E. UK: Women's Budget Group, an NGO consisting of researchers and activists, is in the forefront of putting gender-sensitive budget analysis on the policy agenda. Its core recommendations to the government are the inclusion of a comparative 'gender impact statement' with every budget and public expenditure white paper.

For Gender Budgeting in India, see section 7.11 of chapter 7 of this book.

1.6 Women in Indian History

The Constitution of the Republic of India ensures equality for women and men in every sphere of life and activity. Women in India have been given equality of opportunity in all matters relating to education, employment, and legal status, and they can aspire to grace the highest offices of the State. However, this is indicative of the existing position of women in general in the country. Though legally and constitutionally all women have equal access to and right to venture in every walk of life, a vast majority of them are still illiterate and uneducated. This is a paradoxical situation which must be understood and seen in its historical perspective. The status of women and their activities can be divided into three main historical periods, the ancient, the medieval and the modern.

1.6.1 Ancient Period: From the available documentation, it is revealed that women enjoyed a fair amount of freedom and equality with men in the fields of education and religion during the Vedic period. In the Vedic period, women from higher sections of society were given equal rights in the field of religion, and they attained distinction in the realm of theological studies and philosophy. Distinguished women such as Gargi and Maitrayee are well-known names of this period who excelled as scholars in their own right. During the ancient period, there were icons such as Sita, Damayanti, Draupadi and three of the Panchkanyas, Ahilya, Tara, Mandodari, who are still remembered with great reverence in Indian society. It was in the later period, approximately 500 BC, that the status of women gradually declined with the Smritis and other religious texts giving *diktats* which adversely affected women's freedom and rights. With the rise of Brahaminism and due to conflicting religious and social thoughts, the place of women remained subordinate and unsatisfactory. Buddhism and Jainism, however, continued to give a place of honour to women. Women were eligible for admission to the religious order in both Buddhism and Jainism. Bhikshuni Sanghamitra was one of the main proponents of Buddhism of her time.

1.6.2 Medieval Period: The medieval period saw further deterioration in women's position in society and their subjugation in the religious and legal spheres. This was a period when important scriptures propagated the idea that women were unfit for freedom and deserved no Independence. They should be kept under the authority of men in all stages of life. Due to foreign invasions there was further set back in the position of Indian women. The *purdah* system, which was not practiced as a rule in the Indian society, became prevalent due to uncertain socio-political reasons. The growing incidence of female infanticide, the custom of child marriage, and the inhuman practice of *sati* became a part of the social culture, along with the religious ban on widow remarriage.

Though there are conflicting opinions about the status of women in this period, it was in this period that India saw the floodgates open to social reforms. In spite of many handicaps, the medieval period also had its share of great women in the fields of politics, literature, education and religion. The *Bhakti* movement brought many women poet saints from different social and economic classes to join Vaishnav and other traditions of devotion, and also the Sufi traditions in different parts of India.

1.6.3 Modern Period: In the modern period, the status of Indian women can be divided into two distinct periods, the British Rule, i.e. Pre-Independence India and Post-Independence India.

A. Pre-Independence Period: The British Rule in the 18th century brought in some degree of political orderliness, but the social structure, customs and practices remained unchanged. It was mainly during the 19th century that the reform movement undertaken by enlightened thinkers and leaders of Indian society understood the importance of women's participation that the status of Indian women started changing for the better. Though initially all the leaders were men, women gradually came into the scene and played their role not only in changing history but also the society as a whole, through their efforts in different areas of work such as education, politics, freedom movement and social welfare. Annie Besant, Sarojini Naidu, Kamladevi Chattopadhyay, Nellie Sengupta, and many others gave a direction to Indian womanhood towards change and betterment. Indian women actively participated in the freedom movement which also had different thrusts and ideologies.

The founding of the Indian National Congress in 1885 and Mahatma Gandhi's non-violent movement not only led to political emancipation but also to social and national reconstruction. Women took equal initiatives and participated in all types of struggle for freedom, i.e. non-violent movement advocated by Mahatma Gandhi and the National Congress, as well as in the violent and armed movements advocated by other leaders in different parts of the country. Women's enthusiasm in participating in the armed revolution helped Netaji Subhash Chandra Bose to set up the Rani of Jhansi Regiment of the Indian National Army. Women's participation in the freedom movement was so extensive that the achievers are many in number. Some names of great significance are Kasturba Gandhi, Madam Bhikaji Cama, Sarla Devi, Muthu Lakshmi Reddy, Aruna Asaf Ali, Sucheta Kriplani, Durga Bai Deshmukh, Priti Lata Waddedar, Captain Lakshmi and Janaki Davar of INA, Jahanara Shahnawaz, and Randhabai Subbarayan.

B. Post-Independence Period: In 1947, India won freedom from foreign rule. In 1949 a Constitution was drafted which gave equal rights and status to all Indian citizens. Independent India has seen various reforms and programmes for the uplift of women of all communities. Indian women have played an important role from the very beginning of Independence in different walks of life. Women have taken bold steps in all nation building activities, which started with education and have now blossomed into women's involvement in every activity of India. They have participated in all activities such as education, politics, media, art and culture, services sector, science and technology.

1.7 Female Literacy and Sex Ratio: Census 2011

Government of India released the provisional data of Census 2011 on March 31, 2011. The decadal Census exercise—the 15th headcount of India's population since 1872—is undertaken to create a database on demography, economic activity, literacy and education, housing and household amenities, urbanization, fertility and mortality, social structure, language, religion and migration. The census is the sole data base in India that the Government uses to formulate its policies.

According to the information made available, population of India increased from 103 crore in 2001 to 121 crore in 2011, an increase of 18 crore or 17.6

percent. Out of 121 crore, 62.4 crore were males and 58.6 crore were females.

More precisely, India added 18.1 crore people to its population between 2001 and 2011 against 18.2 crore in the preceding decade. However, even 18.1 crore equals the total population of Brazil, the world's fifth most populous country.

For the first time since Independence in 1947, India added fewer people to its population in the decade just ended than in the previous one. While decadal population growth rates have consistently been declining since the 1960s, the absolute addition in each decade was always higher than in the previous decade. That is now changed.

At 121 crore, India's population is almost equal to the combined population of US, Indonesia, Brazil, Pakistan, Bangladesh and Japan. Mainland China's population is 135 crore.

Uttar Pradesh remains the most populous state (19.95 crore) followed by Maharashtra (11.2 crore) in 2011. These 2 states put together surpass US, the world's third most populous country after China and India, in population.

1.7.1 Literacy Rate: India's literacy rate for people aged 6 and older increased to 74 percent nationwide in 2011, from 65 percent in 2001. However, this is well short of the target set by the Planning Commission to achieve a literacy rate of over 85 percent by 2011-12.

Kerala has the highest literacy rate at 94 percent while Bihar the lowest at 64 percent.

For males, literacy rate rose to 82.2 percent in 2011 from 75 percent in 2001. For females, it went up to 65.5 percent in 2011 from 54 percent in 2001.

In fact, the gap in literacy between men and women got reduced to an all-time low of just 16.7 percentage points in 2011. In 2001, this gap was 21 percentage points.

Provisional data of Census 2011 affirms the India growth story—population growth slowing down and the number of literates growing, especially female literates. The census definition of literacy is the ability to both read and write in any language. The population below 6 years is not counted as they are considered illiterate irrespective of their ability to read or write.

1.7.2 Overall Sex Ratio: Improved medical technology, education and improvement in quality of life during the first decade of the 21st century resulted in the overall gender ratio improving from 933 in 2001 to 940 in 2011. This is in line with general improvement in the overall sex ratio since 1991. Only 3 major states showed a decline in their sex ratio: J&K, Bihar and Gujarat.

Delhi and Haryana are the states with the worst overall sex ratios (866 and 877 respectively). In fact, a healthy sex ratio remains largely a southern phenomenon. Kerala is the only state where women outnumber men (1,084 females for every 1,000 males). Next in order is Tamil Nadu with 995 females for every 1.000 males.

1.7.3 Child Sex Ratio (0-6 years): The data show that the sex ratio for children below 6 years (i.e. number of girls for every 1,000 boys) dropped from 927 in 2001 to a dismal 914 in 2011. This decline is unabated since 1961 Census. Among big states, Chhattisgarh has the highest child sex ratio of 964 followed by Kerala with 959. Haryana is at the bottom (830) followed by Punjab (846). This gender bias draws attention to a lingering societal flaw which economic growth is not being able to correct.

As a result of this declining sex ratio, millions of girls/women are missing in India. It is an alarming scenario and if this trend continues, violence against women would increase and there would be forced polyandry. The demographic balance would be permanently damaged.

One of the reasons for the declining sex ratios is the incidence of sex selection, and or sex determination followed by sex selective abortions. This constitutes a grave form of discrimination against women as women are affected as being part of a social class. This is not a pro-life or pro-choice issue. A woman's right to abortion has to be upheld on grounds of promoting women's rights to equality. The right to abortion is the right to abort any foetus. The abortion of a female foetus following a sex determination test is an act of discrimination. As this act of discrimination cannot be committed without the active intervention of medical professionals, it is essential to strictly enforce laws directed towards regulating the practice of medical professionals. However, keeping in mind the pressures that a woman is subjected to for bearing a male child, the implementation and enforcement of such laws should not lead to the further victimization of women.

The laws regulating sex determination and abortions are provided for in the Pre-conception and Pre-natal Diagnostic Techniques (Prohibition of Misuse) Act and the Medical Termination of Pregnancies Act 1971. In addition, penal provisions on "causing miscarriages" are also provided in Sections 312-316 of the Indian Penal Code.

Sex determination before birth is widely prevalent. Certain districts in Punjab and Haryana account for a substantial drop in the decennial child sex ratio. Richer districts tend to account for a larger decline in the child sex ratio. The incidence of the use of sex determination techniques tends to be more in the most modern and developed districts. This calls into question the argument that the market economy undermines patriarchal authoritarian and male-biased traditional attitudes and spreads egalitarian values. Policy has to address the concern that inculcation of the values of market economy seems to be only enhancing gender inequity as reflected in the female foeticide and infanticide indicators.

There are two important issues of policy associated with this decline in the child sex ratio. One is the obsession with population control, which assumes that all the failures in development can be mono-causally linked to population explosion. The other more recent issue is the intrusion of the two-child norm into the Panchayati Raj Acts of many states, despite its absence from the Population Policy of 2000, leading to disqualification of many elected representatives. Most of the excluded belong to the SCs and STs. Some experts have suggested a link between the imposition of the two-child norm and sex selective abortions. Imposition of the two-child norm, then, cannot be the route to population stabilisation, for it may lead to a disturbingly unbalanced population.

1.8 National Population Policy (NPP), 2000

The alarming growth of India's population calls for a systematic and effective population policy to curb the undesirable trend. The post-Independence population explosion has nullified, to a large extent, the gains of developmental efforts.

The policy of the Government of India to control population has relied excessively on family planning programme. Ever since the launching of the First Five Year Plan (1951-56), family planning has occupied an important place in the development strategy of the Government. Successive plans have allocated more and more resources for the implementation of family planning schemes. In 1966, a separate Department of Family Planning was created in the Union Ministry of Health. However, the results have not been encouraging.

Such dizzying rate of population growth negates whatever gains the nation has been able to achieve in agriculture, industrial and services sectors. Also, this leads to an unbearable burden on health, education, and housing sectors. If this trend is not halted, it will never be possible to render social and economic justice to millions of our masses. The current rate of population growth is simply not sustainable. In nutshell, the population explosion has proved a damper on the developmental efforts of the economy.

National Population Policy (NPP), 2000 outlined the long-term objective of attaining a stable population by 2045, a level consistent with the requirements of sustainable economic growth, social development and environment protection. Apart from implementation of the National Population Policy involving all social sector programmes, the State Governments too will have to play an important role in improving the social, economic and demographic indicators especially in the high fertility regions. In the long-run, it is necessary to have an explicit demographic vision of attaining less than half percent annual growth rate of population by the end of next decade. This would involve significant upgradation of the status of women in the society and attainment of almost 100 percent literacy among adult females.

NPP, 2000 also addressed issues of ensuring universal access to health care options and stabilising population. It recognised links between socio-economic development and health. The hallmark of India's National Population Policy is its emphasis on improving the quality of reproductive health care by working more closely with community-based organisations and women's groups. The policy provides a framework for advancing goals and prioritising strategies to meet the reproductive and child health needs of the people of India and to achieve net replacement levels of total fertility rate by 2010. The immediate objective of the policy is to address the unmet needs of contraception, health infrastructure, health personnel and to provide integrated service delivery for basic reproductive and child health care.

Satisfactorily, the decadal growth of population at 21.34 percent between 1991 and 2001 was the sharpest decline in the rate of growth of population witnessed since Independence, with the average exponential growth rate declining from 2.14 percent per annum during the previous decade to 1.93 percent per annum. The declining trends indicate that the country is entering a phase of rapidly declining fertility in its process of demographic transition.

Sounding a note of optimism on demographic trends in India, the Approach Paper to the Eleventh Five Year Plan (2007-12) remarked, "In the longer run, there is another important potential strength arising from our demographic trends. Our dependency rate (ratio of dependent to working age population) is falling whereas that of industrialised countries and even China is rising. The presence of a skilled young population in an environment where investment is expanding and the industrial world ageing could be a major advantage. It is however important to realise that we can only reap this demographic dividend if we invest massively on human resource development and skill formation and create an economic environment capable of absorbing our relatively young working population in productive employment." [1]

Population stabilisation is crucial for the achievement of the goal of sustainable development and an equitable distribution of resources/opportunities. Though Government initiatives exist in the form of suitable public policies on education, health and family welfare along with economic incentives and facilities for small and micro-families, these measures have had a limited impact on the fertility, net reproduction rates and the family size. Improved access to primary and secondary education extension of basic amenities, the empowerment of women, awareness gene-ration and a better standard of living would ultimately contribute towards inculcation of the required consciousness regarding the desirability of a small family size.

End Note

1. Government of India, Planning Commission, *An Approach to the Eleventh Five Year Plan*, November 2006, p. 5.

2

Constitutional and Legal Safeguards for Women in India

2.1 Constitutional Provisions for Women in India

The Constitution of India adopted on November 26, 1949, became operative on January 26, 1950. It provides for two layers of Government, one at the Central level, and the other at the level of the States.

The Constitution of India recognises the right of women to employment and includes a number of Articles to give direction to the state policy. Article 14 lays down the equality before law of all citizens of the country, and Article 15 prohibits discrimination on the grounds of sex, religion, race etc. Article 16 (1) and (2) emphasises equal opportunities for all in the matter of employment and prohibits discrimination in employment.

Article 15 (3) of the Constitution empowers the state to make special provisions for women and children within the framework of the fundamental rights. Articles 39 and 42 specially refer to women and children. They direct the State to secure health and strength of all workers, men, women and children and not to abuse children for economic gains. Humane and just conditions of work and maternity benefit are assured to women by Article 42.

Thus labour legislation for women in India is rooted in the Indian constitution and is guided by ILO conventions. The objective of these enactments is to protect women from exploitation.

Women as an independent group constitute 48 percent of the country's total population as per the 2001 Census. The importance of women is recognised by the Constitution of India which not only accords equality to women but also empowers the State to adopt measures for positive discrimination in their favour. There are Articles in the Constitution which reiterate the commitment of the nation towards the socio- economic development of women and upholding their political rights and participation in decision-making (Table 2.1).

2.2 Legislations for Protection and Advancement of Women in India

Drawing the strength from the constitutional commitments, the Government of India has been engaged in the continuous endeavour of concretely translating all the rights, commitments and safeguards incorporated in the Indian Constitution for women from *de jure* to *de facto* status.

Table 2.1: Provisions in the Constitution of India for Socio-economic Development of Women

Article	Brief description
Article 14	Men and women to have equal rights and opportunities in the political, economic and social spheres.
Article 15(1)	Prohibits discrimination against any citizen on the grounds of religion, race, caste, sex etc.
Article 15(3)	Special provision enabling the State to make affirmative discriminations in favour of women.
Article 16	Equality of opportunities in matter of public appointments for all citizens.
Article 39(a)	State shall direct its policy towards securing all citizens men and women, equally, the right to means of livelihood.
Article 39(d)	Equal pay for equal work for both men and women.
Article 42	State to make provision for ensuring just and humane conditions of work and maternity relief.
Article 51 (A)(e)	To renounce the practices derogatory to the dignity of women.

2.2.1 Objectives of Women-specific Legislations: The objectives of various legislations enacted include the following:

1. Creating an environment through positive economic and social policies for full development of women to enable them to realize their full potential.
2. Enjoyment of all human rights and fundamental freedom by women on equal basis with men in all spheres—political, economic, social, cultural and civil.
3. Equal access to participation and decision making of women in social, political and economic life of the nation.
4. Equal access to women for health care, quality education at all levels, career and vocational guidance, employment, remuneration, occupational health and safety, social security and public office.
5. Strengthening legal systems aimed at elimination of all forms of discrimination against women.
6. Changing societal attitudes and community practices by active participation and involvement of both men and women.
7. Mainstreaming a gender perspective in the development process.
8. Elimination of discrimination and all forms of violence against women and the girl child.
9. Building and strengthening partnerships with civil society, particularly women's organizations.

2.3 Laws Related to Dowry, Marriage and Divorce: These are the following:

2.3.1 Dowry Prohibition Act, 1961: An amendment brought in 1984 to the Dowry Prohibition Act of 1961 made women's subjection to cruelty a cognizable offence. The second amendment brought in 1986 makes the husband or in-laws punishable, if a woman commits suicide within 7 years of her marriage and it has been proved that she has been subjected to cruelty. Also a new criminal offence of *dowry death* has been incorporated in the Indian Penal Code.

2.3.2 Foreign Marriage Act, 1969: This is an Act to make provision relating to marriages of citizens of India outside India.

2.3.3 Special Marriage Act, 1954: The main reason behind passing this Act was to provide a special form of marriage for the people of India and all Indian nationals in foreign countries, irrespective of the religion or faith followed by either party. The enactment has the following 3 major objectives:

1. To provide a special form of marriage in certain cases.
2. To provide for registration of certain marriages.
3. To provide for divorce.

2.3.4 Christian Marriage Act, 1872: This Act governs the Christian law of marriage in India. Marriage, as is seen in Christian tradition, is not merely a civil contract nor is it purely a religious contract. It is seen as a contract according to the law of nature, antecedent to civil institutions and by itself an institution. A marriage among Christians is traditionally understood as the voluntary union for life of one man and one woman to the exclusion of all others, and Indian law follows suit, so that India does not allow for the possibility of same-sex marriage as it has been celebrated by some churches in other countries in recent years.

2.3.5 Hindu Marriage Act, 1955: Hindu Marriage Act of 1955 amended in 1976 provides the right for girls to repudiate a child marriage before attaining maturity whether the marriage has been consummated or not.

2.3.6 Prohibition of Child Marriage Act, 2006: Child Marriage Restraint Act of 1976 raised the age for marriage of a girl to 18 years from 15 years and that of a boy to 21 years and made offences under this Act cognizable. Child marriages in India have continued unabated despite the enactment of laws for its restraint and prohibition. Early marriages have adverse consequences on women's growth, health, livelihood options and negotiating power within marriages. In addition criminal provisions on kidnapping and abduction can also be used to penalize those involved in child marriages. The status of a child marriage, i.e. whether it is void or voidable, is governed by marriage laws that are applicable to different religious communities.

2.3.7 Marriage (Amendment) Act, 2001 amended the Hindu Marriage Act, Special Marriage Act, Parsi Marriage and Divorce Act, the Code of Criminal

Procedure providing for speedy disposal of applications for maintenance; the ceiling limit for claiming maintenance has been deleted and a wide discretion has been given to the Magistrate to award appropriate maintenance.

2.4 Laws Related to Right to Property

These are as follows:

2.4.1 Hindu Succession Act, 1956: This Act is a law that was passed by the Parliament of India in 1956 to amend and codify the law relating to intestate or unwilled succession, among Hindus. The Act lays down a uniform and comprehensive system of inheritance and applies to persons governed by both the Mitāk□arā and Dāyabhāga schools. It is hailed for its consolidation of Hindu laws on succession into one Act. The Hindu woman's limited estate is abolished by the Act. Any property possessed by a Hindu female is to be held by her absolute property and she is given full power to deal with it and dispose it of by will as she likes. The Act was amended in 2005 by the Hindu Succession (Amendment) Act, 2005.

2.4.2 Muslim Personal Law (Shariat) Application Act, 1937: This is an Act to make provision for the application of the Muslim Personal Law (Shariat) to Muslims.

2.5 Laws Related to Protection of and Crimes against Women

These are the following:

2.5.1 Crimes Identified under the Indian Penal Code (IPC):

1. Rape (Section 376 IPC).
2. Kidnapping and abduction for different purposes (Section 363-373 IPC).
3. Homicide for Dowry, Dowry Deaths or their attempts (Section 302/304-B of IPC).
4. Torture, both mental and physical (Section 498-A of IPC).
5. Molestation (Section 354 of IPC).
6. Sexual harassment (Section 509 of IPC) (referred to in the past as Eve teasing).
7. Importation of girls (up to 21 years of age) (Section 366-B of IPC).

2.5.2 Crimes Identified under the Special Laws

A. Protection from Domestic Violence Act, 2006: Domestic violence against women though pervasive is a largely invisible crime and goes unrecognized, especially since domestic violence is considered as a family matter having an unspoken sanction in patriarchal society. There is very little data on the extent of domestic violence.

Domestic Violence is a term that is difficult to define as the violence occurs against women in intimate relationships. A victim of domestic violence tends to shield the perpetrator of violence in keeping with her socio cultural psyche and value system.

In order to address the phenomenon of domestic violence, which is widely prevalent but remains largely invisible in the public domain, the Protection from Domestic Violence Act, 2006 was enacted by the Parliament. The Act envisages that the Protection Officer would assist the victim of domestic violence to be secure from violence and help her to access shelter homes, health care and legal advice. Harassment relating to dowry has also been covered under this Act.

If we are serious about substantially improving the economic status of poor women working in the informal sector of the economy, we have to devise concrete strategies, which can help to enhance the ownership of and control over productive assets of these women. Perhaps it will be the single most important intervention towards both their empowerment and economic well-being. Some of the assets that women can be given are a plot of land housing, tree pattas, joint ownership of all assets transferred by the State to the family, livestock license, bank accounts, membership of organizations and identity cards.

It would appear from the foregoing discussion that the improvement in the social and economic condition of women calls for fundamental changes in the law regarding the right to property of women generally, and widows in particular.

B. Commission of Sati (Prevention) Act, 1987: The aim of the Act is to protect the dignity of women and prevent violence against them as well as their exploitation.

C. Indecent Representation of Women (Prohibition) Act, 1986: The Act aims to protect the dignity of women and prevent violence against them as well as their exploitation.

D. Immoral Traffic (Prevention) Act, 1956: As amended and renamed in 1986, the Act makes the sexual exploitation of male or female, a cognizable offence. It is being amended to decriminalize the prostitutes and make the laws more stringent against traffickers.

E. Medical Termination Pregnancy Act, 1971: It legalises abortion by qualified professional on humanitarian or medical grounds. The maximum punishment may go up to life imprisonment. The Act has further been amended specifying the place and persons authorized to perform abortion and provide for penal actions against the unauthorized persons performing abortions.

F. Pre-Natal Diagnostic Techniques (Regulation and Prevention of Misuse) Act, 1994: The sex ratio in India has been unfavourable to girls. Legal action to stop female foeticide dates back to the enactment of this Act which was an attempt to reduce the imbalance in sex ratio. Keeping in view the emerging technologies, the Act was amended in 2002 to tighten enforcement.

G. Pre-conception and Prenatal Diagnostic Techniques (Prohibition of Sex Selection) Act, 2003: This Act has broadened the existing ban on sex determination to prompt the use of preconception and pre-implementation gene diagnosis and other technologies for sex selection. Use of ultrasound machines has been brought within the purview of this Act. Other new provisions include maintenance of written records of procedures carried out (not previously required) by doctors, and the vesting in state, district and sub district level authorities of powers equivalent to civil courts to ensure compliance with the law and to follow up reports on violation and misconduct.

Other relevant legislative enactments include amendment to the Medical Termination of Pregnancy Act 1971, (amended in 2002) which includes specific punishments for conduct of illegal abortions by unqualified persons and at places not approved by the concerned authority. Moreover, the authority has been decentralised to District Health Officers.

2.6 Laws Related to Protection of Rights of Working Women

See chapter 6 of this book.

2.7 Legal Aid Services

Guarantees of women's rights to equality can be realized only if women are encouraged to assert their rights in a court of law. In order to achieve this objective, there is need to ensure women's access to legal aid services. Article 39A of the Constitution of India provides that State shall secure that the operation of the legal system promotes justice on a basis of equal opportunity, and shall in particular, provide free legal aid, by suitable legislation or schemes or in any other way, to ensure that opportunities for securing justice are not denied to any citizen by reason of economic or other disability. Articles 14 and 22 (1) also make it obligatory for the State to ensure equality before law and a legal system which promotes justice on a basis of equal opportunity to all. Legal aid strives to ensure that constitutional pledge is fulfilled in its letter and spirit and equal justice is made available to the poor, downtrodden and weaker sections of the society.

2.7.1 Legal Services Authority Act, 1987: Section 12 of the Act includes women as a category eligible for free legal aid in its list of eligible persons. A nationwide network has been envisaged under the Act for providing legal aid and assistance. National Legal Services Authority is the apex body constituted to lay down policies and principles for making legal services available under the provisions of the Act and to frame most effective and economical schemes for legal services. It also disburses funds and grants to State Legal Services

Authorities and NGOs for implementing legal aid schemes and programmes. It also envisages legal service authorities to be constituted at every state, district and taluk levels. These authorities are supposed to give effect to the policies, directions and implement legal aid schemes in their respective areas.

Legal aid to a woman however still remains a distant dream in India. Further, even if a woman decides to approach the court, she is beset with many hurdles like the quality of legal aid, attitude of the implementing bodies and the lengthy period of judicial process.

2.8 Implementation of Women-related Legislations: A Critique

Though a large number of women-related legislations are in place, it is seen that the efficacy of these laws is not satisfactory primarily on account of poor implementation. A major reason for this is the lack of adequate knowledge regarding these special legislations and also absence of gender sensitivity on part of the functionaries such as police, prosecution, medical profession, judiciary etc. The Central and State Governments need to give a very high priority to training and capacity building of these stakeholders not only to educate them about the nuances of the laws but also to inculcate gender sensitivity in the system. The women themselves too need to be made aware of the special legislations that are available for their protection and rights. For this purpose, awareness generation and dissemination of information on a sustained basis is needed with special modules based on the region and group targets.

Thus, while there are a plethora of Acts existing for the protection and socio-economic equality of women, it is only through their effective implementation that women receive the intended benefits. However, gaps still remain and it is essential that specific laws are brought into effect which provide adequate safeguards and protection to women.

Although various provisions regarding employment have been outlined in Indian acts for the betterment and benefit of women, it remains to be seen whether these are being enforced effectively or are merely on paper. The findings of various studies have however, not been very encouraging.

Poor implementation of women-specific legislations does not mean that the conditions of women workers have not undergone any change since the early days of industrialisation. In urban areas and particularly in large factories and establishments women have better conditions and many of the welfare provisions are implemented. However, in rural areas and amongst unorganised workers, much remains to be done. Vigorous efforts by trade unions insisting on the enforcement of law and spreading legal literacy will go a long way towards improving the present conditions.

2.9 India's Commitments to International Conventions on Women Welfare

India has ratified various international conventions and human rights instruments committing to secure equal rights of women. Key among them is the ratification of the Convention on Elimination of All Forms of Discrimination against Women (CEDAW) in 1993. India has ratified the convention with two declaratory statements and one reservation.

Both the declarations relate to marriage. India has declared that the provisions on marriage and family relations in Article 16 (1) of the Convention would be ensured in conformity with its policy of non-interference in the personal affairs of any community without its initiative and consent and that while agreeing to the principle of compulsory registration of marriages, failure to get the marriage registered at the same time will not invalidate the marriage.

India did not agree to Article 29(1) of the Convention, which establishes compulsory arbitration or adjudication by the International Court of Justice of disputes concerning interpretation.

The Mexico Plan of Action (1975), the Nairobi Forward Looking Strategies (1985), the Beijing Declaration as well as the Platform for Action (1995) and the Outcome Document adopted by the UNGA Session on Gender Equality and Development & Peace for the 21st century, titled "Further actions and initiatives to implement the Beijing Declaration and the Platform for Action" have been unreservedly endorsed by India for appropriate follow up.

The Beijing Platform for Action lays down critical areas of concern for the women. The commitments made in the international conventions are as far as possible reflected in the Five Year Plan documents and the National Policy for the Empowerment of Women.

Eight Millennium Development Goals (MDGs) were established in the Millennium Declaration at the General Assembly of the United Nations in the year 2000. These include promoting gender equality and empowerment of women and improving maternal health. Though only these two are explicitly gender specific, gender equality is at the core of achievement of following MDGs:

1. Improving health and fighting disease.
2. Reducing poverty and mitigating hunger.
3. Expanding education and lowering child mortality.
4. Increasing access to safe water.
5. Ensuring environmental sustainability.

3

Institutional Mechanism for Advancement of Women

3.1 Components of Institutional Mechanism

Institutional mechanism for the advancement of women includes institutions of different types—Central, State and Local Governments, non-governmental organisations (NGOs), civil society and other bodies—which support the cause of women's advancement. The various institutional mechanisms that are contributing/will contribute to the achievement of women's empowerment and gender equality as laid down in the Eleventh Five Year Plan (2007-12) are listed below:

1. Government structures with a mandate for women advancement such as Ministries, Departments, focal points, bureaus, cells, desks, coordination units and committees, inter-agency committees etc.
2. Government-sponsored dedicated agencies for women, such as Commissions, Boards, Committees, Councils, Corporations, Women's Resource Centres, Women's Studies Centres, grass roots formations such as Mahila Mandals, Self-help Groups (SHGs) etc.
3. The Parliamentary Committees on the Empowerment of Women.
4. Institutions of local government such as the three-tiered panchayats and urban local bodies which are to be delegated vast administrative, financial and legal powers across the development sectors, including social and women's development.
5. Mechanisms and Plans such as gender budgets, component plans for women, action plans for women, monitoring and assessing instruments such as human development indices, audit systems such as gender and social audit, appraisals and evaluations using tools such as gender analysis, participatory exercises etc. To these can be added grassroots innovations capturing attention such as the Jansunwais (public hearings within an informal space) in the style of courts or other judicial bodies.
6. Women's bodies and groups working for the economic, social and political rights of women, all bearing the *voluntary* and *democratic* label, but with varying emphasis on different belief systems, ideologies and philosophies etc. ranging from academia, research, education, feminism, to action research and advocacy.
7. Federations, trade unions, cooperatives, youth and other age-based groups,

ad-hoc groups formed for short-term objectives, watchdog bodies, local groups etc.

3.2 Role of the Ministry of Women and Child Development (MWCD)

The history of the present Ministry of Women and Child Development—the nodal agency for welfare, development and empowerment of women—is also the history of how women as a specific group were viewed by the successive Governments. The subject of women, prior to 1986, was dealt with by the Ministry of Social Welfare. In the year 1986 a separate Department for Women and Children was constituted under the aegis of Ministry of Human Resource Development, primarily keeping in mind that women were valuable human resources and therefore deserved more focused attention. This also implied a subtle shift from *welfare* to *development* approach for these sections. In January 2006 the Department was elevated to the status of a full-fledged independent Ministry, thus implicitly bringing issues related to women into the forefront with greater focus and a larger mandate. It also meant that the MWCD would enhance its commitment to women through wider range of programmatic interventions and outlays, advocate gender mainstreaming of other sectors.

Due to the wide-ranging facets and nuances of the nature of women' empowerment, the programmatic interventions perforce cannot be restricted to any one particular sector or Ministry/Department. The responsibility has to be shared between sectors and between Ministries/Departments with adequate scope for convergence and inter-sectoral linkages. Thus, the role of MWCD includes policy formulation, conception of innovative programmes and their implementation, coordination with other sectors and State Governments, gender budgeting, training and capacity building, monitoring the status of women and their rights. This requires that appropriate institutional mechanisms are in place both in the MWCD, other sectoral ministries and the State Governments so that implementation, networking, coordination and convergence is possible.

3.3 Programmes/Schemes of the MWCD

The Ministry of Women and Child Development, as the nodal agency for all matters pertaining to welfare, development and empowerment of women, has evolved schemes and programmes for their benefit. These schemes are spread across a broader spectrum such as women's need for shelter, security, safety, legal aid, justice, information, maternal health, food, nutrition etc as well as their need for economic sustenance through skill development, education, and access to credit and marketing.

The schemes/programmes of the MWCD can broadly be categorized into (a) those that contribute to the economic empowerment of women, (b) those that provide rescue and shelter to women in need of care and protection and (c) those that provide gender justice and safeguard the rights of women.

3.3.1 *Swayamsiddha*: After the success of the pilot project *swa-shakti* under which more than 12,000 self-help groups were formed in 10 States, MWCD launched a new scheme *swayamsiddha* on November 29, 2001. This is the flagship scheme of MWCD for women for holistic economic empowerment. This is an integrated scheme for women empowerment through formation of self-help groups (SHGs). The long term objective of the programme is holistic empowerment of women through a sustained process of mobilization and convergence of all the on going sectoral programmes by improving access of women to micro-credit, economic resources, etc. This is a Centrally Sponsored Scheme. The Scheme has been able to provide a forum for women empowerment, collective reflection and united action. The programme is implemented in 650 blocks of the country. 67971 women SHGs have been formed benefiting 9,89,485 beneficiaries. The scheme came to an end in March 2007.

3.3.2 Support for Training and Employment Programme (STEP): This is a Central Scheme launched in 1987. It aims to raise the incomes of rural women by updating their skills in the traditional sectors, such as dairy development, animal husbandry sericulture, handloom and social forestry.

This programme seeks to provide skills and new knowledge to poor and assetless women in the traditional sectors. Under this project, women beneficiaries are organized into viable and cohesive groups or cooperatives. A comprehensive package of services such as health care, elementary education, crèche facility, market linkages etc. are provided besides access to credit. Skill development is provided in ten traditional skills amongst women.

3.3.3 Working Women Hostels and Crèches: In operation since 1972, this scheme provides grants for the construction and expansion of hostel buildings for working women. This scheme is in the nature of support system to help women in their struggle towards economic empowerment. Under the scheme, financial assistance is provided to NGOs, co-operative bodies and other agencies for construction/renting of buildings for working women hostels with day care centre for children to provide them safe and affordable accommodation. This is a central scheme.

The norms and financial pattern of assistance discourage the NGOs for construction of these hostels. At present, the norms are (a) availability of land in prime location so that they get sufficient number of working women, (b) 50 percent of the cost of land (the land has to be acquired before the proposal for the government grant is submitted) and 25 percent of the cost of construction has to be borne by the NGO, (c) construction of the hostel is required to be completed with in two years. Another issue needing review is the fixed percentage of trainees and students as a proportion to working women that is uniformly applicable across the country. There should be some flexibility especially for educationally backward states and regions, where rural girls are not able to find suitable accommodation when entering the portals of higher education.

The objective of the Scheme is to provide cheap and safe hostel accommodation to employment women living out of their homes. The target beneficiaries are single working women, widows, divorcee, separated and working women whose husbands are out of town. Women getting training for employment and girl students studying in post school professional courses are also to stay in the hostel.

3.3.4 Short Stay Homes for Women and Girls: These have been set up to provide shelter and care services for women in distress.

The Government of India launched a programme in 1969 in the Central Sector called the Short Stay Homes for Women and Girls to protect and rehabilitate those women and girls who are facing social and moral danger due to family problems, mental strains, social ostracism, exploitation or other causes. The services extended in these Homes include medical care, case work services, occupational therapy, education-cum-vocational training and recreational facilities.

The need for providing short stay homes for women and girls was felt due to the changing pattern of life, rapid urbanisation and industrialisation and the resulting migration from rural to urban areas. The break-up of social institutions like the joint family, contributes considerably in creating problems of adjustment for women and young girls. Cases of marital conflict and emotional disturbance occur. This effort is made to help the women to rehabilitate themselves within a short period of time. These short stay homes have been established by voluntary organisations.

There is also a provision for some increase in subsequent years on the component of rent and the maintenance cost for residents. Provisions have also been made for upgrading skills and capacities of staff and residents as well as education of the children of residents. The implementation of the scheme has been transferred to the states.

3.3.5 Swawlamban Programme: Swawlamban Programme, previously known as NORAD/Women's Economic Programme, was launched in 1982-83 with assistance from the Norwegian Agency for Development Co-operation (NORAD). NORAD assistance was availed till 1996-97 after which the programme is being run with funds from Government of India. The objective of the programme is to provide training and skills to women to facilitate them to obtain employment or self-employment on sustained basis. The target groups under the scheme are the poor and needy women, women from weaker sections of the society such as Scheduled Castes and Scheduled Tribes etc. In order to ensure more effective implementation and for better monitoring/evaluation of the scheme, it has been transferred to the State governments from 1st April 2006 with the approval of Planning Commission.

MWCD is also implementing a National Plan of Action for the rescue, rehabilitation and reintegration of women and girls trapped in commercial sex.

3.3.6 Swadhar: This Scheme was launched in 2001-2002 for providing relief and rehabilitation to women in difficult circumstances. The main objectives of the scheme are as follows:

1. To provide primary need of shelter, food, clothing and care to the marginalized women/ girls living in difficult circumstances who are without any social and economic support.
2. To provide emotional support and counselling to women.
3. To rehabilitate destitute women socially and economically through education, awareness, skill upgradation and personality development.
4. To arrange for specific clinical, legal and other support for women/girls in need of those interventions by linking and networking with other organizations in both Government and non-Government sectors on case to case basis.
5. To provide Helpline or other facilities.

Beneficiaries covered under the scheme are widows deserted by their families, women prisoners released form jail, women survivors of natural disaster, trafficked women, women victims of terrorist/extremist violence, mentally challenged, and women with HIV/AIDS etc. At present 170 shelter homes are functional in the country.

The number of homes currently functional in the country is grossly inadequate. The requirements of women being catered to by the scheme are different. The needs of mentally challenged women are quite different from that of women rescued from trafficking or women survivors of disasters. The recently introduced Protection of Women from Domestic Violence Act provides that women seeking shelter should be accommodated in the shelter homes. These call for increase in the number of shelter homes in the country. The root cause of most of problems being faced by women is lack of economic independence among women. Providing training and skills in various vocations to women living in shelter homes will facilitate them to obtain employment on sustained basis. Though the scheme in the current form provides for vocational training, no separate funds are being provided for the purpose.

3.3.7 Rajiv Gandhi National Crèche Scheme for Children of Working Mothers: Working women from the economically weaker sections are provided support services in terms of substitute care through crèches for children in the age group of 0-6 years. They are provided day care services, supplementary nutrition, health care services and early childhood education.

The scheme for the children of working mothers was revamped on January 1, 2006 and is being implemented by the Central Social Welfare Board (CSWB) with two national level voluntary organisations. The Scheme provides crèche services to children in age group of 0-6 years and includes supplementary nutrition, emergency medicines and contingencies.

The combined monthly income of both the parents should not exceed ₹ 12,000 for availing of the facilities.

3.4 Compensation to Rape Victims

The Supreme Court in Delhi Domestic Working Women's Forum vs. Union of India and others writ petition (CRL) No. 362/93 had directed the National Commission for Women to evolve a "scheme so as to wipe out the tears of unfortunate victims of rape." The Supreme Court observed that having regard to the Directive principles contained in the Article 38(1) of the Constitution, it was necessary to set up Criminal Injuries Compensation Board, as rape victims besides the mental anguish, frequently incur substantial financial loss and in some cases are too traumatized to continue in employment.

The Court further directed that compensation for victims shall be awarded by the Court on conviction of the offender and by the Criminal Injuries Compensation Board whether or not a conviction has taken place. The Board shall take into account pain, suffering and shock as well as loss of earnings due to pregnancy and the expenses of child birth if this occurs as a result of rape. Accordingly NCW has drafted a scheme titled "Relief to and Rehabilitation of Rape Victims".

3.5 Protection of Women from Domestic Violence Act (PWDVA), 2006

In order to address the phenomenon of domestic violence, which is widely prevalent but remains largely invisible in the public domain, PWDVA, 2006 was enacted by the Parliament. The Act envisages that the Protection Officer would assist the victim of domestic violence to be secure from violence and help her to access shelter homes, health care and legal advice.

In the Eleventh Plan, it is proposed to take up the following for effective implementation of the PWDVA:

1. Set up the required infrastructure and requirements to make the Act effective.
2. Provide training, sensitization and capacity building of Protection Officers, Service Providers, members of the judiciary, police, medical professionals, counsellors, lawyers, etc on the issue of domestic violence and the use of law (PWDVA and other criminal and civil laws) to redress the same.
3. Monitoring the appointment of Protection Officers by regular feedback from the various states.
4. Set up an effective MIS to monitor its implementation.
5. Give wide publicity to the Act.

A number of women specific and women related laws have been enacted to protect them from social discrimination and to give them equal opportunity. Ministry of Women and Child Development is the administrative ministry for implementation of many of these Acts like Commission of Sati (Prevention) Act, Dowry Prohibition Act, Indecent Representation of Women (Prohibition) Act, Immoral Traffic Prevention Act and Protection of Women from Domestic Violence Act. In spite of some of these Acts being in place since a long time, these crimes against women continue unabated. Implementation of these Acts is very poor. The knowledge about the existence of these Acts is also very low among the public and other stake holders. Similarly, though the country is a signatory to the UN convention on elimination of discrimination against women and the convention was ratified as long back as in 1992, its dissemination has been very poor.

Further, to achieve gender equality and to stop crime against women, what is needed is a change in the people's attitude, both of men and women. Having any number of legislations, policies and programmes will not take us towards the desired goals unless the thinking, perception and attitude of the society changes.

Bringing about attitudinal change in the society as well as dissemination about the laws, policies, programmes etc of the Government can be achieved only through an effective multi-media publicity campaign through electronic media, print media and outdoor publicity tools.

3.6 Autonomous Organisations under MWCD

MWCD has 4 autonomous organizations, viz. National Institute of Public Cooperation and Child Development (NIPCCD), Rashtriya Mahila Kosh (RMK), Central Social Welfare Board (CSWB) and Central Adoption Resource Agency (CARA) working under its aegis. NIPCCD, RMK and CARA are societies registered under the Societies Registration Act, 1860. CSWB is a charitable company registered under section 25 of the Indian Companies Act, 1956. These organizations are fully funded by the Government of India and they assist the Ministry in its functions including implementation of programmes/schemes. In addition to these, National Commission for Women was constituted as a national apex statutory body in 1992 for protecting and safeguarding the rights of women. Similarly, National Commission for Protection of Child Rights (NCPCR) was set up in 2007 to protect and safeguard the rights of children.

3.6.1 National Institute of Public Cooperation and Child Development (NIPCCD): NIPCCD is a successor to the Central Institute of Research and Training in Public Cooperation which was sponsored by the Planning Commission and registered under the Societies Registration Act, 1860 as an autonomous organisation on February 28, 1966. NIPCCD functions under the aegis of the Department of Women and Child Development with its Headquarters in New Delhi.

The objectives of NIPCCD are to (a) develop and promote voluntary action in social development, (b) take a comprehensive view of child development and develop and promote programmes in pursuance of the National Policy for Children, (c) develop measures for coordination of governmental and voluntary action in social development and (d) evolve framework and perspective for organising children's programmes through governmental and voluntary efforts.

With a view to achieving the above objectives, NIPCCD (a) organises training programmes, seminars, workshops, conferences, (b) conducts research and evaluation studies and (c) provides documentation and information services in the field of public cooperation and child development. NIPCCD is the apex body for training of functionaries of the Integrated Child Development Services (ICDS) programme. It provides technical advice and consultancy to government and voluntary agencies in promoting and implementing policies and programmes for child development and voluntary action. In addition, it collaborates with regional and international agencies, research institutions, universities and technical bodies.

3.6.2 Rashtriya Mahila Kosh (RMK): RMK was established in 1993 to provide micro-credit in a quasi-formal manner to the poor women for income generating, production, skill development and housing activities in order to make them economically independent. RMK mainly channelises its support through NGOs, Voluntary agencies, States Women Development Corporations, Cooperative societies, State government agencies, Urban Women Co-op Banks etc. to the women SHGs. It is an innovative mechanism for reaching credit to poor women. Through access to credit, it aims to raise the capacity of women by enhancing through productivity and economic self-reliance.

3.6.3 Central Social Welfare Board (CSWB): CSWB was set up on 12th August 1953 by a Resolution of Government of India to act as an apex body at national level for welfare and development of women and children. State Social Welfare Boards were established in 1954 in all State capitals to support CSWB in achieving its objectives.

3.6.4 Central Adoption Resource Agency (CARA): CARA has initiated various steps for the promotion of in-country adoption. These include strengthening the Voluntary Coordinating Agencies (VCAs) by providing them grants-in-aid.

3.6.5 National Commission for Women (NCW): NCW was set up in 1992 to protect and safeguard the rights of women. The activities of the Commission include receiving complaints or suo moto enquiring in cases of deprivation of rights of women, providing counselling, conducting Parivarik Lok Adalats and legal awareness programmes and organising public hearings.

NCW being the nodal agency for protection of the rights of women needs to be strengthened. The NCW Act needs to be suitably amended to give the Commission more power.

NCW, a statutory body, set up under the National Commission for Women Act, 1990 has a mandate to safeguard the rights and interests of women. The Commission pursues its mandated activities, namely review of laws, interventions into specific individual complaints of atrocities and remedial action to safeguard the interests of women, whatever appropriate and feasible. The Commission has accorded highest priority to securing speedy justice to women.

The Commission has been instrumental in introducing fresh ideas, innovative model, training, packages, model for speedy justice etc. The Commission has, before it, apart from looking into the law and legislation for effecting improvement to ensure speedy justice, thrust areas in the realm of:

1. Organising through NGOs Parivarik Mahila Lok Adalats throughout the length and breadth of the country on a continuous basis;
2. Launching of programmes on legal awareness;
3. Sensitisation programmes for police, NGOs, officials for better implementation of safeguards and laws for the benefit of women;
4. Release and rehabilitation of women prisoners;
5. Rehabilitation of prostitutes and their children;
6. Rehabilitation of widows and land support to anti arrack movement;
7. Custodial justice for women prisoners;
8. Participation of women in the electoral process;
9. Issue of violence on women;
10. *Dahej Mukti Abhiyan*;

11. Technological empowerment of women in agriculture;
12. Rights of minority women.

The Commission maintains the Complaints Cell/counselling Cell which is a Core Unit of the Commission and processes various categories of written/oral complaints and also take suo-moto notice of matters relating to deprivation of women's rights, non implement of laws enacted to provide protection to women, non compliance of policy decisions, guidelines or instructions aimed at mitigating hardships to women and taking up issues arising out of such matters with appropriate authorities. The complaints received relate to harassment for dowry, dowry deaths, torture, desertion, bigamy, rape, refusal to register FIR by the police, discrimination in employment, domestic violence, incest and cruelty by husbands and in-laws.

3.6.6 National Commission for Protection of Child Rights (NCPCR): As envisaged in the Commission for Protection of Child Rights Act 2005, notified in the Gazette of India on January 20, 2006 as Act No. 4 of 2006, the Government set up NCPCR with effect from March 5, 2007.

The women's movements and a wide-spread network of non-government organisations (NGOs)—which have strong grassroots presence and deep insight into women's concerns)—have contributed in inspiring initiatives for the empowerment of women. However, there still exists a wide gap between the goals enunciated in the Constitution, legislations, policies, plans, programmes and related mechanisms on the one hand and the situational reality of the status of women in India, on the other.

Gender disparity manifests itself in various forms, the most obvious being the trend of continuously declining female ratio in the population in the last few decades. Social stereotyping and violence at the domestic and societal levels are some of the other manifestations. Discrimination against girl children, adolescent girls and women persists in parts of the country. The underlying causes of gender inequality are related to social and economic structure, which is based on informal and formal norms, and practices. Consequently, the access of women)—particularly those belonging to weaker sections including Scheduled Castes/Scheduled Tribes/Other backward Classes and minorities, majority of whom are in the rural areas and in the informal, unorganized sector)—to education, health and productive resources, among others, is inadequate. Therefore, they remain largely marginalized, poor and socially excluded.

4

Categorisation of Vulnerable Groups of Women

Polices, programmes and schemes for women are generally formulated as if they are comprised of one composite and homogenous group. In reality, there are many layers of heterogonous groups of women with differing degrees of vulnerabilities, depending on their socio-economic and geo-political backgrounds. Therefore, specific strategies and programmes need to be developed to address the unique problems of specific groups.

Amongst vulnerable groups, the women belonging to socially backward communities—such as Scheduled Castes (SCs), Scheduled Tribes (STs) and Other Backward Classes (OBCs)—face double discrimination of being a woman and also from a backward community. Similarly women with disabilities have specific problems even when compared to men with disability. There are women who are victims of violence or sexual abuse such as trafficked women, rape victims who need a very different but specialized rehabilitation package. Adolescent girls are a highly vulnerable group as they are subject to a number of atrocities like trafficking, rape, and child marriage. Child marriages are increasingly taking place and witch hunting is now increasingly linked not only to women's property rights but also to bigamy. Non-participation in the traditional decision-making forums, increase in the incidence of alcoholism and the resulting domestic violence are other problems of women.

The following illustrates a list of categories of women who are in difficult circumstances. These categories of women find themselves more vulnerable on account of their unique social, cultural circumstances or because they are victims of violence or abuse. These groups require special interventions to address their needs. The possibility of developing pilot projects suitably formulated to address specific requirements may be examined.

4.1 Women Impacted by Internal Displacement, Disasters and Migration

4.1.1 Women Affected by Internal Displacements: There are problems associated with displacement caused by the introduction of huge development projects—like dams and special economic zones (SEZs)—in tribal and rural areas. Women have taken part in many of the agitations surrounding these projects. The loss of livelihoods has led to tribal women's increasing dependence on migration. Their work load has increased with the loss of traditional rights.

They are also subjected to sexual violence, exploitation and trafficking. They are in conflict with many powers and interests, ranging from the state agencies to builders and landlords.

4.1.2 Disaster-affected Women: Experiences have shown that effects of disasters (floods, droughts, riots) are profoundly discriminatory. Wherever they hit, pre-existing structures and social conditions determine that some members of the community pay a higher price. Among the differences that determine how people are affected by such disasters is that of gender. Lower status of women in general results in various kinds of exclusions and vulnerabilities in a disaster setting. Low mobility and lower access to information implies that women are often the last to receive relief resources. Women are disproportionately represented within the informal and agricultural sectors, which are the most adversely affected by disasters. This adversely affects their claim to relief and rehabilitation. Thus, women experience high rates of unemployment, further decreasing their bargaining power within households and communities. Unlike men, they are the primary household caretakers and thus are not able to migrate for work. All these factors involving structural biases and gender discrimination result in the compensation amounts awarded being directed invariably at men.

Furthermore, domestic violence against women sharply increases after disasters and women face additional kinds of physical and sexual violence in relief camps. Disasters in which men die or migrate or are injured, women are left to lead households and communities, with few marketable skills and opportunities and even more vulnerability to violence and extortion. Women take on the responsibility for both caring for families and meeting livelihoods while having the least access to information, resources and opportunities.

Disasters create the potential to engage in longer-term rights and equity-based development through practical strategies for gender empowerment. Successfully incorporating women within disaster management is one way to increase women's social, political and economic status in general, and to minimize the currently disproportionate impact of disasters on women. Strengthening the marketable skills of women, promoting livelihood options, enhancing women's leadership in micro-planning, relief and disaster mitigation and increasing their role in local governance are some of the strategies for adoption.

Practically, women have immense knowledge of their local environments and information about how to mitigate risks that lead to disasters. This knowledge can be transformed into actionable expertise by involving women within disaster management. Furthermore, women are the most effective in mobilizing communities, networks and institutions to pool resources, respond to disaster and create safety mechanisms. Women are also most knowledgeable about those living within their communities, in terms of identifying marginalized groups and community trends.

Thus, a gender perspective must be incorporated whenever disaster prevention, mitigation and recovery strategies are being developed and implemented.

4.1.3 Migrant Women: Internal short-term migration for work (which may be seasonal) is now a widespread feature of rural India and reflects the continuing crisis of inadequate livelihood opportunities in rural areas. Increasingly, women are moving for work, not only with husbands or male members of families, but even on their own or in groups in search of work. Since the consequences of such migration are highly gendered, policies generating greater and more prolonged job opportunities for men and women within particular rural areas must be considered.

The migrant labourers generally work at whatever they can find, mostly contract work or casual work. The condition of migrant workers away from their homes is often pitiable. They get paid very less. They do not have access to clean water, sanitation, healthcare, public distribution system and have to buy their essentials at open market prices. Their children travel around with them and do not get education.

A. Impact of Male Migration on Women: Male out-migration, when the families are left behind, affects the work burden of the women in rural areas. Women have to put in extraordinary amount of time to eke out a living, working in the field for wages or for subsistence, in addition to fetching fuel and fodder. The absence of men adds to material and psychological insecurity, leading to pressures and negotiations with wider family. Women may have to cope with a number of problems which are exacerbated due to the uncertainty of the timing and magnitude of remittances on which the precarious household economy depends. This, in turn, pushes women and children from poor labouring households to participate in the labour market under adverse conditions. The impact of male migration can be especially adverse for girls who often have to bear additional domestic responsibilities and take care of younger siblings. The absence of male supervision further reduces their chances of acquiring education. Incidence of women-headed households may also increase and it is to be noted that female-headed households are generally poorer than male-headed households.

The wages of the migrant husbands are either too infrequent or insufficient for constant sustenance of the family left behind. In fact, it is the free and hard work of women in sustaining the domestic economy, which helps to keep a large number of men working in town and cities at extremely low wages. Mobility and migration of workers make them more vulnerable, as a result of separation from spouse and release of social sanctions leading to high-risk sexual practices and consequently may contract HIV, which in turn is carried to their spouses and to their children. Public policy with respect to migration should cover issues affecting households of migrant workers, who are left without adult caregivers. It should also cover issues of protection and basic needs of migrant workers at their destination. Since women migrant workers face much greater threats to security and possibilities of violence, special measures should address this problem.

4.2 Women with Health Problems

4.2.1 Women Affected by HIV/AIDS: The rapid progression of the HIV/AIDS pandemic, particularly in the developing world, has had a devastating impact on women. Responsible behaviour and gender equality are among the important prerequisites for its prevention. There is also the need for more effective strategies to empower women to have control over and decide freely and responsibly on matters related to their sexuality, to protect themselves from high risk and irresponsible behaviour leading to sexually transmitted infections including HIV/AIDS and to promote responsible, safe and respectful behaviour by men and to also promote gender equality.

The burden of care for people living with HIV/AIDS and for children orphaned by HIV/AIDS falls particularly on women, as infrastructures are inadequate to respond to the challenges being posed. Women with HIV/AIDS often suffer from discrimination and a stigma and are often victims of violence.

4.2.2 Women with Disability: The 2001 Census estimated that there were over 9 million women with disabilities in India constituting 3.5 percent of the population. The majority of women with disabilities in India suffer the *triple discrimination of being female, being disabled and being poor*. Indeed not only are they a socially invisible category but their plight is worse than both men with disabilities and other non-disabled women.

While being a man and being disabled are very incongruous, being female and being disabled also implies a certain level of continuity as both are to varying degrees associated with notions of weakness, passivity and dependence. But the likeness is only superficial because a disabled woman is also considered incapable of fulfilling the normative feminine roles of homemaker, wife and mother. Then, she also does not fit the stereotype of the normal woman in terms of physical appearance. Since women embody family honour, disabled girls are kept hidden at home by families and denied basic rights to mobility, education and employment. They are less likely to be given in marriage than disabled men.

Doubts around the capacity of women with disabilities to be sexual partners, homemakers and mothers abound. They are not considered capable of performing household chores efficiently, having meaningful sexual relationships or producing and rearing healthy children. Under these circumstances, they may be married off to older already married or men in poor health. In short, women with disabilities do not have the same options of marriage and motherhood as non-disabled women.

Women with disabilities face violations of their rights at every level. They are considered a financial burden and social liability by their families; they are denied opportunities to movement outside the home and access to education; they are viewed as asexual, helpless and dependant; their vulnerability to physical, sexual and emotional abuse is enormous; their aspirations for marriage and parenthood often denied; they grow up ensconced with the walls of home or special institutions isolated and neglected with no hope of a normal life.

A. Elderly Women with Disabilities: Needs of elderly women with disabilities—many of whom may be widows—deserve special mention. The combination of physical/mental disability and widowhood raises the spectre of a very precarious existence. Being powerless, isolated and anonymous women with disabilities are extremely vulnerable to abuse and violence. In addition, care-giving involving activities of daily living like dressing, eating and other bodily activities renders the disabled woman more vulnerable to abuse both at home and in institutions. She will be less able to defend herself in a risky situation because she may not be able to run or scream for help. Then, persons with developmental disabilities may be too trusting of others and hence may be easier to trick, bribe or coerce. They may not understand differences between sexual and non-sexual tactile behaviour. Persons with speech and hearing difficulties may have limited communication skills to report abuse. Furthermore since disabled persons are often taught to be obedient, passive and control their behaviour, this will render them easy victims.

Although a rights-based approach has entered the disability rights movement, the specific concerns of women with disabilities have found a place neither in the government policies and programmes nor the voluntary sector. Ironically or expectedly, the disabled rights movement all over the world including India is male dominated. It may even be blatantly sexist. Even within the women's movement, women with disabilities rarely figure as a distinct group.

4.3 Women in Border Trade Areas

Women are the most vulnerable section of society in border trade centres and areas—which are adjacent to international borders and normally a *no-man's land*

—controlled by anti-social elements and organizations that are inimical to the interests of the country. Under the circumstances, women, who are the major component in border trades, especially in agriculture and allied activities, are under severe threat. Matters are compounded by problems of infrastructure and facilities, which are either most rudimentary or simply do not exist. Access to health, education, drinking water, and sanitation is almost impossible, which adversely affect health.

Border trade centres/areas—besides normally being hot beds of smuggling, particularly of narcotics—are also centres of trafficking of women and children. Women are rendered vulnerable to all kinds of diseases, especially HIV/AIDS. Women are also used or forced into smuggling of narcotics, which makes them further vulnerable to law-enforcing agencies that are not sensitized to dealing with women law-breakers. The circle gets more vicious for women in these areas, many of whom are either illiterate or have received only rudimentary education and cannot be expected to be aware of their fundamental, human, legal and other rights. Problems of communication, organized marketing and non-implementation of labour laws also adversely affect women's economic power, which in turn reinforces them to play subservient roles and their empowerment continues to remain illusionary and elusive.

It is therefore necessary that some mechanism is set-up in border trade centres and areas to enforce the law of the land, as also to implement and monitor all fundamental, human, legal and other rights to ensure that no citizen of this country is denied and deprived of them.

Enhancing the utilization of the region's local and rich natural resources with appropriate technology for producing and marketing herbal products and processed food/fruits is another avenue to meet with the challenge posed by anti-social elements. Cold storages can be located in appropriate areas of the region, to sustain perishable items before they are transported to larger markets.

4.4 Women Left Behind due to Suicide by Farmer Husbands

Another highly vulnerable group are women who are left behind to take care of their children when their farmer husbands commit suicide on account of failure of crops or heavy indebtedness. These women face a whole host of problems –the possibility that they may not inherit the land holding; even if they did, they may not have the wherewithal to till the land as they do not have the necessary resources or access to credit, seeds, fertilizers etc. The problem of inheriting debts which cannot be repaid may lead to distress sale of land without alternative livelihood options. The possibility of these women and their children being exploited or trafficked for nefarious purposes is very probable. There is an immediate need to develop a special package for women whose farmer husbands have committed suicide. The package should contain a comprehensive input of programmes of various sectors like agriculture, rural development, rural industries along with adequate support from micro credit facilities.

4.5 Other Vulnerable Groups of Women

4.5.1 Adolescent Girls: Adolescent girls are one of the most vulnerable sections of society as they are subject to a number of problems:

1. Discrimination in terms of nutrition and food (malnutrition and anaemia rates for adolescents are quite significant).
2. School drop out.
3. Forced into sibling care.
4. Households work or even farm labour.
5. Domestic labour.
6. Trafficked for sexual exploitation.
7. Subjected to child marriages.
8. Frequent child bearing etc.

This is also the period during which girls can be truly empowered to make life-changing decisions and chart the course of their life in a most productive way. At present the programmatic interventions for adolescent girls are limited and sporadic and do not address the needs and requirements as an integrated whole. It is necessary to draw up a special package for their development which will take into account inter sectoral inputs.

4.5.2 Violence-affected Women:

1. Women who are victims of domestic violence.
2. Rape victims.
3. Trafficked-victim women.
4. Women who are labelled as witches.
5. Women who are victims of acid attacks.

4.5.3 Women as Labourers:

1. Women who work as domestic help.
2. Women who are bonded labour.
3. Destitute women who are homeless.

4.5.4 Women in Agriculture:

1. Landless women.
2. Marginal women farmers.
3. Women who work as agricultural workers.

4.5.6 Women from Minority Community: The main issues of Muslim minority women stem from three major factors: (a) insecurity, (b) exclusion and

(c) poverty.

4.5.7 Single Women:

1. Adolescents.
2. Widows.
3. Women whose husbands are absent due to conflict, economic migration etc.
4. Divorcees.

4.5.8 Others

1. Women in Border Trade Areas.
2. Slum dwellers.
3. Women prisoners.
4. Women belonging to ethnic and religious minorities (especially Muslims).

4.6 The *Missing* Girl Child

This group consists of the unborn girl children in their mothers' wombs, who are deliberately disposed of (in contravention of existing laws) before birth only because they are female. Their disposal is an instance of the most extreme instance of gender discrimination, (forbidden both by domestic and international laws and conventions), but seldom regarded as such, it being more commonly referred to as a social issue.

The burgeoning size of this *missing* group is now receiving attention as a factor crucial to the health of the social fabric and to the well-being of communities. The high numbers of missing girls seriously affect the status of the living girls and women and their prospects for a safe and secure life. Less realized is the strong possibility that increasing numbers of 'missing' girl children are also inimical to the safety and health (including mental and psychological health) of mothers. Repeated abortions weaken the reproductive health system and increase the risk of infections.

Women from lower socio-economic strata are also being trafficked from *supply centres* (e.g. Kerala) to *demand centres* (e.g. Haryana) to make up for the deficit of females in the marriageable age groups. All such women are treated as merchandise, as *inferior* wives and many of them are abandoned as soon they carry out their apportioned task of giving birth to children.

In *deficit areas*, there is also some evidence emerging of increased surveillance over young girls and their physical movements at the village and local level, by traditional male-dominated councils such as the khap panchayats. The incidence of violence against women is on the rise, giving the lie to the myth that lesser numbers of women means better and more humane treatment, resulting in higher status.

Factors responsible for female feticide are many, complex and interlinking. A succinct summarization is given below:

1. Obsession to have a son.
2. Discrimination against the girl child.
3. Socio-economic and physical insecurity of women.
4. Evil of dowry prevalent in our society.
5. Worry about getting girls married as there is the stigma attached to being an unmarried woman.
6. Easily accessible and affordable procedures for sex selection during pregnancy.
7. Failure of medical ethics.
8. Two-child norm policy of certain State Governments.

The two-child norm implies that the State promotes two children per family and has a system of incentives and disincentives/punishments for achieving it. A two child norm has the potential to cause immense harm to women's health in the existing social situation where son preference is high and women's status is very low. One of the gravest risks includes increase in sex selective abortion and consequent reduction in the numbers of girl children. The compulsion to have no more than two children would result in increased female feticide. This happened in China when Government declared that no couple should have more than one child. There are lessons to be learnt from the Chinese experience.

There are two important issues of policy associated with the decline in the child sex ratio. One is the obsession with population control, which assumes that all the failures in development can be linked to population explosion. The other more recent issue is the intrusion of the two-child norm into the Panchayati Raj Acts of many States, leading to disqualification of many elected representatives. Most of the excluded belong to the SCs and STs. Some experts have suggested a link between the imposition of the two-child norm and sex selective abortions. Imposition of the two-child norm then cannot be the route to population stabilization, for it may lead to a disturbingly unbalanced population.

Women are victims of iniquitous gender relationships. If they fail to produce sons, they face desertion, humiliation and witch hunts. Yet, they are also deemed to be the wrong doers when they attempt to dispose of the female children in the foetal stage or in infancy. In almost all cases, this action is collaborative, taken in consultation with other family members, both male and female. In certain parts of the country, women are punished under the law for committing female infanticide and are imprisoned. The compulsions behind these acts by the women can be imagined. The act of giving birth to girls becomes a justified ground for abandonment of the mothers. In some cases, the *guilty* women themselves, opt out of the marriage, locating a sister or any close relation or a stranger to take her place, who would produce a child of the *right* gender.

Within the Government of India's Rules of Business, subjects such as women's physical and mental health, sex ratios, the two child norm, violence against women, population control and stabilization programs, trafficking and prostitution, child health and nutrition, abortion rights, female feticide, child survival etc. do not fall neatly into the purview of one or the other government ministries or departments. A number of agencies (both at the central and state level) are responsible for these and other allied subjects. It is difficult to fix accountability for the safe survival, healthy development and well being of the girl child and the mother at a single point. Inter-agency coordination is the mechanism that is conventionally resorted to; yet, inter-agency coordination has been one of the weakest links in government working, where the system tends to function in hierarchies, leaving little space for lateral thinking or action. Plans of action for the girl child at national and regional levels, in which effective level coordination has been the key requirement, have therefore not been either successful or effective.

The entity of Girl Child was brought into public focus only since the late 1980s. Prior to this, a *gendered* view of childhood was seldom taken. Public agencies and most child lobbies saw childhood for both boys and girls as a uniformly vulnerable and critical period, when children needed the same levels and types of services such as nutrition, health care, education, cognitive stimulation, shelter, play opportunities etc. This general, non-gendered view remained predominant, even though data collected by researchers from the field did show that girls had less access to breast milk and were less often likely to be taken to public hospitals when ill as compared to boys.

Similarly, the girl child tended to remain invisible in the eyes of women's rights groups and women's development agencies. Here, the tendency was to identify *women* only in terms of adult age groups and to deal with patriarchal oppression and exploitation of women who had reached the child bearing age. In other words, the girl child fell between the two stools of age and gender and remained submerged. There were no separate planning provisions for the girl child either amongst children or amongst women. The gendered links with childhood or womanhood were also not apparent.

From the 1990s, MWCD has included the girl child on its agenda and in its programming and budget allocations. It has accepted that discrimination against the girl child is not merely a result of poverty and illiteracy, but is rooted in traditionally ingrained attitudes and mindset. The perspective that is now needed has to be a much larger one and has to take on board not only State Governments, but other organizations such as local bodies, media, medical doctors and lawyers etc. Also, MWCD has to play a continuous gender monitoring and auditing role in terms of keeping in touch with the field on the repercussions of coercive polices such as the two child norm and incentives and disincentives being offered by several State Governments in favour of this norm.

To sum up, women are not homogenous categories. They belong to diverse castes, classes, communities, economic groups, and are located within a range of geographic and development zones. Consequently, some groups are more vulnerable than others. Mapping and addressing the specific deprivations that arise from these multiple locations is essential for the success of planned interventions. Thus, apart from the general programme interventions, special targeted interventions, catering to the differential needs of these groups, should be undertaken.

5

National Policy for Empowerment of Women (NPEW), 2001

Progress towards gender equality and women's empowerment in India has been built upon strong commitments by the government and unflagging effort by the women's movement. India's commitment to gender equality is further evidenced by the fact that it is a signatory to Convention on the Elimination of All Forms of Discrimination against Women (CEDAW), which was ratified on June 25, 1993 (with one reservation and two declaratory statements). India is also a signatory to the Convention on the Rights of the Child. The first report to the UN Committee of Experts on the Rights of the Child was submitted in 2000 and the second report in 2004.

In pursuance of the avowed objective of empowering the *women* as agents of socio-economic change, the National Policy on Empowerment of Women was adopted in April 2001. Gender inequality arising out of social norms and cultural traditions has been addressed through a range of direct and indirect measures, and the aim of the NPEW has been to bring about social change—changes in attitudes towards women, and women's empowerment. The policy itself reflects the aspirations of women and the women's movement. The effort is to bring gender justice and make *de jure* equality into *de facto* equality. Several State Governments have also formulated a policy for women's empowerment.

On the basis of NPEW, the National Plan of Action is being implemented which includes the following strategies:

1. To create an enabling environment for women to exercise their rights both within and outside their homes.
2. To reserve one-third of seats for women in the Lok Sabha and State Legislative Assemblies.
3. To adopt a special strategy for Women Component Plan to ensure that at least 30 per cent of funds and benefits flow to women from all development sectors.
4. To organize women in self-help groups as a mark of the beginning of empowering them.
5. To accord high priority and ensure easy access to maternal and child health services.

6. To initiate steps for eliminating gender bias in all educational programmes; further to institute plans for free education of girls up to college levels including professional levels.
7. To equip women with necessary skills in modern upcoming trades which would make them economically independent and self-reliant.
8. To increase women's access to credit through setting up of Development Bank for women entrepreneurs in small and tiny sectors.

Various aspects of NPEW are as under.

5.1 Introduction

The principle of gender equality is enshrined in the Indian Constitution in its Preamble, Fundamental Rights, Fundamental Duties and Directive Principles of State Policy. The Constitution not only grants equality to women, but also empowers the State to adopt measures of positive discrimination in favour of women. Since Independence in 1947, there has been a marked shift in the approach to issues related to welfare, development and empowerment of women. Within the framework of a democratic polity, India's laws, development policies, schemes/programmes under Five Year Plans have aimed at advancement of women in different spheres. In recent years, the empowerment of women has been recognized as the central issue in determining the status of women. The National Commission for Women was set up by an Act of Parliament in 1990 to safeguard the rights and legal entitlements of women. The 73rd and 74th Amendments to the Constitution of India provided for reservation of seats for women in panchayats and municipalities, laying a strong foundation for their participation in decision-making at the local levels.

India has also ratified various international conventions and human rights instruments committing to secure equal rights for women. Key among them is the ratification of the Convention on Elimination of All Forms of Discrimination against Women (CEDAW) in 1993.

The Mexico Plan of Action (1975), the Nairobi Forward Looking Strategies (1985), the Beijing Declaration as well as the Platform for Action (1995) and the Outcome Document—adopted by the General Assembly Session of the United Nations on Gender Equality and Development and Peace for the 21st Century—titled "Further Actions and Initiatives to Implement the Beijing Declaration and the Platform for Action" have been unreservedly endorsed by India for appropriate follow up.

5.2 Objectives of the Policy

National Policy for Empowerment of Women, 2001 was formulated for bringing about advancement, development and empowerment of women in all spheres of life through creation of a more responsive judicial and legal system sensitive to women and mainstreaming a gender perspective in the development process. The strengthening and formation of relevant institutional mechanisms and implementation of international obligations/commitments and co-operation at the international, regional and sub-regional level was another commitment.

The primary objective of NPEW was to bring about the advancement, development and empowerment of women. Specifically, the objectives of this Policy included the following:

1. Creating an environment through positive economic and social policies for full development of women to enable them to realize their full potential.
2. The *de-jure* and *de-facto* enjoyment of all human rights and fundamental freedom by women on equal basis with men in all spheres—political, economic, social, cultural and civil.
3. Equal access to participation and decision-making of women in social, political and economic life of the nation.
4. Equal access to women to healthcare, quality education at all levels, career and vocational guidance, employment, equal remuneration, occupational health and safety, social security and public office etc.
5. Strengthening legal systems aimed at elimination of all forms of discrimination against women.
6. Changing societal attitudes and community practices by active participation and involvement of both men and women.
7. Mainstreaming a gender perspective in the development process.
8. Elimination of discrimination and all forms of violence against women and the girl child.
9. Building and strengthening partnerships with civil society, particularly women's organizations.

5.3 Various Elements of NPEW

5.3.1 Politico-legal Empowerment of Women

A. Legal-Judicial System: Legal-judicial system would be made more responsive and gender sensitive to women's needs, especially in cases of domestic violence and personal assault. New laws would be enacted and existing laws reviewed to ensure that justice is quick and the punishment meted out to the culprits is commensurate with the severity of the offence.

At the initiative of and with the full participation of all stakeholders including community and religious leaders, NPEW would aim to encourage changes in personal laws such as those related to marriage, divorce, maintenance and guardianship so as to eliminate discrimination against women.

The evolution of property rights in a patriarchal system has contributed to the subordinate status of women. NPEW would aim to encourage changes in laws relating to ownership of property and inheritance by evolving consensus in order to make them gender just.

B. Decision-making: Women's equality in power sharing and active participation in decision making, including decision-making in political process at all levels would be ensured for the achievement of the goals of empowerment. All measures would be taken to guarantee women equal access to and full participation in decision-making bodies at every level, including the legislative, executive, judicial, corporate, statutory bodies, as also the advisory commissions, committees, boards, trusts etc. Affirmative action such as reservations/quotas, including in higher legislative bodies, will be considered whenever necessary on a time-bound basis. Women–friendly personnel policies will also be drawn up to encourage women to participate effectively in the developmental process.

C. Mainstreaming a Gender Perspective in the Development Process: Policies, programmes and systems would be established to ensure mainstreaming of women's perspectives in all developmental processes, as catalysts, participants and recipients. Wherever there are gaps in policies and programmes, women-specific interventions would be undertaken to bridge these. Coordinating and monitoring mechanisms will also be devised to assess, from time to time, the progress of such mainstreaming mechanisms. Issues and concerns related to women would be specifically addressed and reflected in all concerned laws, sectoral policies, plans and programmes of action.

5.3.2 Economic Empowerment of Women:

A. Poverty Eradication: Since women comprise the majority of the population below the poverty line and are very often in situations of extreme poverty—given the harsh realities of intra-household and social discrimination, —macro economic policies and poverty eradication programmes would specifically address the needs and problems of such women. There would be improved implementation of programmes which are already women-oriented with special targets for women. Steps would be taken for mobilization of poor women and convergence of services, by offering them a range of economic and social options, along with necessary support measures to enhance their capabilities

B. Micro Credit: In order to enhance women's access to credit for consumption and production, establishment of new and strengthening of existing micro-credit mechanisms and micro-finance institution would be undertaken so that the outreach of credit is enhanced. Other supportive measures would be taken to ensure adequate flow of credit through extant financial institutions and banks so that all women below poverty line have easy access to credit.

C. Women and Economy: Women's perspectives would be included in designing and implementing macroeconomic and social policies by institutionalizing their participation in such processes. Their contribution to socio-economic development as producers and workers would be recognized in the formal and informal sectors (including home-based workers) and appropriate policies relating to employment and to her working conditions would be drawn up. Such measures could include the following:

1. Reinterpretation and redefinition of conventional concepts of work wherever necessary (e.g. in the census records), to reflect contribution of women as producers and workers.
2. Preparation of satellite and national accounts.
3. Development of appropriate methodologies for undertaking (1) and (2) above.

D. Globalization: Globalization—the gender impact of which has not been evaluated fully—has presented new challenges for the realization of the goal of women's equality. It is evident that there is a need for re-framing policies for access to employment and quality of employment.

Benefits of the growing global economy have been unevenly distributed leading to wider economic disparities, the feminization of poverty, increased gender inequality through deteriorating working conditions and unsafe working environment especially in the informal economy and rural areas. Strategies would be designed to enhance the capacity of women and empower them to meet the negative social and economic impacts, which may flow from the globalization process.

E. Women and Agriculture: In view of the critical role of women in the agriculture and allied sectors as producers, concentrated efforts would be made to ensure that benefits of various programmes/schemes reach them in proportion to their numbers. The programmes for training women in soil conservation, social forestry, dairy development and other occupations allied to agriculture (like horticulture, livestock including small animal husbandry, poultry, fisheries etc.) would be expanded to benefit women workers in the agriculture sector.

F. Women and Industry: The important role played by women in electronics, information technology, food processing, agro industry and textiles has been crucial for the development of these sectors. They would be given comprehensive support in terms of labour legislation, social security and other support services to participate in various industrial sectors.

Women at present cannot work in night shift in factories even if they wish to. Suitable measures will be taken to enable women to work on the night shift in factories. This would be accompanied with support services for security, transportation etc.

G. Support Services: The provision of support services for women—like child care facilities, including crèches at work places and educational institutions, homes for the aged and the disabled—would be expanded and improved to create an enabling environment and to ensure their full cooperation in social, political and economic life. Women-friendly personnel policies would also be drawn up to encourage women to participate effectively in the developmental process.

5.3.3 Social Empowerment of Women:

A. Education: Equal access to education for women and girls would be ensured. Special measures would be taken to eliminate discrimination, universalize education, eradicate illiteracy, create a gender-sensitive educational system, increase enrolment and retention rates of girls and improve the quality of education to facilitate life-long learning as well as development of occupation/vocation/technical skills by women. Reducing the gender gap in secondary and higher education would be a focus area. Sectoral time targets in existing policies would be achieved, with a special focus on girls and women, particularly those belonging to weaker sections including the Scheduled Castes/Scheduled Tribes/Other Backward Classes/Minorities. Gender sensitive curricula would be developed at all levels of educational system in order to address sex stereotyping as one of the causes of gender discrimination.

B. Health: A holistic approach to women's health which includes both nutrition and health services would be adopted and special attention would be given to the needs of women and the girls at all stages of the life cycle. The reduction of infant mortality and maternal mortality, which are sensitive indicators of human development, is a priority concern. NPEW reiterated the national demographic goals for Infant Mortality Rate (IMR), Maternal Mortality Rate (MMR) set out in the National Population Policy, 2000. Women should have access to comprehensive, affordable and quality health care. Measures would be adopted that take into account the reproductive rights of women to enable them to exercise informed choices, their vulnerability to sexual and health problems together with endemic, infectious and communicable diseases such as malaria, TB, and water-borne diseases as well as hypertension and cardio-pulmonary diseases. The social, developmental and health consequences of HIV/AIDS and other sexually transmitted diseases would be tackled from a gender perspective.

To effectively meet problems of infant and maternal mortality, and early marriage, the availability of good and accurate data at micro level on deaths, birth and marriages is required. Strict implementation of registration of births and deaths would be ensured and registration of marriages would be made compulsory.

In accordance with the commitment of the National Population Policy, 2000 to population stabilization, NPEW recognized the critical need of men and women to have access to safe, effective and affordable methods of family planning of their choice and the need to suitably address the issues of early marriages and spacing of children. Interventions such as spread of education, compulsory registration of marriage should impact on delaying the age of marriage so that by 2010 child marriages are eliminated.

Women's traditional knowledge about health care and nutrition would be recognized through proper documentation and its use would be encouraged. The use of Indian and alternative systems of medicine would be enhanced within the framework of overall health infrastructure available for women.

C. Nutrition: In view of the high risk of malnutrition and disease that women face at all the three critical stages, viz. infancy and childhood, adolescent and reproductive phase, focussed attention would be paid to meeting the nutritional needs of women at all stages of the life cycle. This is also important in view of the critical link between the health of adolescent girls, pregnant and lactating women with the health of infant and young children. Special efforts would be made to tackle the problem of macro and micro nutrient deficiencies especially amongst pregnant and lactating women as it leads to various diseases and disabilities.

Intra-household discrimination in nutritional matters vis-à-vis girls and women would be sought to be ended through appropriate strategies. Widespread use of nutrition education would be made to address the issues of intra-household imbalances in nutrition and the special needs of pregnant and lactating women. Women's participation would also be ensured in the planning, superintendence and delivery of the system.

D. Drinking Water and Sanitation: Special attention would be given to the needs of women in the provision of safe drinking water, sewage disposal, toilet facilities and sanitation within accessible reach of households, especially in rural areas and urban slums. Women's participation would be ensured in the planning, delivery and maintenance of such services.

E. Housing and Shelter: Women's perspectives would be included in housing policies, planning of housing colonies and provision of shelter both in rural and urban areas. Special attention would be given for providing adequate and safe housing and accommodation for women including single women, heads of households, working women, students, apprentices and trainees.

F. Environment: Women would be involved and their perspectives reflected in the policies and programmes for environment, conservation and restoration. Considering the impact of environmental factors on their livelihoods, women's participation would be ensured in the conservation of the environment and control of environmental degradation. The vast majority of rural women still depend on the locally available non-commercial sources of energy such as animal dung, crop waste and fuel wood. In order to ensure the efficient use of these energy resources in an environmental friendly manner, NPEW would aim at promoting the programmes of non-conventional energy resources. Women would be involved in spreading the use of solar energy, biogas, smokeless chulahs and other rural application so as to have a visible impact of these measures in influencing eco system and in changing the life styles of rural women.

G. Science and Technology: Programmes would be strengthened to bring about a greater involvement of women in science and technology. These would include measures to motivate girls to take up science and technology for higher education and also ensure that development projects with scientific and technical inputs involve women fully. Efforts to develop a scientific temper and awareness would also be stepped up. Special measures would be taken for their training in areas where they have special skills like communication and information technology. Efforts to develop appropriate technologies suited to women's needs as well as to reduce their drudgery would be given a special focus too.

H. Women in Difficult Circumstances: In recognition of the diversity of women's situations and in acknowledgement of the needs of disadvantaged groups, measures and programmes would be undertaken to provide them with special assistance. These groups include women in extreme poverty, destitute women, women in conflict situations, women affected by natural calamities, women in less developed regions, the disabled widows, elderly women, single women in difficult circumstances, women heading households, those displaced from employment, migrants, women who are victims of marital violence, deserted women and prostitutes etc.

I. Violence against Women: All forms of violence against women, physical and mental, whether at domestic or societal levels, including those arising from customs, traditions or accepted practices shall be dealt with effectively with a view to eliminate its incidence. Institutions and mechanisms for assistance would be created and strengthened for prevention of such violence—including sexual harassment at work place—and for the rehabilitation of the victims of violence and for taking effective action against the perpetrators of such violence. A special emphasis would also be laid on programmes and measures to deal with trafficking in women and girls.

J. Rights of the Girl Child: All forms of discrimination against the girl child and violation of her rights shall be eliminated by undertaking strong measures both preventive and punitive within and outside the family. These would relate specifically to strict enforcement of laws against prenatal sex selection and the practices of female foeticide, female infanticide, child marriage, child abuse and child prostitution etc. Removal of discrimination in the treatment of the girl child within the family and outside and projection of a positive image of the girl child would be actively fostered. There would be special emphasis on the needs of the girl child and earmarking of substantial investments in the areas relating to food and nutrition, health and education, and in vocational education. In implementing programmes for eliminating child labour, there would be a special focus on girl children.

K. Mass Media: Media would be used to portray images consistent with human dignity of girls and women. NPEW would specifically strive to remove demeaning, degrading and negative conventional stereotypical images of women and violence against women. Private sector partners and media networks would be involved at all levels to ensure equal access for women, particularly in the area of information and communication technologies. The media would be encouraged to develop codes of conduct, professional guidelines and other self-regulatory mechanisms to remove gender stereotypes and promote balanced portrayals of women and men.

5.4 Operational Strategies of NPEW

5.4.1 Action Plans: All Central and State Ministries would draw up time bound Action Plans for translating NPEW into a set of concrete actions, through a participatory process of consultation with Central/State Departments of Women and Child Development and National/State Commissions for Women. The Plans would specifically include the following:

1. Measurable goals to be achieved by 2010.
2. Identification and commitment of resources.
3. Responsibilities for implementation of action points.
4. Structures and mechanisms to ensure efficient monitoring, review and gender impact assessment of action points and policies.
5. Introduction of a gender perspective in the budgeting process.

In order to support better planning and programme formulation and adequate allocation of resources, Gender Development Indices (GDI) would be developed by networking with specialized agencies. These could be analyzed and studied in depth. Gender auditing and development of evaluation mechanisms would also be undertaken along side.

Collection of gender disaggregated data by all primary data collecting agencies of the Central and State Governments as well as research and academic institutions in the public and private sectors would be undertaken. Data and information gaps in vital areas reflecting the status of women would be sought to be filled in by these immediately. All Ministries/Corporations/Banks and financial institutions etc would be advised to collect, collate, disseminate and maintain/publish data related to programmes and benefits on a gender disaggregated basis. This would help in meaningful planning and evaluation of policies.

5.4.2 Institutional Mechanisms: Institutional mechanisms, to promote the advancement of women, which exist at the Central and State levels, would be strengthened. This would be done through appropriate and would relate to, among others, provision of adequate resources, training and skills to effectively influence macro-policies, legislations, programmes etc. to achieve the empowerment of women.

National and State Councils would be formed to oversee the operationalisation of the Policy on a regular basis. The National Council would be headed by the Prime Minister and the State Councils by the Chief Ministers and would be broad in composition having representatives from the concerned Departments/Ministries, National and State Commissions for Women, Social Welfare Boards, representatives of non-government organizations, women's organisations, corporate sector, trade unions, financing institutions, academics, experts and social activists. These bodies would review the progress made in implementing the Policy twice a year. The National Development Council would also be informed, from time to time, of the progress of the programme undertaken under the policy for advice and comments.

National and State Resource Centres on women would be established with mandates for collection and dissemination of information, undertaking research work, conducting surveys, implementing training and awareness generation programmes etc. These Centres would link up with Women's Studies Centres and other research and academic institutions through suitable information networking systems.

While institutions at the district level would be strengthened, women would be helped by Government at the grassroots level through its programmes to organize and strengthen self-help groups (SHGs) at the anganwadi/village/town levels. The women's groups would be helped to institutionalize themselves into registered societies and to federate at the panchyat/municipal level. These societies would bring about synergistic implementation of all the social and economic development programmes by drawing resources made available through Government and non-government channels, including banks and financial institutions and by establishing a close Interface with the panchayats/ municipalities.

5.4.3 Resource Management: Availability of adequate financial, human and market resources to implement NPEW would be managed by concerned departments, financial credit institutions and banks, private sector, civil society and other connected institutions. This process would include the following:

1. Assessment of benefits flowing to women and resource allocation to the programmes relating to them through an exercise of gender budgeting. Appropriate changes in policies would be made to optimize benefits to women under these schemes.
2. Adequate resource allocation to develop and promote the policy outlined earlier based on (1) above by concerned Departments.
3. Developing synergy between personnel of health, rural development, education and women and child development department at field level and other village level functionaries.
4. Meeting credit needs by banks and financial credit institutions through suitable policy initiatives and development of new institutions in coordination with the Department of Women and Child Development.

The strategy of Women's Component Plan adopted in the Ninth Five Year Plan (1997-98 to 2001-02) ensuring that not less than 30 percent of benefits/funds flow to women from all Ministries and Departments would be implemented effectively so that the needs and interests of women and girls are addressed by all concerned sectors. The Department of Women and Child Development being the nodal Ministry will monitor and review the progress of the implementation of the Component Plan from time to time in terms of both quality and quantity in collaboration with the Planning Commission.

Efforts would be made to channelize private sector investments also, to support programmes and projects for advancement of women.

5.4.4 Legislation: The existing legislative structure would be reviewed and additional legislative measures taken by identified departments to implement the Policy. This would also involve a review of all existing laws including personal, customary and tribal laws, subordinate legislation, related rules as well as executive and administrative regulations to eliminate all gender discriminatory references. The process would be planned over a time period 2000-03. The specific measures required would be evolved through a consultation process involving civil society, National Commission for Women, and Department of Women and Child Development. In appropriate cases the consultation process would be widened to include other stakeholders also.

Effective implementation of legislations would be promoted by involving civil society and community. Appropriate changes in legislations would be undertaken, if necessary. In addition, following other specific measures would be taken to implement the legislation effectively:

1. Strict enforcement of all relevant legal provisions and speedy redressal of grievances would be ensured, with a special focus on violence and gender related atrocities.
2. Measures to prevent and punish sexual harassment at the place of work, protection for women workers in the organized/unorganized sector and strict enforcement of relevant laws such as Equal Remuneration Act and Minimum Wages Act would be undertaken.
3. Crimes against women, their incidence, prevention, investigation, detection and prosecution would be regularly reviewed at all crime review fora and conferences at the Central, State and District levels. Recognised, local, voluntary organizations would be authorized to lodge complaints and facilitate registration, investigations and legal proceedings related to violence and atrocities against girls and women.
4. Women's cells in police stations, women police stations, family courts, mahila courts, counselling centres, legal aid centres and nyaya panchayats would be strengthened and expanded to eliminate violence and atrocities against women.
5. Widespread dissemination of information on all aspects of legal rights, human rights and other entitlements of women, through specially designed legal literacy programmes and rights information programmes would be done.

5.4.5 Gender Sensitization: Training of personnel of executive, legislative and judicial wings of the State—with a special focus on policy and programme framers, implementation and development agencies, law enforcement machinery and the judiciary, as well as non-governmental organizations—would be undertaken. Other measures would include the following:

1. Promoting societal awareness of gender issues and women's human rights.
2. Review of curriculum and educational materials to include gender education and human rights issues.
3. Removal of all references derogatory to the dignity of women from all public documents and legal instruments.
4. Use of different forms of mass media to communicate social messages relating to women's equality and empowerment.

5.4.6 Panchayati Raj Institutions: The 73rd and 74th Amendments to the Indian Constitution have served as a breakthrough towards ensuring equal access and increased participation of women in political power structure. The PRIs would play a central role in the process of enhancing women's participation in public life. The PRIs and the local self-governments would be actively involved in the implementation and execution of NPEW the grassroots level.

5.4.7 Partnership with the Voluntary Sector Organizations: The involvement of voluntary organizations, associations, federations, trade unions, non-governmental organizations, women's organizations, as well as institutions dealing with education, training and research would be ensured in the formulation, implementation, monitoring and review of all policies and programmes affecting women. Towards this end, they would be provided with appropriate support related to resources and capacity building and facilitated to participate actively in the process of the empowerment of women.

5.4.8 International Cooperation: NPEW would aim at implementation of international obligations/commitments in all sectors on empowerment of women such as the Convention on All Forms of Discrimination Against Women (CEDAW), Convention on the Rights of the Child (CRC), International Conference on Population and Development (ICPD) and other such instruments. International, regional and sub-regional cooperation towards the empowerment of women would continue to be encouraged through sharing of experiences, exchange of ideas and technology, networking with institutions and organizations and through bilateral and multi-lateral partnerships.

6

Women Workers in India

6.1 Double Burden of Work for Women

The problems of women workers in general and in the unorganised sector in particular deserve special emphasis and focus in view of their marginalised position within the class of workers. Even when women are not employed in the sense of contributing to the national output, a considerable share of their time is consumed by socially productive and reproductive labour. This is what is called the *double burden of work* that distinguishes women from men. For women workers in the informal economy, the double burden of combining the tasks of production and reproduction is even more arduous because they are already engaged in activities that require long hours to obtain a subsistence wage.

Thus, while women workers constitute a marginalised category within the class of workers in general, there are layers of subordination determined by structural factors such as the initial conditions of social status and economic sector to which they belong. This is quite evident in the case of women workers in the unorganised sector.

6.2 Characteristics of Women's Work in India

Employment of women in the organised or the unorganised sector is not a new phenomenon, though opportunities have certainly increased in the post-Independence period. Government and public sector undertakings are the major employers. The conditions of employment have been carefully laid down in various regulations enacted from time to time. As these regulations are uniformly applicable to men and women and as most women going for employment in the Government or public sector have some education, they get the benefits without any discrimination. In other words, knowledge puts them at an advantage. The same does not hold true of employment in the other sectors.

Women's work participation rates reflect the twin characteristics of their work, double burden of productive and reproductive responsibilities and being confined to non-conventional spaces of work. These features together with the poor access to human and physical capital lead to much lower participation of adult women in the workforce than men. The disparity in work participation across rural and urban areas is also large. While nearly half the rural adult women participate in the workforce, only a little more than one-fifth of the urban women do so. This is partly explained by the self-employment on land or engagement in livestock related activities (e.g. taking care of cattle) in the rural areas.

However, the work participation rates for women belonging to SCs/STs are significantly higher than women in general. Such a high work participation rate for rural women does not mean that their economic condition is better than their counterparts in the urban areas. In fact, the reality is to the contrary, given the low level of wages in rural areas, highly restricted work opportunities (mostly in agriculture and related activities) and the social constraints imposed especially on those who come from the bottom layer of the social hierarchy. A higher work participation rate in such a context is more likely the result of economic hardships than the availability of work opportunities. This is also corroborated by the low level of education of rural women workers.

The low level of education is a serious handicap for not only women workers in general but rural women in particular. Here again the bottom layer is the rural women belonging to SC/ST categories.

6.2.1 Volatility of Employment: In recent years, there has been a massive shift of women's labour into the paid workforce. The new forms of employment are fragile and insecure. Women's livelihoods in rural areas have been affected by the agrarian crisis. Most women employed are engaged in agriculture either as workers in household-owned farms or are taken on tenant contracts by their families, or as wage workers on farms owned by others. Most of the primary sector activities offer subsistence employment.

In the industrial sector, women are mostly concentrated in the informal sector, which offers no security of either the employment or conditions at work. Within manufacturing, they predominate in certain industries such as garments, textiles, food and electronics. The seasonality of work in this sector and the lack of other avenues of work make them vulnerable to a range of exploitative practices. They remain the most vulnerable and the poorest. And yet they are economically active and contributing to the national economy.

The most important trend as regards women's employment is the considerable increase in the share of tertiary sector in recent years. In this sector women are found largely in the trading, retailing and caring activities which do not offer much in terms of remuneration or skill endowment.

Volatility of employment in the export-oriented units is well-known.

6.2.2 Self-employed Service Work: Women are generally engaged in informal work, characterized by greater reliance on casual contracts. There has been a substantial increase in self-employed low-end service work, especially in domestic and retail trade.

6.2.3 Subsidiary Status Work: Another prominent characteristic of women's work force participation is that even within the low participation of women, a large part is of subsidiary work status, nearly a quarter of the women workers. Subsidiary status workers are non-workers or the unemployed persons engaged in an economic activity for part of the year.

Again the societal compulsions and double responsibilities would partly explain this phenomenon. The interesting feature is that it is mainly the self-employed women who engage in work in a subsidiary capacity and, to some extent, women casual workers, who perhaps tend to have fewer employment opportunities. In the case of the casual workers it would be the compulsions and pressures of survival that make them work in their principal capacity. In marked contrast, a negligible proportion of men work as subsidiary workers.

6.2.4 Women's Migration for Work: Internal migration has increased. Migrant workers have few rights, and governments rarely think about ensuring their protection.

6.2.5 Home-based Work: A large number of women work as home-based workers. Home-based workers refer to the general category of workers who carry out remunerative work with in their homes or in the surrounding grounds. Women turn to home-based work for a number of reasons. Lack of necessary qualifications and formal training, absence of childcare support, social and cultural constraints and absence of alternatives are some of the reasons. Families need cash incomes for their survival. Loss in formal employment and reduced returns from agriculture often result in men migrating to urban centres, leaving behind women and children. With home-based work being the only alternative available to poorest communities, it is not confined only to women but also involves children, especially girls.

The home workers are dependent on the sub-contractor for supply of work, raw material and sale of finished goods. They are also isolated from their fellow women workers in the same trade. This dependence on the contractor together with the isolation undermines their ability to bargain for higher piece-rates, timely payments or overtime pay. The home workers are paid piece-rate wages for the work delivered. Delayed payments and arbitrary cuts in wages on the pretext of poor quality also add to the hidden costs.

Changing as well as complicated designs due to fashions when no training is provided for adds to the costs since one has to learn the new work from family friends or neighbours utilizing valuable time of both the informal trainers and trainees. Some not so hidden costs are the cost of inputs such as thread for the garment workers and maintenance of equipment. All these are often not factored into the wages leading to extremely low net wages per day.

There are positive aspects to home-based work also. It gives women the opportunity to combine work with domestic chores, flexible and sometimes better working conditions. While designing strategies to meet the challenges, it is important to retain the positive aspects of home-based work.

6.2.6 Unpaid Work: The impact of the decline in the public provision of many basic goods and services has meant a substantial increase in unpaid work by women.

6.2.7 Crisis of Livelihoods in Agriculture: Trade liberalization in recent years has been accompanied by a decline in world agriculture prices. Agriculture constitutes the main employer of women in the developing world and the basic source of income for most of the poor in the world.

6.3 Problems of Women Workers

6.3.1 Double Burden of Work: The reproductive role of women is less visible and less recognized by the society. She engages in multiple livelihood activities to fulfil her productive and reproductive role. The Central Statistical Organisation of the Government of India provided official visibility to this double burden of work through a pilot study of utilization of time by men and women in 6 states in 1998. The report classified the activities based on the 1993 System of National Accounts (SNA) into three categories: (i) those coming under economic activities that are included in the SNA; (ii) those that are not currently included in the SNA but are characterised as extended SNA, which include household maintenance and care for the children, old and the sick in the household and (iii) non-SNA consisting of the social and cultural activities, leisure and personal care. Since productive and reproductive roles performed by women are equally necessary for the well-being and regeneration of the society, the study found that women spend a disproportionate amount of time in what is called extended SNA. On the other hand, men spend a much greater time in SNA activities than women. As for non-SNA activities, the difference was not as striking as in the case of extended SNA.

Women undertake a number of activities that help their household to save incomes, if not to directly earn it. Fetching water and free collection of firewood, including preparation of cow-dung cakes, are the predominant activities in rural areas. In urban areas, these are fetching water, sewing and tailoring and tutoring children free of cost. Many of these activities are included in the count of extended SNA activities as discussed above. If all these were to be included as economic activities, the participation rates of women would be considerably higher than what has been currently estimated.

What it means is the absence of recognition of the kind of work, which although not in the realm of monetisation, is important to the sustenance of the family as well as the economy. Recognition of the women's contribution to extended SNA could, and should, lead to greater appreciation of public policies for the welfare of women.

In spite of the stress from the double burden of work, the economic condition forces many women to be available for additional work.

6.3.2 Non-conventional Place of Work: The fact that women workers have restricted mobility because of which their capacity to engage in economically productive work is restricted is clearly brought out by their place of work. The conventional idea of a workplace is the office, factory or an institution.

Lack of a clear-cut employer-employee relationship in the case of the self-employed and outworkers/home workers and lack of a designated place of work for the majority, particularly of women, adds to the problem of invisibility of such enterprises. It also makes it difficult for such units to approach the formal financial institutions such as banks for credit.

Workers engaged in enterprises on a casual basis tend to change employers frequently. It is relatively easy for the employer then not to recognize the workers and then to deny them any additional benefits. The problem is compounded if the workers are engaged in the enterprises based in the employers' home.

Unorganised workers, in both self-employed and wage employed categories , remain, by and large, legally unrecognised as workers, which implies that the existing laws related to minimum wages or social security are not applied to them. Besides the lack of legal recognition, lack of a designated "business place" also works to increase their vulnerability and exposes them to exploitation by the authorities. Further, the dispersed nature of workplace makes organisation of these workers and enterprises more difficult, further adding to their invisibility.

6.3.3 Sexual Division of Labour: Discrimination on the lines of gender is not always overt. It appears in very subtle forms such as in the nature of work performed, the skills required to perform the work and the valuation of these skills and the technology used by men and women.

A number of national and international studies have documented the sex-typing of jobs and occupations by women. Occupational segregation represents a form of discrimination when large segments of the labour force are in essence restricted from entering many occupations.

The sexual division of labour in the society is reflected in the division of labour in the workplace. Sexual division of labour has implications for the wages earned, permanency in the job and the possibilities for upward mobility in the industry.

Thus, sexual division of labour is often used as a justification for dubbing women's work as low skilled. It is observed that in most industry groups there is a hierarchy of jobs where the women are placed at the bottom. This hierarchy of jobs is then used to value the jobs where women are concentrated as low skilled even if it involves exceptional talent and years of informal training.

The consequence of this sex-typing of jobs is two fold: even women with requisite skills find it difficult to get into the so called *male jobs* and the ones in which the women are concentrated are categorised as *low skilled* and receive lower wages.

That women are comparatively less suited for heavy work, and are more vulnerable to situations in industry which produce fatigue, are used as arguments to justify views which are often held in support of lower wages for them. They are either given lower jobs or the jobs they handle traditionally become women's jobs and carry lower salaries. Simply because women's abilities are different does not necessarily mean that they constitute a lower class of workers.

A. Textile Industry: In the occupations related to the textile industry, the jobs of supervisors and machine operators are male dominated, while the preparatory work of making of fibre and yarn, spinning and winding are dominated by women. In the garment industry women tailors are not too few, but it is the kind of garments that they stitch that makes the difference in valuation. Sewing and embroidery works are clearly dominated by women.

Women receive lower wages and have limited job mobility in the hierarchy of the knitwear industry.

In the textile and wearing apparel industry all jobs done by hand and involving minimal or low level equipment is delegated to the women. The myth of "nimble fingers" is also used to relegate much of the work done by hand to women. So while women sew the buttons, do the hemming and hand stitching, they also do the embroidery work, zardosi and stitching of sequences to the dresses. This latter is a very skilled activity, but is valued very low because it is seen as women's work.

B. Health Sector: In the health sector, women are clearly concentrated as nurses, midwives and para-health workers, all likely to get lower wages than men who are concentrated as physicians or in particular jobs even within the category of para-health workers.

C. Education Sector: In the education sector, the occupational segregation is very clear. Men are prominently in the higher education sector, and women in rural areas are mainly in pre-primary. A lot of them are likely to be anganwadi workers, ayahs etc. In urban areas women workers are prominently primary school teachers.

D. Construction Industry: In the construction industry, a very large proportion of men and women are concentrated as casual workers. Women are clearly categorized as unskilled workers in a broad 'others' category. Women do have some presence among the brick-layers and stone masons and tile setters.

E. Ceramic Industry: In the ceramic industry or in brick-kilns, preparation of the mud or clay is a skilled activity. If the consistency of this raw material is not correct, the pottery will disintegrate and the houses built of the brick would collapse. This work is done by women but is valued as one of the lowest. Women in this activity are paid the least, well below minimum wages.

F. Agricultural Sector: In the agricultural sector, while the men undertake ploughing and harvesting, the women do the weeding. While ploughing is important, weeding involves back-breaking work. The gender discrimination is such that while minimum wages are fixed separately for ploughing and harvesting, there is most often no minimum wage fixed for weeding.

6.3.4 Sexual Harassment: Sexual harassment is a problem faced by women workers in all walks of life. It is of particular significance when the relationship between man and woman is that of an employer and employee.

Verbal and physical violence against women has been an age-old method of subjugating women. This is used in the workplace to further strengthen the sexual division of labour and keep women at the bottom of the work hierarchy. Such harassment leads to stress and reduces the productivity of the workers. It can also be used to curb upward mobility and inhibit growth of women-operated enterprises.

Recently, the International Confederation of Free Trade Unions has taken great interest in the problem and has issued guidelines to its affiliated unions on how to deal with these cases.

6.3.5 Female Domestic Workers: Female and child domestic workers constitute a large portion of migrant worker population. Most of them are at the risk of exploitation and human rights abuse. Working in the unregulated domain of a private home, mostly without the protection of national labour legislation, allows for female domestic workers to be maltreated by their employers with impunity. Women are often subjected to long working hours and excessively arduous tasks. They may be strictly confined to their places of work. They are frequently the victims of sexual harassment and, in the very worst cases, rape and torture.

Thus, women as well as children working as domestic servants are often forced to work in sub-human conditions with no job security, no benefits and no dignity. The increasing demand for domestic workers in all big cities and towns of the country played a major role in the migration of women from rural or tribal areas. Most of them are from poor families and are illiterate. Due to the lack of education and skill they become easy victims of exploitation.

The biggest problem faced by the domestic workers across the country is their non-recognition as workers. The domestic workforce is excluded from labour laws that look after important employment-related issues such as conditions of work, wages, social security, provident funds, old age pensions, and maternity leave.

Women, though they make half the world's population, constitute the largest group which is excluded from the benefits of development. Work participation rate of women is much less than that of men. The multiple roles of women and the meagre ability to access resources and available assets are areas of concern. It is important to emphasise that women require adequate security and protection to be self-reliant.

Special attention has to be paid to women workers because of problems peculiar to them. Comparatively speaking, they are much less organised. They also suffer from certain social prejudices and physical disabilities.

6.4 Categorisation of Laws Pertaining to Women Workers

The laws which are applicable to women workers in India can be broadly divided into three categories.

6.4.1 Category I Laws: Laws of this category include laws which are exclusively meant for women, the important ones being the following:

A. Maternity Benefit Act (MBA), 1961: Performance of the biological role of child bearing necessarily involves withdrawal of a woman from the workforce for some period. During this period she not only cannot work for her living but needs extra income for her medical expenses. In order to enable the woman worker to subsist during this period and to preserve her health, the law makes a provision for maternity benefit so that the woman can play her productive and reproductive roles efficiently.

One of the earliest conventions adopted by International Labour Organization (ILO) was the Maternity Protection Convention, 1919 the purpose of which was to provide protection to women workers in certain conditions. All the member countries of ILO were directed to pass suitable legislation to extend certain benefits to women during pregnancy and after childbirth. India being one of the founder members of ILO was expected to pass such legislation without delay.

It was the Government of the State of Bombay that enacted the first maternity benefit legislation in the year 1929. The Act provided for a leave of 7 weeks and an allowance of 50 paise per day during the leave period, for any woman worker who was due for delivery. To be eligible to receive this benefit the woman should have worked in that factory or establishment for at least a period of 6 months. This legislation was regarded as very progressive. Soon some other states followed the example of Bombay state and enacted similar laws with some minor variations.

It was in the year 1961 that the Central Government with a view to bringing some uniformity in the provisions of various maternity protection acts, passed what is known as the Maternity Benefit Act, 1961. Article 42 of the Constitution of India requires that the State should make provision, inter alia, for maternity relief.

MBA, 1961 applies to all factories, establishments, plantations, mines, and shops where 10 or more persons are employed. Maternity benefits are also provided under the Employees State Insurance (ESI) Act, 1948 and an insured woman is entitled to maternity benefit in the form of periodical payments in case of confinement, miscarriage or sickness arising out of pregnancy. They are also entitled to medical care under the ESI Scheme for maternity, and where medical facilities are not available they are paid a specified sum for the purpose. The provisions in the ESI Act for medical benefit are more comprehensive than those under the MBA 1961, in so far as they include medical care, and pre and post-natal care. The factories or the establishments to which the provisions of the ESI Scheme apply are excluded from the purview of the Act of 1961.

MBA, 1961 is administered by State Governments. There are comprehensive regulatory provisions. Women employees who complete 80 days of work prior to delivery are entitled to maternity benefits.

MBA, 1961 provides for payment of cash maternity benefits for certain periods before or after confinement, grant of leave and other medical facilities. This benefit is available in case of confinement, miscarriage, sickness arising out of pregnancy and premature birth of the child. In 1995, MBA, 1961 was amended to extend the benefits to women undergoing tubectomy, medical termination of pregnancy (MTP) and for any illness arising out of MTP or tubectomy.

(a) Working of MBA, 1961: In order to claim the benefit, continuous service for a certain period was required. Earlier the employers, wanting to avoid the expenditure, kept a large number of women as temporary or casual labour. Thus these workers were not able to fulfil the obligatory requirement of having worked for 160 days in the preceding one year. Sometimes employers caused a break in the service on the slightest pretext in order to save on maternity benefits.

As a result of these practices, a very small percentage of women were able to obtain these benefits. To check this malpractice, MBA, 1961 was amended in 1988 to reduce the eligibility criterion for claiming maternity benefits from 160 days to 80 days. In computation of 80 days the period of lay off and paid holidays is also included. Employers have thus been prevented from escaping their obligation by causing a break in service.

The law of maternity benefit was enacted to ensure the health and well-being of the working mother and the child. It was meant to provide support to a woman worker as mother, and to remove any discrimination faced by her because of a biological condition. All these good intentions seem to have backfired since employers often refuse to employ married women in order to avoid paying maternity benefits. In some cases marriage itself is a disqualification while in others pregnancy acts as a bar to employment.

(b) Marriage: A Bar to Employment: Various organisations refuse to employ married women because marriage creates obligations and difficulties which adversely affect the efficiency of women. The Supreme Court of India has in a number of cases held that such practices are unconstitutional. The requirement of being unmarried is not only confined to employment opportunities but also extends to training courses which are offered to *unmarried women* or *widows without encumbrances*. Married women or women with children are thereby excluded.

The greatest weakness of the Act lies in its limited application to the state of women workers during pregnancy. The Act prohibits dismissal or discharge of a woman during or on account of leave granted under it. However, if a woman is dismissed during pregnancy it only safeguards her right to claim maternity benefits. It does not protect her service by forbidding discharge or dismissal of a pregnant woman. The Act completely glosses over the discrimination which pregnant women face at the time of recruitment and the widely prevailing practice of dismissing them during pregnancy.

The three main provisions of MBA, 1961 relate to (a) eligibility conditions, (b) period for which the benefit is paid and (c) rate of benefit.

(i) Eligibility: No woman employee is entitled to maternity benefits until and unless she has actually worked in an establishment of the employer, from whom she claims maternity benefits, for a period of at least 80 days in the 12 months immediately preceding the day of her expected delivery.

(ii) Period of Benefit: The maximum period for which any women is entitled to maternity benefit is 12 weeks, i.e. 6 weeks up to and including the day of her delivery and 6 weeks immediately following the day.

(iii) Rate of Benefit: Payment of maternity benefits to the women employees is made at the rate of average daily wage for the period of their actual absence immediately preceding and including the day of their delivery and for 6 weeks immediately following that day. For this purpose the average daily wage is calculated on the basis of wages payable to her for the days on which she worked during the period of 3 calendar months immediately preceding the day from which she absents herself on account of maternity, subject to the minimum of one rupee per day.

Maternity protection in India is provided by some other legislations/schemes too, such as Beedi and Cigar Workers (Conditions of Employment) Act, 1966, Beedi and Cigar Workers Welfare Fund, Working Journalists and other Newspaper Employees (Conditions of Service) and Miscellaneous Provisions Act 1955. A National Maternity Benefit Scheme (1995) also exists under National Social Assistance Programmes (NSAP) to provide financial assistance to women who are below the poverty line. Many State Governments too have their own maternity assistance schemes.

B. Equal Remuneration Act (ERA), 1976: ERA, 1976 provides for the prevention of discrimination on the ground of sex against women in the matter of employment and for matters connected therewith or incidental thereto. It also prohibits discrimination while recruiting men and women workers for the same or similar nature of work except where the employment of women in such work is restricted or prohibited by or under any law for the time being.

Till 1975, there was no specific legal provision mandating payment of equal wages to women even though discrimination against women in the payment of wages was widely rampant. Such discrimination was practised not only by private employers but by the instruments of the state as well. The First National Commission on Labour (1969) had found that in agriculture and small industries—the large sectors where women were employed—some State Governments had been fixing differential wages rates.

This situation continued in spite of the fact that Article 15 of the Constitution specifically prohibits discrimination against women. The provision relating to *equal pay for equal work* is not an enforceable fundamental right but is issued as a directive to the state in Part IV of the Constitution. By this, the state was obliged to secure such social and economic freedoms for the citizens which could not be guaranteed at the time when the Constitution was framed due to the then prevalent socio-economic conditions.

In 1951, ILO passed a convention called Equal Remuneration Convention (No. 100), the full title of which is "Equal Remuneration for Men and Women Workers for Work for Equal Value." With a view to honour this ILO convention and also to implement Article 39 (equal pay for equal work, for both men and women) of the Indian Constitution, the President of India promulgated an ordinance in September 1975 (i.e. in the International Women's Year) called Equal Remuneration Ordinance. After receiving the consent of the parliament it was turned into Equal Remuneration Act of 1976 according to which if a man and a woman do the same kind of work, they must get equal wages. It does not mean only work which is identical in all respects but also work which can broadly be considered to be same or similar in nature to the other work.

ERA, 1976 places duty on the employer to pay equal remuneration to men and women workers employed by him in an establishment or employment for performing same or similar nature of work. It forbids discrimination against women workers either at the time of recruitment or in any condition of service subsequent to recruitment such as promotion, training or transfer. This protection does not extend to places where the employment of women is prohibited or restricted by any other law in force.

In order to promote employment opportunities for women, ERA 1976 provides for setting up advisory committees and appropriate authorities to hear and decide claims and complaints arising out of the Act. With the aim of providing increasing options for women including part-time employment, the advisory committees are required to inform the government of the extent to which women may be employed in specified establishments duly considering the nature and hours of work and suitability of women for that employment. The inclusion of this provision shows recognition of the need to look into the quantitative aspect of women's employment.

6.4.2 Category II Laws: This category covers those laws which are not exclusively for women but are meant for all workers, and yet contain certain sections or provisions especially for women. These sex-neutral laws include the following:

A. Factories Act, 1948: This Act is the principal legislation for regulating various aspects relating to safety, health and welfare of workers employed in factories. It aims at protecting workers employed in factories from industrial and occupational hazards. The Act prescribes a 48-hour week for adult workers and forbids employment of children under 14 years of age in any factory. Minimum standards of lighting, ventilation, safety and welfare services which employers must provide in their factories have also been laid down.

The Act is important as it contains certain provisions regarding the nature of work to be given to women workers, hours of work for them, etc. It also makes arrangements for certain welfare amenities.

(a) Background: In the early period of industrialisation, working conditions of workers in factories were extremely miserable. Men, women and children worked from sunrise to sunset without rest and without any break to eat food. The working places were closed and unventilated. Children were also employed in the factories.

These miserable conditions of Indian workers were brought to the notice of

Lord Shaltesburg, the Secretary of State, by some social workers in England. He tried to bring the issue of the factory legislation for Indian workers before the British Parliament but did not succeed. Ultimately after a lot of initial resistance, the first Indian Factory Act was passed in 1881. This prohibited the employment of children under 7 years of age and limited the working hours to 9 per day for children between 7 to 12 years. However, the Act had no special provisions for women.

In 1890, the Government of India appointed the Second Factory Commission to look into the conditions of the factory workers and make recommendations for their improvement. The Commission in its report recommended 11 hours of work for women, prohibition of night work for women, limit of minimum 14 years for employment of children and Sunday as a weekly off day. On the basis of the recommendations, the Factory Act was amended in 1891.

(b) Main Provisions: Broadly speaking, the following provisions are enshrined in the Factories Act, 1948.

(i) Night Work: The Act prohibits the employment of women between 7 p.m. to 6 a.m. Section 66 (1) (a) of the Act provides that no exemption can be granted from provisions related to daily hours. Section (1) (b) states that no women shall be required or allowed to work except between the hours of 6 a.m. to 7 p.m. Section 66 (1) (c) mentions that these limits may be varied by the State Government but no variation shall be authorised for exemption of women between 5 a.m. to 10 p.m. Also, there shall be no change of shifts except after a weekly holiday or any other holiday. State Governments by notification in the official gazette, may vary the limits in case of certain factories or groups of workers, but the limits cannot be extended beyond 5 a.m. and 10 p.m.

Exemption from this rule may be given by the State Governments for women working in fish curing or fish canning factories in order to prevent damage or deterioration of product.

(ii) Maximum Permissible Weight of Load: The Act does not allow women workers to handle excessively heavy weights. The Act authorises the State Governments to fix the maximum weights which can be lifted, carried or moved by men, women and children. However, the regulations made in this regard in certain cases are very general.

(iii) Crèche Facilities: Factories Act, 1948 is one of the earliest Acts to make provisions for crèche facilities. Sections 48 (1) and (2) of the Act state that in all factories with more than 30 women workers, adequately lighted and ventilated room in clean and sanitary condition, for children under the age of 6 years of such women must be maintained under the charge of women trained in the care of children and infants. Originally, this provision was meant for factories employing more than 50 women. However, an amendment to the provision was made in 1976 by which the number 50 was reduced to 30.

(iv) Unhealthy Employment: The Act prohibits the employment of women in any part of a factory for pressing cotton in which a cotton opener is at work. There is also a provision under which no woman worker is allowed to clean, lubricate or adjust any part of the prime mover or of any transmission machinery while it is in motion or to clean, lubricate or adjust any part of any machine if such work exposes the woman worker to risk of injury from any moving part either of that machine or of any adjacent machinery.

State Governments have been authorised to prohibit or restrict the employment of women in any operation which exposes them to a serious risk of bodily injury, poisoning or disease.

Provisions also exist for separate enclosed latrines and urinals for males and females which must be adequately lighted and ventilated, and maintained in clean and sanitary condition.

(v) Welfare Facilities: The Act makes provisions for a number of welfare facilities for workers. Most of these are meant for both male and female workers, but there are some provisions especially for women, e.g. separate and adequately screened washing facilities have to be provided in every factory for the use of female workers [Section 42 (b)].

B. Plantation Labour Act, 1951: Plantation is an important industry as far as employment of women is concerned.

The Act lays down conditions for the registration of plantations by the owners and also has provision regarding health, safety and welfare of the workers. A peculiar feature of employment in plantations is that the entire family of a worker is employed. The worker usually lives on the site and he, his wife, and adolescent children all work in the plantations in different capacities. Hence the unit of employment is the family, not the individual. Women mainly work as pluckers in tea and coffee plantations.

The Act defines the term *family* as follows: The worker, his or her spouse, legitimate or adopted children depending on him who have not completed 18 years of age, and where the worker is a male, his parents dependent on him.

Every plantation has to be registered and it is mandatory on the owner to provide certain health facilities and housing for all workers. The following are the provisions for health.

1. Cool drinking water must be provided near the sites where the workers are working.
2. Separate latrines and urinals must be provided for male and female workers.
3. Medical facilities must be made available for the worker and his family. In

case the employer does not provide these, the Chief Inspector of Plantations should arrange to provide them and make the employer pay the cost.

The following are the provisions for welfare of workers.

Canteen facility must be provided in every plantation which employs 150 or more workers.

Wherever 50 or more women (including women workers employed by contractors) are employed or were employed on any day in the previous 12 months, or where the number of children under 6 years of women employed in the plantation exceeds 20, a fully equipped crèche must be provided by the owner. Even if the number of women employees is less than 50, the State Governments may order that a separate room should be provided for their children.

Every plantation must provide certain recreational facilities for the workers and their families. The details of the requirement would be laid down by the State Government concerned.

When children between 6 and 10 years on any plantation exceed 25, the owner must provide educational facilities for them. The details of the requirement should be specified by the State Government concerned.

Housing has to be provided for every worker and his family residing in the plantation, and for every worker and his family residing outside the plantation but wanting to stay on the plantation, provided such worker has been working in the plantation for at least 6 months.

In case the house provided by the management collapses resulting in an injury to the worker or his family, adequate compensation must be paid by the management.

The Act also lays down that women and children must not be employed for night work. They should work only between 6 a.m. and 7 p.m.

A fitness certificate must be obtained from a doctor by all children and adolescents who desire to work on the plantation.

Women working in plantations are also covered by the Maternity Benefit Act of 1961. Hence they are also eligible to get full pay leave for 6 weeks together with the medical bonus.

As in all the other laws, in this Act also there is a provision for inspectors who are to visit the plantation estates and see that the Act is being implemented. Penalties are also provided for the violation of the provisions.

C. Mines Act, 1952: It provides for safety, health and welfare of workers employed in mines. Provisions of the Act and the rules and regulations framed under it are enforced by the Ministry of Labour through the Directorate General of Mines Safety. The main functions of the Directorate General are: inspection of mines, investigation of all fatal accidents, approval of mines/safety equipment, exemptions and relaxations in respect of various mining operations.

Although gender-neutral, the Act has some provisions especially for women.

Mines are of two types, surface and underground. Every underground mine also has some aspects of the work which is carried out on the surface. When the ore is taken out from the deep mines it is to be loaded on trucks or wagons etc. Women are employed in this loading operation. Women also do the same type of work in open quarries. Sometimes they are employed for breaking stones.

In the Act, apart from the usual sections regarding the licensing of mines, inspection, penalties etc., the following provisions are especially meant for women.

1. Separate latrines and urinals are to be provided for men and women working in mines. The number of latrines and urinals is fixed by the State Government according to the size of the employment at that mine.
2. No woman or child is to work below ground. They must be given work only on the surface.
3. No night work is allowed for women. They have to work only between 6 a.m. and 7 p.m. In special cases or for some special type of work, the State Government may relax the time limit up to 10 p.m. at night and 5 a.m. in the morning.

Under the Act, the Central Government is authorised to make rules requiring the mines to maintain crèches if a certain number of women workers are employed in the preceding 12 months. Thus, the Mines Crèche Rules, 1966 makes it obligatory for the owner, agent or manager of every mine, wherein women are employed or were employed on any day of the preceding 12 months, to provide a crèche at his colliery. Each crèche is required to have a trained nurse and the prescribed set of equipment. Supply of food to the children attending crèche is also obligatory on the part of the management. No limit of the number of woman employees is stated. However, the State Government may grant exemption to some employers if it is found that the number of women of children is very small, or the place where the mine is situated is not at all suitable.

Four types of crèches have been specified as A, B, C and D according to the size of the room or rooms to be provided and the equipment and facilities. Details of latrines, bathrooms, furniture, medicines, first aid, toys, uniforms for the staff etc., have been given in the schedule. Cool water, milk and medicines are to be provided for children. There has to be a medical examination of the child every month, and of the nursing mothers after every 2 months. Records of medical examination must be kept for which formats are specified. Crèche must be supervised by a competent and trained person and it is to remain open day and night.

As in any other industry, women working in mines are also covered by the Maternity Benefit Act of 1961 and are eligible to get the maternity benefits.

6.4.3. Category III Laws: This category consists of laws which are neither meant exclusively for women nor contain any special provisions for women, yet they are of great significance to women workers in the unorganised sector. These are the following:

A. Minimum Wages Act, 1948: This Act empowers the Government to fix minimum wages for employees working in specified employments. Payment of overtime in scheduled employments is also governed by this Act.

Based on the recommendations of the Central Advisory Board, the Central Government recommends a National Minimum Wage and all states are requested to ensure fixation of wages in all the scheduled employments at a rate not below the recommended national minimum wage.

The Act is applicable to the workers engaged in the scheduled employments and provides for fixing minimum rates of wages in certain employments. It is applicable both to agricultural, non-agricultural and to rural as well as urban workers. The Government may, however, increase the scope of this Act by adding schedules. Units employing even one worker are covered by the Act. Thus, the Act covers wage worker, home worker but not the self-employed. Supreme Court in the case of Bandhua Mukti Morcha (1984) held that even a piece-rated worker is entitled for minimum wages.

Under the Act, the appropriate government fixes the minimum rates of wages payable to employees in a specified employment and reviews the rates at such intervals as it may think fit, such intervals not exceeding 5 years. The Government also fixes a minimum rate of wages for time-rated work, a minimum rate of wages for piece work, a minimum rate of remuneration to apply in the case of employees on piece-work for the purpose of securing to such employees a minimum rate of wages on a time work basis, a minimum rate (whether a time rate or a piece rate) to apply in substitution for the minimum rate which would otherwise be applicable, in respect of overtime work done by employees.

Different minimum rates of wages may be fixed for (a) different scheduled employments, (b) different classes of work in the same scheduled employment, (c) adults, adolescents, children and apprentices and (d) different localities. Similarly, minimum rates of wages may be fixed by the hour, day, month, or by such other larger wage period as may be prescribed. Any minimum rate of wages fixed or revised by the Government in respect of the scheduled employments may consist of a basic rate of wages and cost of living allowance or a basic rate of wages with or without the cost of living allowance, and the cash value of the concessions in respect of supplies of essential commodities at concessional rates, or, an all-inclusive rate allowing for the basic rate, the cost of living allowance and the cash value of the concessions.

Minimum wages are generally payable in cash unless authorised by the Government considering the prevailing custom or practice. Further, the Government may (a) fix the number of hours of work which shall constitute a normal working day, inclusive of one or more specified intervals, (b) provide for a day of rest in every period of 7 days which shall be allowed to all employees or to any specified class of employees and for the payment of remuneration in respect of such days of rest and (c) provide for payment for work on a day of rest at a rate not less than the overtime rate. Under the Rules, Sunday is the weekly day of rest ordinarily. For an adult 9 hours and for a child 4½ hours constitute a normal working day. Overtime is payable at 1½ times the wage in agriculture and double the rate in other cases of scheduled employment.

The subject of national minimum wages has been considered by several bodies in the past. The National Commission on Labour (1969) was of the view that such a wage in the sense of uniform minimum monetary remuneration for the country as a whole is neither feasible nor desirable.

B. Contract Labour (Regulation and Abolition) Act, 1970: It provides for regulation of employment of contract labour in certain establishments and for its abolition in certain circumstances. It fixes responsibility on the principal employer for payment of wages in case of defaults.

This Act is applicable to every establishment in which 20 or more workmen are employed or were employed on any day of the preceding 12 months as contract labour and to every contractor who employs or who employed 20 or more workmen on any day preceding 12 months. However, the appropriate government may, after giving not less than 2 months' notice and by notification in the Official Gazette, apply the provisions of this Act to any establishment or contractor employing less than 20 workmen. This Act does not apply to establishments in which work of only an intermittent or casual nature is performed. Workman means any person employed in or in connection with the work of any establishment to do any skilled, semi-skilled or unskilled manual, supervisory, technical or clerical work for hire or reward, whether the terms of employment be express or implied. It does not include any person employed mainly in a managerial or administrative capacity; or a person employed in a supervisory capacity drawing wages exceeding ₹ 500 per month or an out-worker (home worker).

Under the Act, the appropriate government may prohibit employment of contract labour in any process, operation or other work in any establishment, having regard to the conditions of work and benefits provided for the contract labour in that establishment and other relevant factors, such as whether nature of work is incidental or necessary to the main operation, whether it is of perennial nature, that is to say, it has sufficient duration, whether it is done ordinarily through regular workmen in that/other establishment(s), and whether it is sufficient to employ considerable number of whole time workmen.

The Act also provides for licence to be taken subject to such conditions including, in particular, as to hours of work, fixation of wages and other essential amenities in respect of contract labour. The Act also contains provisions regarding welfare and health of contract labour, e.g. canteens, rest rooms, other facilities such as drinking water, urinals and, first aid facilities. For security of payment of wages the Act provides for its payment by the contractor, and in case of failure by the principal employer.

C. Beedi and Cigar Workers (Conditions of Employment) Act, 1966: The Act is applicable to the workers engaged in beedi and cigar establishments. It regulates the conditions of their work. It applies to wage workers and home workers but not to self-employed workers/persons in private dwellings/houses.

The Act provides for cleanliness of industrial premises free from effluvia arising from any drain, privy or other nuisance. It seeks to maintain cleanliness including white washing, colour washing, varnishing, or painting. In order to prevent injury to the health of the workers, the industrial premise has to maintain proper lighting, ventilation and temperature. To prevent overcrowding, the Act prescribes at least four and a quarter cubic metres of space for every person in the workroom. It also provides for sufficient supply of wholesome drinking water, sufficient latrine and urinal accommodation, adequate washing facilities, crèches, adequate first aid facilities and canteens. It also provides for working hours in any one day and in any week, overtime, interval for rest, spread over in any day, weekly holidays, substituted holiday etc. There is prohibition of employment of children altogether and prohibition of employment of women during hours except between 6 a.m. and 7 p.m. It also contains provisions regarding annual leave with wages and wages during the leave period.

The Act applies to the entire country except the state of Jammu & Kashmir. Any person who wants to start this industry in his place or any other place, must first obtain a license from the government. The license is granted only if the authorities are satisfied that the place is suitable and that the employer would be able to take care of the welfare of the workers employed.

This Act is of special significance for women in the unorganised sector as a large number of women work in this industry. In fact, there are more women than men. The Act also contains some special provisions for women workers.

Three provisions in the Act are important as far as women workers are concerned. In the first place, while defining the word *employer*, the Act includes *home workers,* i.e. those workers whom the contractor supplies raw material which they process in their homes. Due to the inclusion of *home workers* in the definition, those workers who roll beedis at home are also entitled to same benefits which a worker in the factory gets. Hence this provision in the Act is of importance to women.

The second important provision is for a crèche for the infants and babies of women workers. The Act stipulates that every industrial premises, where more than 60 female employees are ordinarily employed, should maintain a crèche which is clean and well-ventilated and which is under the charge of a trained woman.

The third provision is a restriction on night work. No woman or child is to be asked to work before 6 a.m. or after 7 p.m. Of course, this provision applies only to those women workers who work in a factory or premises of the employer. If they are home workers, their working at night is not restricted.

In addition to this Act, there is a Beedi Workers Welfare Act also which prescribes provision for hospital etc. for beedi workers and their families.

D. Inter-State Migrant Workmen (Regulation of Employment and Conditions of Service) Act, 1979: The Act is applicable to every establishment in which 5 or more inter-state migrant workmen are employed and to every contractor who employs 5 or more inter-state migrant workmen. The establishments engaging less than 5 interstate migrant workmen are not covered under this Act. For the purposes of this Act, *workman* means any person employed in or in connection with the work of any establishment to do any skilled, semi-skilled or unskilled, manual, supervisory, technical or clerical work for hire or reward, but does not include any person who is employed mainly in a managerial or administration capacity; or who, being employed in a supervisory capacity, draws wages exceeding ₹ 500 per month.

The Act provides that the wage rates, holidays, hours of work and other conditions of service of an inter-state migrant workman shall be the same as those applicable to such other workman performing the same or similar kind of work and cannot be less that the wages fixed under the Minimum Wages Act, 1948 and are payable in cash. It also provides for payment of displacement allowance and journey allowance. The contractor has the liability to (a) make regular payment of wages, ensuring equal pay for equal work irrespective of sex, (b) ensure suitable conditions of work, (c) provide and maintain suitable residential accommodation to such workmen during the period of their employment, (d) provide the prescribed medical facilities to the workmen free of charge, (e) provide protective clothing to the workmen and in case of fatal accident or serious bodily injury to any such workman to report to the specified authorities of both the states and also the next-of-kin of the workman. The primary responsibility for payment of wages is on the contractor and on his failure on the principal employer.

6.5 Enforceability of the Acts

Although various provisions regarding employment have been legislated for the betterment and benefit of women, it remains to be seen whether these are being enforced effectively or are merely on paper. Studies, from time to time, have revealed that the statutory provisions in this regard are not being strictly implemented. For instance, the provision of a crèche of a prescribed standard for children under the age of 6 years is a statutory obligation in mines employing women workers irrespective of their number. However, it has been observed that most of the mines are not adequately complying with the statutory provisions contained in the Mines Crèche Rules.

There are several reasons for poor implementations of labour laws. In the first place compared to the number of factories and establishments to be inspected, the number of inspectors is inadequate. Secondly, very often the establishments to be inspected are small and scattered and in rural areas often at a long distance from one another. The inspectors are not usually provided with vehicles. So they visit the nearest places to complete their quota of inspections. Thirdly, apart from his regular work of inspections, an inspector has several other duties like attending the court cases, collecting data for assembly questions, attending election duties etc.

It has also been observed that out of various welfare laws and provisions, the least enforced are those meant for women and children. The general apathy of society towards women is responsible for this situation. If a woman suffers and works in unhealthy conditions, it is attributed to her fate. Due to this attitude, a woman often comes across unsympathetic and indifferent bureaucratic authorities.

Moreover, women usually are docile workers (unless they are organised by trade unions). They have neither the time, nor the inclination to fight for their rights. Trade unions also are not very keen to take up women's issues.

Lack of education in general, and of labour laws in particular, amongst women workers is also responsible for their conditions. This, however, does not mean that the conditions of women workers have not changed since the early days of industrialisation. In urban areas, and particularly in large factories and establishments, women have better working conditions and many of the welfare provisions are implemented. However, in rural areas, and amongst unorganised workers, much remains to be done. Vigorous efforts by trade unions insisting on the enforcement of women-related laws and spreading legal literacy will go a long way towards improving the present conditions of women.

The post-Independence period has witnessed the enactment of social security and welfare legislation in a large measure, but the unfortunate story is that most of the workers, male and female, are not well conversant with them. The problem of women is two fold. First, as a wage earner, they have certain problems in the matter of in-house conditions of employment which have to be taken care of so as to enable them to perform their duties with a reasonable degree of efficiency and without tension.

Further, they have to be aware of the special legislations enacted for them so that they do not suffer from discrimination. Second, a woman, as the wife of a primary wage earner, should be aware of the various social security measures to which she would be entitled if something happens to her husband. Most of the women are not aware of these provisions and therefore have to do without the benefits due to them. This is particularly so in the non-governmental organised and unorganised sectors, where innocent women do not get the provident fund, gratuity and other benefits. Thus, law itself cannot offer protection unless there is a sense of awareness of its existence among the concerned people. However, it is heartening to note that presently this awareness among the women is much greater than what it used to be in the early days of Independence.

The special cares and duties which fall to women necessarily place them under some handicap as industrial workers. Special provisions for protecting them are, therefore, made in various statutes, but their effective implementation is essential. In particular, women should be protected against injurious work, should receive maternity benefits, and work places should provide crèche facilities for children. Nursing mothers should be entitled to paid rest intervals for feeding infants. The principle of equal pay for equal work needs to be more vigorously implemented and the tendency to scale down the jobs traditionally handled by women has to be guarded against. Training facilities should be provided for them so that they can compete for higher jobs. In addition, the possibility of increasing opportunities for their part-time employment should be explored.

The protection extended so far relates to prohibition of employment of women in underground coal units/mines, also in certain other hazardous occupations, provision of certain welfare facilities like crèches, maternity benefits and ensuring equal wages for equal work for both male and female labour. While social services like health services, education etc. are required by all labour, male and female, the employment of female labour calls for special attention.

Though India has created protective legislation for women, the enactments have not been easy to implement. The very vastness of the country, the scattered nature of women workers, their lack of education and legal literacy, the indifferent attitude of the government bureaucracy and the general status of women in society have caused vulnerability in women. This is true not only of rural unorganised women, but to an extent of the urban women workers also.

Inadequate enforcement, unclear provisions leading to legal battles, inadequate penalties, hostile and indifferent adjudicating machinery, authorities far removed from workers homes lead to loss of time and wages etc.

Although the provisions enshrined in the Constitution might not have been implemented fully in their letter and spirit, yet it is a fact that law itself cannot offer protection unless there is a sense of awareness of its existence among the concerned people. However, it is heartening to note that today this awareness among the women is much greater than what it used to be in the early 1950s.

In a semi-industrialised country like India, the working class is destined to be one of the weaker sections of society. Moreover, society being male-dominated, female labour receives poor recognition or value. It is not that there are no statutory provisions. In fact, the Constitution of India provides equal rights and opportunities to both the genders. In addition there are specific provisions for protection and welfare of working women in many of the labour laws. However, most of these statutes do not cover the units in small and informal sectors which are the predominant workplaces of women. Even where they are covered by the statutes, the poor enforcement practically nullifies the provisions. There is one more tragic factor that has to be noted. The very laws which are meant for working women are paradoxically turned against their interests by unscrupulous employers. If the employers find it difficult to bypass these provisions, they get rid of the women workers and thus strike at the economic base of their livelihood. All these factors need to be studied in depth while drafting policy and legal provisions for the working women in order to plug all possible loopholes.

For the reasons mentioned above, as also for the benefit of working women, their union leaders and for all those who are interested in the welfare of women workers, knowledge of existing provisions of labour laws is very essential. Women's emancipation is part of our general developmental plans but government action can be neither effective nor adequate unless women themselves become more aware of their rights and the corresponding responsibilities. Every woman is a working woman, whether she works in the home or outside it. Many women work to earn money. Working women must know that they have some basic rights which are given by the law.

7

Economic Empowerment of Women

7.1 Women and the Economy

The extent of empowerment of women in the national hierarchy is determined largely by three factors: their economic, social and political identity. These factors are deeply intertwined and interlinked with many cross cutting linkages. However, if efforts in even one dimension remain absent or weak, outcomes generated by the other components are adversely affected. Women can be truly empowered only when all the three factors are simultaneously addressed and made compatible with each other. In other words, for holistic empowerment of woman to happen, economic, social and political aspects impacting women's life must converge effectively.

It is a well-acknowledged fact that the thrust on social and human development is an important plank of next generation policy reforms. The efforts are being complemented by a steep jump in budgetary outlays for social sectors, along with dedicated initiatives for removing poverty and increasing employment. Participation of women in productive activities reduces poverty, enhances economic growth and hence benefits society at large.

Women's lack of economic empowerment, on the other hand, not only impedes growth and poverty reduction, but also has a host of other negative impacts including less favourable education and health outcomes for children. Thus, it is extremely important to ensure that women are economically empowered.

Women's contribution to the economy remains significantly invisible in national accounts. Although a certain degree of statistical invisibility of women in the economy is a global phenomenon, it is particularly predominant in India and other South Asian nations due to their orthodox socio-cultural milieu. The United Nations Statistical Division has been active in extending the production boundary of the Systems of National Accounts (SNA), 1993 and this has led to the inclusion of the unpaid work of women in the care economy in the national accounting system as satellite accounts. This extended production boundary of SNA, 1993 provides a better understanding of women's contribution to the economy.

7.2 Vicious Circle of Poverty and Gender Inequality

Poverty and gender inequality thrive on each other. In other words, there exists a two-way link between economic growth and poverty, and gender inequality. At one level, poverty and the lack of growth exacerbate gender disparities. Inequalities between girls and boys in access to schooling or adequate health care are more acute among poor people than among those with higher incomes. While poor people have less access to such productive resources as land and credit, poor women generally have the least access of all. Similarly, health and schooling of girls and women are more vulnerable to economic downturns than those of boys and men. At another level, gender inequalities undermine the prospects for poverty reduction in fundamental ways. While disparities in basic rights, access to schooling, credit and jobs, and the ability to participate in public life take their most direct toll on women and girls, the evidence shows that gender inequality ultimately hinders economic growth.

The rationale for economically empowering women is compelling both for its own sake and for other spill over benefits. Economic participation of women—their presence in the workforce in quantitative terms—is important not only for lowering the disproportionate levels of poverty among women, but also as an important step toward raising household income and encouraging economic development in a country. Education, employment and ownership rights of women have a powerful influence on their ability to control their environment and contribute to economic development. However, participation alone is not enough because quality of women's work is also important. A key challenge is to overcome a situation where women may gain employment with relative ease, but where their employment is either concentrated in poorly paid or *unskilled job ghettos*, characterized by the absence of upward mobility and opportunity. For example, women are often concentrated in *feminized professions* such as nursing and teaching, office work, care of the elderly and disabled—termed *horizontal occupational segregation*—where they tend to remain in lower job categories than men. Since these activities are carried out by women, they are the lowest paid, in addition to offering limited or no opportunity for advancement. The term *feminization of poverty* is often used to illustrate the fact that a substantial percentage of poor are women and that the gap between women and men in poverty has not lessened, but may well have widened in recent years.

7.2.1 Gender Discrimination in Wages: Discriminatory practices in the labour market are reflected in the wages of women workers. They are not only concentrated in low-paid occupations in the unorganised sector but are subjected to discrimination in payment. In terms of wage-workers, for all categories of employment considerable differentials prevail in both rural and urban areas. The increase in gender disparity in wages in the urban areas is quite marked and it usually results from employment of women in lower-paying activities in the aggregate. For the majority of women engaged in paid economic activity, the fact of being female means being paid less than men for their work. It is most evident in respect of agricultural labourers. Agricultural daily wages are in general low, though they vary by type of agricultural operation (ploughing, sowing, weeding, harvesting, etc.), by the prosperity of a state or region, and by gender. Some operations such as ploughing do not involve women at all, whereas others such as weeding are women-intensive.

From the various categories of industrial work, the manufacturing sector is the most discriminatory. Coupled with gender discrimination in wage differentials is inequality in access to superior positions and promotions. Men are seen confined to regular and more managerial or technically-oriented jobs while women are often given technically inferior positions where they are mostly hired as contract workers. Women get lower pay despite longer working hours and the conditions of work are substandard. Discrimination exists not only in terms of wages but also in terms of access to employment. Often women are found concentrated in occupations where the wage rates, as well as working conditions, are poor and substandard.

The reasons for gender discrimination in wages may not be specific to India but the cultural context also is an important factor. The implicit assumptions that women should be paid less then men include the following: (a) low levels of skill on entry, (b) lack of access to on-the-job training, (c) employment histories punctuated by time spent bearing and raising children, (d) time off to care for family members and (e) the assumption that men are the primary earners.

7.3 Strategies for Economic Empowerment of Women

7.3.1 Sound Macroeconomic Policies: Gender inequalities manifest as women and men have different access to resources, roles and responsibilities, both in the market and at the household. In the Indian context, fiscal policies are being increasingly examined through gender sensitive-budgeting exercises, although the focus still remains on expenditures in *soft sectors*, with several aspects like taxation, trade, capital flows etc. remaining largely an unstudied domain. Macroeconomic policies are formulated and implemented in areas such as trade, fiscal management, debt financing, social welfare and other sectors without a comprehensive assessment of their potential gender impacts. All these issues would be particularly important if the analysis of the sources of growth were to suggest that influencing the distribution of income and assets by gender might have a beneficial effect. Some policies—particularly those promoting health and education, or promoting greater women's property rights and control over assets or access to credit, technology, and transport—are likely to be win-win policies in terms of higher growth, greater gender equality, and reduced susceptibility of women to economic shock.

7.3.2 Improvement in Infrastructure: Development of infrastructure was previously assumed to be gender neutral, with both sexes benefiting equally from well-designed projects. The new thinking asserts that gender-responsive infrastructure interventions can free up women's time, thereby increasing girls' enrolment in schools and facilitating women's participation in income-generation and decision-making activities.

A. Transport: In the area of transport, men and women have varying transport needs and constraints and are affected differently by transport interventions. Rural transport projects that build roads for motorized transport often do not benefit rural women, who mainly work in and around the village and travel on foot. Urban transport systems that transport people to and from employment centres are sometimes inadequate for women, who must combine income-generating activities with household and familial activities, such as taking children to school and health centres and visiting the market. Poor women, who balance productive, social, and reproductive roles in societies, often have higher demands on their time than poor men.

B. Energy: Women are disproportionately impacted by a lack of access to energy given their prominent role in domestic, low paid and unpaid work. In rural India women spend considerable time in gathering fuels and processing them, i.e. chopping, drying, turning, storing, stacking and handling. This work is done almost exclusively by women. Since this energy system is managed by women, they need to be substantially supported through investment, management and technology inputs to be able to continue to manage the systems in sustainable ways and with minimum hardship. Thus, the focus should be not only on meeting cooking energy needs but also on enhanced livelihood options. Both rural and urban women need adequate energy supplies for their small and medium scale enterprises and home industries. Hence, there is a commercial motivation to improve the efficiency of the entire process.

C. Information and Communication Technology (ICT): ICT has delivered enormous benefits around the world. However, much of their potential remains untapped—particularly for groups facing severe time constraints, suffering from social isolation, or lacking access to knowledge and productive resources. Women in developing countries are among the most important of these groups. Although women account for nearly a third of information technology workers in developing countries, they are concentrated in lower-level jobs (data entry, call centres etc.) and paid smaller salaries than men. Few are project managers. With supportive policies from employers, complemented by enlightened national labour laws, women can move up the professional ladder. Low enrolment of girls and women in science and technology education is one of the main obstacles to higher-level employment in information technology.

In India, where software services are major exports, women have been targeted by government initiatives promoting the growth of the ICT workforce. Supported by gender-sensitive human resource development policies and training strategies, women in India are being trained to provide basic services such as data processing. They are also encouraged to develop their skills in order to go beyond back-office work and become website designers, network managers or ICT service consultants. The idea is to make them suitable for enhanced work opportunities, on equal terms with men. It is worth mentioning here that certain software companies offer crèche facilities to working women.

7.3.3 Gender-sensitive Agricultural Policies: Rural women form the most important productive work force in the Indian economy. Beyond the conventional market-oriented narrower definition of *productive workers*, almost all women in rural India can be considered as *farmers* in some sense, working as agricultural labourers, unpaid workers in the family farm enterprise, or combination of the two. Moreover, several farm activities traditionally carried out by men are also being undertaken by women as men are pulled away into higher paying employment. Thus, rural India is witnessing a process which could be described as feminization of agriculture.

Despite significant contribution of women in the production process, an all pervasive bias of development planners in treating them primarily as consumers of social services rather than producers, kept them away from the development programmes in agriculture and allied sectors. As men and women have different roles and needs and face gender-specific constraints, women may not automatically benefit from development activities, but may remain excluded.

In spite of the key role of women in crop husbandry, animal husbandry, fisheries, forestry and post-harvest technology, those in-charge of formulating packages of technologies, services and public policies for rural areas have often tended to neglect the productive role of women. Consequently, the developments of technologies, specifically tailored to women-specific occupations and the involvement of women in technology development and transfer have received inadequate attention from both scientific and administrative departments of Government.

Women have traditionally been discriminated in their access to productive resources and have been denied ownership of land, cattle, trees, harvest and shelter. They have even been discriminated in access to credit and marketing facilities for their economic activities. It is, thus, essential to develop strategies and mechanism to improve women's access to agricultural support services.

It has been recognized that for an accelerated socio-economic development of any community, the active participation of women in the entire process is very essential. In a social set up like ours, the participation of women in the development process has to be ensured through tangible measures, taken at various levels, which result in empowerment of women in the real sense. In view of the above, government has taken a conscious view to make adequate provisions in its policies and programmes through which it is to be ensured that the women of the country are empowered and they become the active participants in the development process.

The absence of faster diversification is partly due to the lack of new economic opportunities for women. While men migrate as well as take up new employment opportunities in rural areas, women find themselves at a disadvantage.

There appears to be a faster rate of occupational mobility out of agriculture among men than among women. The latter remain more bound to rural areas and to agriculture due to socio-cultural and structural causes.

A. Importance of Land for Women: Land is important for women due to following reasons:

1. Land access can reduce a household's risk of poverty, but for persistent gender inequalities land solely in men's hands need not guarantee female welfare.
2. Direct land transfers to women are likely to benefit not just women but also children. Evidence, both from India and from many other parts of the world, shows that women, especially in poor households, spend most of the earnings they control on basic household needs, while men spend a significant part of theirs on personal goods, such as alcohol, tobacco etc.
3. Women with assets such as land have greater bargaining power, which can lead to more gender-equal allocations of benefits even from male incomes.
4. Women without independent resources are highly vulnerable to poverty and destitution in case of desertion, divorce, or widowhood. In parts of western and north-western India, rural women even from rich parental and marital families, deprived of their property shares when widowed, can be found working as agricultural labourers on the farms of their well-off brothers or brothers-in-law. The fate of deserted and divorced women is worse.
5. Tenure security, and especially titles, can empower women to assert themselves better with agencies that provide inputs and extension services.
6. Women in many parts of South Asia are often better informed than men about traditional seed varieties and the attributes of trees and grasses. If they have greater control over land and farming, this knowledge can be put to better use.

B. Sources of Land for Women: There are three main sources of land for women:

1. Direct government transfers.
2. Market purchase/lease.
3. Inheritance or gifts from families.

To enhance women's land access from all three sources, a range of initiatives are needed, including land titles to women in all government land transfers, credit support to poor women to purchase or lease in land from the market, raising legal awareness and legal support about women's inheritance rights.

It will also need a new approach to enable women to retain the land they get by strongly encouraging a *group approach* in land cultivation and investment in productive assets. It is now well-recognized that the poor are best empowered if they function as a group rather than as individuals. This lesson should be incorporated in the creation of all productive assets in women's hands.

Agricultural policies are of prime importance in gender budgeting exercises as there is a growing feminization of agriculture in recent years with out-migration of men to urban areas in search of work. The number of women-headed households in the agricultural sector is also increasing. The prosperity of agriculture therefore will largely depend on how effectively these women are empowered.

Enhancing women's rights to land, providing infrastructure support to women farmers and advancing legal support on existing laws are some of the policy interventions needed. However, critical problems persist. The lack of formal titles to women on the land they cultivate is a big drawback. This adversely affects their access to credit, inputs and marketing outlets. It also reinforces women's position as unpaid farm labourers, which reduces their incentives to invest in the land. It further excludes them from receiving agricultural extension services, new production techniques etc.

The lack of appropriate women-friendly tools and agricultural implements is another drawback. Also, the co-operatives of farmers basically comprise of men and therefore disadvantageous to women in terms of mindset and location and services profile. The agricultural policy, therefore, needs to be reviewed to provide a gender-friendly perspective.

Policies for non-farm sector and information are another highly important area that has to be seriously reviewed keeping in view the gender perspective. As women tend to remain in the rural sector they also undertake non-farm activities, which significantly contribute to the family's income. In times of agricultural stress, it is these non-farm activities of women that support the family. Therefore, the requirements of women in this sector need to be identified and appropriate support facilities in terms of access to raw materials, micro credit, skill development, training, market linkages etc. have to be ensured.

C. Hindu Succession (Amendment) Act, 2005: It made significant amendments in the Hindu Succession Act, 1956 correcting existing inequities in women's rights to agricultural land, Mitakshara joint family property, parental dwelling house and certain widow rights. This has brought woman on par with men in relation to agricultural land.

In short, the absence of faster diversification is partly due to the lack of new economic opportunities for women. While men migrate as well as take up new employment opportunities in rural areas, women find themselves at a disadvantage.

There appears to be a faster rate of occupational mobility out of agriculture among men than among women. The latter remain more bound to rural areas and to agriculture due to socio-cultural and structural causes.

The faster shift out of agriculture among male workers compared to female workers is expected to result in what is termed as feminization of the agricultural workforce.

7.3.4 Self-help Groups (SHGs) and Empowerment of Women: The emergence and rapid multiplication of Self-help Groups (SHGs) based on micro credit is a phenomenon that is gaining increasing importance in the development scenario. SHGs are being viewed by governments and NGOs as a strategy for both women's empowerment as well as poverty reduction. SHGs are a conduit for routing a wide range of government-sponsored development messages and schemes. NGOs have increasingly been adopting SHGs as a strategy to bring women together, at a faster pace and larger scale than the collective building processes adopted by them earlier. A number of powerful players like MFIs, NGOs, corporations and donors—all of whom have a significant and growing interest in the SHG phenomenon which centres on poor women—have entered the arena. Credit is a right that poor women must have access to. The experience of SHGs has shown that they have provided improved access to credit. Poor women are now perceived by the mainstream financial sector as creditworthy. Women have used savings and credit for needs such as those related to education and health, and in particular for crisis related needs. Participation in SHGs has meant opportunities related to mobility and a legitimate space in the public realm for leaders of SHGs. Notwithstanding all the positive achievements, the overall picture is uneven and raises following concerns related to gender justice and livelihoods:

1. Despite the increased access to credit, there continue to be several hurdles faced by women when they want to access credit from banks. These include

huge amounts of paperwork and the fact that women are often pressurized by banks to recover loans made earlier to men in the village as an unwritten conditionality before loans are released to them.

2. It is increasingly being reported that SHG members have limited control over financial resources that they borrow despite being the conduit for access to such credit through their groups. The burden of repayment of such loans falls almost exclusively on the women. As SHGs are almost exclusively women-only, often women become proxy to husband's demands without the men taking up the responsibility for repayment or proper utilization of these loans.
3. Many of the micro enterprise activities undertaken have tended to be unviable. Low levels of credit absorption capacity, low skill base and low asset base have been challenges to the SHG movement, which are yet to be addressed. Moreover, lack of skills, experience and technical support services to promote livelihoods and build sustainable interventions among the intermediary organizations especially NGOs etc does not enable sustainable livelihood options to be developed.
4. Access to credit as the focus of the micro credit programmes looses sight of the fundamental issues of access and control over common resources such as water forests etc which are the mainstay of occupations of a large number of the rural poor. The fundamental livelihood concerns related to the existing economic realities of poor women's lives remain largely unaddressed in the process.

7.3.5 Skill Development: With the advent of globalisation and liberalization, new technologies and fast changing markets tend to make existing skills obsolete, requiring upgradation of existing skills and adoption of new skills and multi-skilling. Globalisation often puts a premium on skills, requiring high levels of education, often out of the reach of the unorganised sector workers. On the other hand, it opens up new markets which workers can reach by adopting existing or traditional skills.

Women workers are usually at the lowest-paid end of any sector. They are usually termed as unskilled, even though very often their work, though low-paid, requires a certain level of technique. Furthermore, many of the skills that women learn are those that are in some way connected to care and reproduction, which are often not regarded as skills at all. For example, women in forest areas have a skill of recognizing and using herbal plants. However, this skill is not regarded as skill at all, either by the person who is documenting the skills, or even by the women themselves.

Similarly, the potential marketability of a particular skill is never recognized. This refers to a woman's skills which currently are not being marketed but which have a good market potential like embroidery or knowledge of herbs. The *care skills* of the women can no longer be sidelined. These would include knowledge of child-care, care of the sick and particular skills such as mid-wifery. One unfortunate tendency that has been noticed in the desperate search for employment that goes on in the unorganised sector is the tendency towards deskilling. Workers lose their traditional or acquired skills when they cannot find employment with these skills.

7.3.6 Gender Mainstreaming in the Corporate Sector: While so far the focus of gender budgeting has been on public expenditure of Government only, an increasing quantum of funds is being invested by the corporate sector in their businesses as well as in fulfilling their corporate social responsibility. The development of the corporate sector as an employer has grown tremendously in the wake of liberalization and globalization, especially with its entry in those sectors which were hitherto the domain of the Government. Therefore the time has come to apply the strategy of gender budgeting to the private sector. There is a three fold responsibility that rests with the corporate sector:

1. Extending the scope of employment opportunities to more and more women.
2. Providing them with level playing fields (equal wages and promotion opportunities).
3. Supporting skill building, training, vocational courses etc.
4. Fulfilling social obligations towards women employees in terms of (a) extending maternity benefits, (b) protection from occupational hazards and sexual harassment, (c) provision of facilities like crèches, toilets, sanitation and hygiene, (d) allowing formation of women's associations and (e) legal protection etc.

The civil society organizations whether NGOs or other community-based organizations are partnering government in formulation and implementation of government policies and programmes. Thus their voice and views have an important bearing on shaping economic or social issues pertaining to women. They have to function as *watchdogs* ensuring that gender budgeting and mainstreaming is actually taking place right at the grassroots levels and helping in implementing gender concerns effectively.

7.3.7 Gender-friendly Insurance Schemes: The possibilities of gender differentials for social security *insurance* schemes is another area that needs to be examined, as there is an urgent need for low-cost and gender-friendly insurance systems that cater to the specific life cycle needs of women. It must be acknowledged that a safety net/social security in the informal sector is almost non-existent. As women comprise a large proportion of the informal sector, this implies that they are excluded from the insurance framework and therefore not protected against social, medical or economic emergencies. More importantly, it is absolutely necessary to put in place a well-designed *Health Insurance* scheme for women in view of their inability to access medical facilities. Also pension policies need a relook in view of the large number of widow population in the country.

7.3.8 Gender Sensitization of Trade Policy: United Nations Conference on Trade and Development (UNCTAD) organized an International Conference on Moving towards Gender Sensitization of Trade Policy in New Delhi from February 25 to 27, 2008.

The conference provided a forum for Indian and international trade and gender experts to discuss and raise awareness on trade performance and gender linkages in India and globally and propose actions and directions towards enhanced and more effective gender sensitisation of trade policy with particular reference to India and generally to developing countries.

Equitable distribution of gains from trade among the genders is a development objective which needs to be addressed through trade policies and trade agreements. Women are significant stakeholders in the process of trade, growth and development. This must be recognized and harnessed by Government to make globalization more inclusive with pro-poor impact. Women's groups must be consulted to a greater extent and in a systematic and structured manner, in the formulation of trade policies or negotiating positions, so as to integrate the gender dimension, he suggested.

Broadly, the Conference deliberations suggested a strong and direct relationship between trade performance, gender empowerment and development, explicit and specific attention to gender issues in policy and operational actions, as well as in attitudes, are key conditions for maximizing the gains for gender empowerment through trade and minimizing the costs that can arise. This is important because overall the situation in India and in many developing countries presently is that there is progress towards gender empowerment through trade. Moreover, a gender-sensitive approach to trade must involve a vision of trade as an integral component of wider development efforts to eradicate poverty and promote inclusive, people-centred development.

7.3.9 Right to Maintenance: Maintenance is a civil right that enables needy persons to receive economic support from those who are liable to protect and maintain their spouse, children, parents etc. By law, parents are bound to maintain minor children, major children their parents, husband his wife and vice versa. The quantum of maintenance varies depending on the economic status of the parties. The various personal laws such as the Hindu Marriage Act, 1955, the Hindu Adoption and Maintenance Act 1955, the Indian Divorce Act 1859, the

Parsi Marriage Act, 1954, the Shariat Laws etc. provide for maintenance, also known as alimony or allowance. Civil courts take a long time to dispose off cases. Even if a competent civil court passes a judgement and decree, execution takes months and even years due to cumbersome legal procedures. Even before the maintenance is realised the decree holder may die of starvation.

Realising the above, the right to maintenance has been incorporated in Chapter IX of the Criminal Procedure Code (Cr.P.C.). It is entitled 'order for maintenance of Wives, Children and Parents.' Under Section 125 of the Cr.P.C., 'if any person having sufficient means neglects to maintain (a) his wife, unable to maintain herself, or (b) his legitimate or illegitimate minor child, whether married or not, unable to maintain itself, or (c) his legitimate or illegitimate child (not being married) who has attained majority, where such child is, by reason of any physical or mental abnormality or injury unable to maintain itself, or (d) his father or mother, unable to maintain himself or herself, a magistrate, of the first class, may upon proof of such neglect or refusal, order such person to make a monthly allowance for the maintenance of his wife or such monthly rate not exceeding five hundred rupees on the whole, as the magistrate thinks fit, and to pay the same to such person as the magistrate may from time to time direct.' A ceiling of Rs. 500 per month towards maintenance will not prevent vagrancy though that is the object of the provision. Various women and civil rights organizations and other activists have raised their voice against this ceiling. In West Bengal the amount was raised to ₹ 1,500. Through an amendment to Section 125 of the Cr.P.C, the Government of India enhanced the interim maintenance limit for an estranged wife from ₹ 500 to ₹ 5,000.

7.3.10 Research and Development: Research and development should also be geared with a view to identify technological needs of women and develop and adapt technology especially to reduce the drudgery of women, facilitating her health and also income generating activities. The information technology policy should also be women-oriented imparting skills and strengthening the knowledge base of girls and women in the field of computer software and hardware especially in rural areas. Dissemination of information in local languages on socio-economic and legal issues concerning women would encourage better awareness and instil confidence. Information technology kiosks should be opened for women which would facilitate the Self Help Groups in using internet facilities to purchase raw material designing and marketing of their products.

7.4 Mahatma Gandhi National Rural Employment Guarantee Act (MGNREGA), 2005

MGNREGA was notified on September 7, 2005. The Act came into force on

February 2, 2006 when 200 selected districts of the country were brought under its purview (Phase I, 2006-07). MGNREGA was extended to additional 130 districts in Phase II during 2007-08. The remaining rural areas were notified with effect from April 1, 2008.

7.4.1 Objectives and Significance of MGNREGA: The objective of the MGNREGA is to enhance the livelihood security of unorganised workers in rural areas by guaranteeing 100 days of wage employment in a financial year to a rural household whose members volunteer to do unskilled manual work. The Act further aims at creating durable assets and strengthening the livelihood resource base of the rural poor. The choice of works suggested in the Act address causes of chronic poverty like drought, deforestation, soil erosion, etc. so that the process of employment generation is on a sustainable basis.

The significance of MGNREGA lies in the fact that it creates a right-based framework for wage employment programmes and makes the Government legally bound to provide employment to those who seek it. In this way the legislation goes beyond providing a social safety net, and towards guaranteeing the right to employment. By prioritizing natural resource management and emphasizing the creation of durable assets it holds the potential of becoming a growth engine for sustainable development of an agriculture-based economy.

Under MGNREGA, employment is dependent upon the worker exercising the choice to apply for registration, obtain a job card and then to seek employment through a written application for the time and duration chosen by her. The legal guarantee has to be fulfilled within the time limit prescribed and this mandate is underpinned by the provision of unemployment allowance. The Act is thus designed to offer an incentive structure to the States for providing employment as ninety percent of the cost for employment provided is borne by the Centre, and there is a concomitant disincentive for not providing employment, if demanded, as the States then bear the double indemnity of unemployment and the cost of unemployment allowance. Earlier wage employment programmes were allocation based. However, MGNREGA is not supply driven but demand driven. Resource transfer under MGNREGA is based on the demand for employment and this provides another critical incentive to States to leverage the Act to meet the employment needs of the poor. The delivery system has been made accountable, as it envisages an Annual Report on the outcomes of MGNREGA to be presented by the Central Government to the Parliament and to the State Legislature by the State Government.

7.4.2 Funding of the Programme: The Central Government bears the costs on the following items:

1. The entire cost of wages of unskilled manual workers.

2. 75 percent of the cost of material, wages of skilled and semi skilled workers.
3. Administrative expenses as may be determined by the Central Government, which will include inter alia, the salary and the allowances of the Programme Officer and his supporting staff, work site facilities.
4. Expenses of the National Employment Guarantee Council.

The State Government bears the costs on the following items:

5. 25 percent of the cost of material, wages of skilled and semi-skilled workers (As a ratio of 60:40 is to be maintained for wages of the unskilled manual workers and the material, skilled/semi-skilled workers' wages, the State Government has to bear only 25 percent of the 40 percent component, which means a contribution of 10 percent of the expenditure).
6. Unemployment allowance payable in case the State Government cannot provide wage employment on time.
7. Administrative expenses of the State Employment Guarantee Council.

7.4.3 Expression of Demand for Employment: Since MGNREGA is a right-based programme, expression of demand for employment by the rural poor is the basic premise of its operation, especially if the wage seekers are illiterate and unorganized. Generating awareness about the programme among local rural communities becomes critical for enabling the rural poor to express demand. States have adopted various methods for communication and social mobilisation that include preparation of communication material on MGNREGA processes in simple local language, orientation of sarpanches/ward members, convening gram sabhas, using district teams for village level interactions, local vernacular newspapers, TV and radio spots, pamphlets and brochures, local cultural forums, fixing a Rozgar Day in a week and establishing a helpline. The full knowledge of the rights that MGNREGA confers on the rural poor is the most important pre-requisite to enable them to seek employment as per their choice of time and duration.

7.4.4 Labour Budget, Inventory of Projects and Perspective Plan: MGNREGA guarantees providing employment within 15 days of demand and the instrument for providing employment is unskilled manual work selected from the list of permissible works. This legal guarantee has implication for the way in which works have to be planned.

A labour budget, as stipulated under the Act, is required to be prepared to facilitate advance planning, whereby districts estimate their labour demand for the ensuing financial year by December end.

National Guidelines indicate the way in which the annual shelf of projects may be prepared to meet the estimated labour demand. Districts should keep a list of works ready to meet employment demand. Estimated benefits in terms of person days need to be assessed, so that the employment expected to be generated through the works planned may be clearly matched with the estimated employment demand. Physical improvement envisaged (land/water conservation etc.) has to be quantified so that the focus remains on creating durable and productive assets that support further self-sustaining employment. Displaying the list of approved works at the Gram Panchayat Office and the details of works taken up on the work site has been stipulated so that the workers know the work opportunities locally available.

National Guidelines lay down the broad principles of preparing a Five Year District Perspective Pan that must have the following components, viz. village mapping of natural resources and social infrastructure, identification of gaps and works that can be taken up as per MGNREGA permissible list, assessment of works that respond to what local people want, what will build a livelihood base to enable them to move out of MGNREGA to sustainable employment and assessment of labour demand.

7.4.5 Work Record, Payment of Wages and Preventing Bogus Muster Rolls: The legal guarantee of MGNREGA mandates that wages due to workers be paid within 15 days of work completion. This requires that a fair record be maintained for the work done. To ensure that authentic muster rolls are used, numbered muster rolls are to be issued for each sanctioned work by programme officer and maintained on the work site by the executing agency. Muster rolls must mention job card numbers of workers, days worked, quantum of work done, amount paid and must have space for recording inspections.

Muster rolls should be read out on the work site during measurement and wage payment to prevent bogus records. Entries of the muster roll should be correspondingly recorded in the job cards of the workers. Updating of muster roll data at the block level computers in a 15 days cycle needs to be ensured. Regular measurement and supervision of works should be done by qualified technical personnel on time.

7.4.6 Women Empowerment: MGNREGA stipulates that priority shall be given to women. In terms of implementation it mandates that a minimum of one-third of the beneficiaries shall be women who have registered and have requested for work.

7.4.7 Vigilance and Transparency: Vigilance and transparency have been strongly emphasized in MGNREGA. The field verification of MGNREGA processes is through external and internal agencies and the feedback is shared with the States for follow up. Independent concurrent studies have also been taken up. Monitoring at the State level is required and States are expected to ensure 100 percent verification at block level, 10 percent at district level and 2 percent at the state level, especially of work muster rolls, and records. Guidelines for muster roll verification have been evolved. The setting up and training local vigilance and monitoring committees is also required for bringing in lateral transparency.

A web-enabled MIS www.nrega.nic.in has been developed that seeks to place all information in public domain. It is a household level database and has internal checks for ensuring consistency and conformity to normative processes. All critical parameters get monitored in public domain.

Since the MIS places all critical data on the web and this data is software engineered, it has significant advantages in terms of transparency as it allows cross verification of records and generation of reports on any parameter of the Act.

7.4.8 Public Accountability: MGNREGA contains specific provisions for public accountability. This has to be accomplished through the provisions made in the Act and guidelines regarding right to information, proactive disclosure of information and a transparent social audit process. The right to information should be followed in both letter and spirit in all matters relating to MGNREGA. Section 17 of MGNREGA provides for social audit of all works in a Gram Panchayat (GP) by the Gram Sabha and the Gram Panchayat has to provide records for social audit.

7.4.9 Grievance Redressal: Enforcement of the right to employment requires setting up an effective grievance redressal system. MGNREGA vests the responsibility for grievance redressal with the programme officer. To ensure prompt grievance redressal, certain basic arrangements must be ensured, such as setting up a grievance redressal cell at the Programme Officer (PO)/District Programme Co-ordinator (DPC) offices, preferably with a toll free helpline. The PO and DPC must review the disposal of complaints on a monthly basis and the persons concerned must be informed.

7.4.10 Financial Management: A non-lapsable Central Employment Guarantee Fund has been set up to ensure that availability of funds match working season demands. Districts have dedicated accounts for MGNREGA funds and submit their proposals based on clearly delineated guidelines so that funds may be devolved efficiently at each level, and adequate funds may be available to respond to demand. The funds are released on the basis of demand for employment received in a district and are based on an appraisal of both financial and physical indicators of outcomes.

7.4.11 Other Processes of MGNREGA:

A. Right-based Framework:

1. Adult members of a rural household who are willing to do unskilled manual

work may apply for registration to the local Gram Panchayat, in writing, or orally.

2. Gram Panchayat after due verification will issue a job card. The job card will bear the photograph of all adult members of the household and is free of cost.
3. A job card holding household may submit a written application for employment to the Gram Panchayat, stating the time and duration for which work is sought.

B. Time-bound Guarantee:

1. Gram Panchayat will issue a dated receipt of the written application for employment, against which the guarantee of providing employment within 15 days operates. If employment is not provided within 15 days, daily unemployment allowance in cash has to be paid. Liability of payment of unemployment allowance is of the States.
2. Work should ordinarily be provided within 5 km. radius of the village or else extra wages of 10 percent are payable.
3. Wages are to be paid according to minimum wages. Disbursement of wages has to be done on weekly basis and not beyond a fortnight.

C. Work Site Facilities:

Work site facilities such as crèche, drinking water, shade have to be provided.

D. Labour-intensive Works:

A 60:40 wage and material ratio has to be maintained. Contractors and use of labour displacing machinery is prohibited.

E. Permissible Works:

1. Water Conservation,
2. Drought Proofing (including plantation and afforestation),
3. Irrigation Canals,
4. Minor Irrigation, horticulture and land development on the land of SC/ST/BPL/IAY and land reform beneficiaries,
5. Renovation of traditional water bodies,
6. Flood Protection,
7. Land Development,
8. Rural connectivity, and
9. Any other work that may be notified by the Central Government in consultation with the State Government.

F. Rozgar Jagaran Puruskar: The objective of the award is to acknowledge the outstanding and exemplary contribution made by a registered Civil Society Organizations (CSO) in the effective implementation of the MGNREGA at state, district, block and gram panchayat levels. The award includes a medal, scroll and cash (gram panchayat, ₹ 1,000; intermediate panchayat, ₹ 2,000; district panchayat, ₹ 5,000 and State level, ₹ 25,000).

7.4.12 MGNREGA: A Review: Enactment of MGNREGA was a historic step in the Indian context.

MGNREGA is visualized as a first step towards the realization of the economic right to work as envisioned in the Directive Principles of State Policy in the Constitution of India. It recognizes Article 39 of the Constitution, according to which the State must ensure that "citizens, men and women equally, have the right to an adequate means to livelihood" and Article 41 whereby "the State, shall within the limits of its economic capacity and development, make effective provision for securing Right to Work..."

The potential of the MGNREGA to lead the economy towards a labour-intensive growth path needs to be emphasized in this context. The wage-work programme needs to be seen in a long-term perspective, with a strong planning component, dovetailing it with the ongoing development efforts, incorporating decentralised planning and implementation, skill training, maintenance of public assets and eventually absorbing wage-earners into mainstream employment. The path towards full employment lies in strengthening the sectors where the poor are located and stabilizing their incomes, improving their asset base, constructing basic socio-economic infrastructure at the local level, enabling access to paid work opportunities and exerting an upward pressure on market wages. MGNREGA as a programme is expected to create conditions for realisation of the above outcomes.

According to some recent studies, the performance of MGNREGA varies significantly across the States. There are some States where MGNREGA has managed to achieve its key outcomes very well and which have indeed innovated in many respects. In others, performance has been unimpressive and lack lustre. Given that the overall framework for MGNREGA is similar across the States, the variations in performance depend on factors such as political and administrative will of the governments, historical background of the state as well as the nature of civil society and public actions around MGNREGA State Governments have the responsibility of framing the rules as well as overseeing the actual implementation of the scheme on the ground. There is a lot of scope for State Governments to innovate and adapt the scheme according to the local requirements. State-specific experiences are important sources for innovations which in turn provide valuable lessons for replication. The relative success of the scheme in some regions, and failure in others highlights the need to properly understand the reasons for inter- and intra-state variations and to replicate and adopt features of implementation of the better performing states.

In a number of states, low participation of women in the programme is not due to the lack of demand from women but to the social norms that restrict work participation outside the home, especially in states like Uttar Pradesh and Bihar. Thus, there are still several hurdles in most of the states for enhancing women's participation in the programme. One of the stated objectives of MGNREGA is to foster a sense of gender equality and encourage women's participation in the economic domain. However, such exclusion only leads to reinforcement of the existing social biases against women and goes against the spirit of MGNREGA. Fostering gender equality also implies that the state must step in to lighten the women's role in the *care economy.*

Overall, even within the existing framework and limitations, many of the problems can be substantially overcome if the political and administrative leadership at the state and local levels plays a more proactive role in implementing the objectives of the MGNREGA.

Several violations of the basic entitlements of workers under the scheme are routinely reported. At the same time, these entitlements become more difficult to safeguard due to low levels of awareness among the workers in several parts of the country. Violations of MGNREGA norms are with respect to issues such as setting up of proper work application process and receipt of applications, payment of minimum wages, delays in payments, and lack of basic facilities at work places. While some of the violations occur due to procedural lapses like over-exacting or non-transparent schedule of rates, defective measurements, and weaknesses/gaps in the implementation system, there are also instances of wilful denial of entitlements by the officials.

7.4.13 Recommendations of the National Commission for Enterprises in the Unorganised Sector (NCEUS) to Improve the Functioning of MGNREGA: The Commission in its final report entitled *Challenge of Employment in India: An Informal Economy Perspective*, submitted in April 2009, reviewed the working of MGNREGA and made a number of recommendations to improve its functioning. Some important recommendations are as under:

1. Limit to employment days under MGNREGA be expanded. The cap of 100 days of employment should be removed in districts where 50 percent of the working population belong to Scheduled Castes and Scheduled Tribes.
2. Employment guarantee should be made applicable for each individual rather than per household.
3. MGNREGA activities should be taken up in class B and C municipalities as that would enhance employment opportunities in semi-urban localities.
4. The scheme guidelines should make provision for upgradation of skills of women and men workers so that they are able to take up skilled jobs in the

implementation apparatus of the programme.

5. To strengthen the administrative and operational efficiency, the administrative expenditure limits of MGNREGA funds be enhanced to 6 percent.
6. Awareness generation about MGNREGA should be a key component so as to increase the number of beneficiaries and to make the scheme more transparent.
7. Steps should be taken to provide opportunities for *light work* at every worksite for persons who are unable to meet the standard productivity norms due to old age, disability, illness, pregnancy and related conditions.
8. Proactive measures by the State Governments for fulfilling the mandate of 33 percent norm of women's share of MGNREGA.

7.4.14 Twelfth Five Year Plan (2012-17) on MGNREGA: Commenting on the performance of MGNREGA, the Approach Paper to the Twelfth Plan observed, "With a people-centred, demand-driven architecture, completely different from the earlier rural employment programmes, MGNREGA has directly led to the creation of 987 crore person-days of work since its inception in 2006-07. In financial year 2010-11, MGNREGA provided employment to 5.45 crore households generating 253.68 crore person-days. It has also successfully raised the negotiating power of agricultural labour, resulting in higher agricultural wages, improved economic outcomes leading to reduction in distress migration. This is not to deny that with better project design, implementation leakages could be greatly reduced; and the assets so created could make a larger contribution towards increase in land productivity.

Reforms in implementation of Plan schemes are a priority and should receive focussed attention in the Twelfth Plan. There is need for more flexibility in the design of the schemes to reflect the ground realities across the States. Additional provisions should be considered for encouraging innovation; also special efforts to promote convergence at the level of implementation to prevent duplication and to create synergies that improve the quality of outcomes." [1]

The Plan Document further stated, "Experience thus far suggests that while MGNREGA is generating employment, the technical soundness of design and quality of works undertaken in MGNREGA falls short of what is needed to ensure land productivity enhancement. There appear to be two critical areas in regard of MGNREGA that need to be addressed and resolved in the Twelfth Plan.

First, the technical capacity at the local level has to be significantly enhanced. This is in regard to planning, design and quality of works, as well as of their maintenance. Planning for MGNREGA on a mini-watershed and aquifer basis would improve outcomes. To strengthen the demand-driven character of the scheme and guarantee legal entitlements, it is important to record applications for work. There is a clear case for establishing a pool of local 'barefoot' engineers/technical assistants who could be trained up through an appropriate mechanism, enabling them to fulfil the need for technical and managerial capacity in MGNREGA, as well as in other rural infrastructure projects.

Second, it is important that the selection of works reflects the needs, aspirations and priorities of the local people, without which the community will not necessarily have a sense of ownership of the project. The latter is a vital component of the concept of rural infrastructure creation. The training of a pool of local youth in technical skills must also incorporate their ability to act as social mobilizers and ensure the involvement of Panchayati Raj Institution (PRI) representatives at every level of the process. They would be guided in this process by a dedicated team of technical professionals (to be created) at each cluster of around 30 villages that broadly correspond to the boundaries of a mini-watershed and aquifer. Madhya Pradesh and Maharashtra have already initiated work in this direction.

Delays in wage payments have emerged as the most frequently heard complaint under MGNREGA. At times payments have not been made even after nine months and workers are rarely being paid compensation for the delay. The major reason for delay is that measurements of work are not being made on time, mainly due to lack of adequate technical staff at the block level. There are also bottlenecks in the flow of funds through the system, at times because data on the Management Information System (MIS) is not being filled up on time. Better use of information technology, as in Andhra Pradesh, is worth emulating. The tightly integrated, end-to-end computer network in Andhra Pradesh identifies delay in execution of any work registered online and takes corrective action immediately. Free availability of payment information facilitates public scrutiny and transparency.

There is a need to involve NGOs who could support gram panchayats in planning, implementing and conducting of social audits of MGNREGA works. There are good examples of such successful models across the country. There is a need to disseminate the learnings from these experiences in the field and improve the functioning of the programme.

Rural India has a large population of artisan families, many of whom are from the minority and tribal communities. Most of these artisan farmers do not own any land and many find themselves in a difficult condition with poor access to market linkages and to remunerative livelihoods. Thought must be given as to how the MGNREGA in conjunction with the NRLM programme can help these artisan communities to obtain a decent living while at the same time conserving the base of craftsmanship, which is India's cultural heritage."[2]

7.5 National Rural Livelihoods Mission (NRLM)

Swarnjayanti Gram Swarozgar Yojana (SGSY) has been restructured as National Rural Livelihoods Mission (NRLM) to implement it in a mission mode and in a phased manner for targeted and time-bound delivery of results.

NRLM aims to reduce poverty by enabling the poor households to access gainful self-employment and skilled wage employment opportunities, resulting in appreciable improvement in their livelihoods on a sustainable basis, through building strong grassroots institutions of the poor.

Universal social mobilization through formation of Self-help Groups (SHGs) under NRLM will ensure that at least one member of each rural BPL family, preferably a woman member, is covered under SHG net. With a view to form strong peoples institutions, NRLM focuses on setting up of federations of SHGs from village panchayat to district levels. NRLM proposes to ensure universal financial inclusion by facilitating opening of savings accounts of all its beneficiaries, simultaneously encouraging thrift and credit activities, facilitating access to credit from banks etc. There is a provision to utilize 10 percent of allocation under the programme for training and capacity building of the intended beneficiaries to take up the micro enterprises for enhancing their incomes. In addition to self-employment, NRLM also focuses on supporting rural BPL youth for accessing skilled wage employment through placement-linked skill development projects.

The two major strategic shifts under NRLM, vis-à-vis SGSY, are (a) NRLM is a demand-driven programme and the states will formulate their own poverty reduction action plans under it based on their past experience, resources and skills base and (b) NRLM provides for a professional support structure for programme implementation at all levels from national to sub-district level in different streams.

In order to ensure a holistic approach towards income enhancement of the rural poor, NRLM focuses on 4 streams of livelihoods which are as follows:

1. Coping with Vulnerabilities: Debt bondage, food insecurity, migration, health checks.
2. Existing Livelihoods: Stabilising and expanding, making them sustainable.
3. Self-employment: Micro enterprise development, skilled wage employment.
4. Opportunities in growing sectors of the economy.

7.5.1 Main Provisions of NRLM:

A. Universal Social Mobilization: To begin with, NRLM would ensure that at least one member from each identified rural poor household, preferably a woman, is brought under the self-help group (SHG) network in a time bound manner. Subsequently, both women and men would be organized for addressing livelihoods issues, i.e. farmers' organizations, milk producers' cooperatives, weavers' associations etc. All these institutions are inclusive and no poor would be left out of them. NRLM would ensure adequate coverage of vulnerable sections of the society such that 50 percent of the beneficiaries are SC/STs, 15 percent are minorities and 3 percent are persons with disability, while keeping in view the ultimate target of 100 percent coverage of BPL families.

B. Promotion of Institutions of the Poor: Strong institutions of the poor such as SHGs and their village level and higher level federations are necessary to provide space, voice and resources for the poor and for reducing their dependence on external agencies. They empower them and also act as instruments of knowledge and technology dissemination, and hubs of production, collectivization and commerce. NRLM, therefore, would focus on setting up these institutions at various levels.

In addition, NRLM would promote specialized institutions like Livelihood Collectives, producers' cooperatives/companies for livelihood promotion through deriving economies of scale, backward and forward linkages, and access to information, credit, technology, markets etc. The Livelihoods Collectives would enable the poor to optimize their limited resources.

There are existing institutions of the poor women formed by governments and NGOs. NRLM would strengthen all existing institutions of the poor in a partnership mode.

C. Training, Capacity Building and Skill Building: NRLM would ensure that the poor are provided with the requisite skills for managing their institutions, linking up with markets, managing their existing livelihoods, enhancing their credit absorption capacity and credit worthiness etc. A multi-pronged approach is envisaged for continuous capacity building of the targeted families, SHGs, their federations, government functionaries, bankers, NGOs and other key stakeholders. Particular focus would be on developing and engaging community professionals and community resource persons for capacity building of SHGs and their federations and other collectives. NRLM would make extensive use of information technology to make knowledge dissemination and capacity building more effective.

D. Revolving Fund and Capital Subsidy: Subsidy would be available in the form of revolving fund and capital subsidy. The revolving fund would be provided to the SHGs (where more than 70 percent members are from BPL households) as an incentive to inculcate the habit of thrift and accumulate their own funds towards meeting their credit needs in the long-run and immediate consumption needs in the short-run. Subsidy would be a corpus and used for meeting the credit needs of members directly and as catalytic capital for leveraging repeat bank finance. Capital subsidy fund would be given directly to the SHGs or would be routed to the SHGs through the federations, wherever the SHGs desire such an arrangement.

E. Universal Financial Inclusion: NRLM would work towards achieving universal financial inclusion, beyond basic banking services to all the poor households, SHGs and their federations. NRLM would work on both demand and supply side of financial inclusion. On the demand side, it would promote financial literacy among the poor and provide catalytic capital to the SHGs and their federations. On the supply side, it would coordinate with the financial sector and encourage use of information technology-based financial technologies, business correspondents and community facilitators. It would also work towards universal coverage of rural poor against loss of life, health and assets. Further, it would work on remittances, especially in areas where migration is endemic.

F. Provision of Interest Subsidy: The rural poor need credit at low rate of interest and in multiple doses to make their ventures economically viable. In order to ensure affordable credit, NRLM has a provision for subsidy on interest rate above 7 percent per annum for all eligible SHGs, who have availed loans from mainstream financial institutions, based on prompt loan repayment (This would not be applicable when a SHG avails capital subsidy. Interest subsidy would be provided to this SHG, when they avail a fresh loan after repaying the capital subsidy-linked loan). This subsidy would be available to SHGs, where at least 70 percent of the members are from BPL households, till a member accesses credit, through repeat cumulative loaning, up to ₹ 1 lakh per household.

G. Infrastructure Creation and Marketing Support: NRLM would seek to ensure that the infrastructure needs for the major livelihood activities of the poor are met with. It would also provide support for marketing to the institutions of the poor. The range of activities in marketing support includes market research, market intelligence, technology extension, developing backward and forward linkages, building livelihood collectives and supporting their business plans. NRLM would encourage and support partnerships with public and private organizations and their networks/associations for these activities, particularly for market linkages. 20 percent of the programme outlay of a state (25 percent in case of North-Eastern States and Sikkim) is reserved for this purpose.

H. Skills and Placement Projects: NRLM would scale up the existing skill and placement projects through partnership mode as one of the best investments in youth, and provide impetus to livelihood opportunities in emerging markets. For strengthening this, various models of partnerships with public, private, non-government and community organizations would be developed. A strong relationship would also be developed with industry associations and sector specific employers' associations. National Skill Development Corporation (NSDC) would be one of the leading partners in this effort. 15 percent of the central allocation under NRLM is earmarked for this purpose.

I. Rural Self-employment Training Institutes (RSETIs): NRLM encourages public sector banks to set up RSETIs in all districts of the country. RSETIs transform unemployed rural youth in the district into confident self-employed entrepreneurs through need-based experiential learning programme followed by systematic handholding support. Banks are completely involved in selection, training and post-training follow-up stages. RSETIs partner with others, including institutions of the poor, to realize their mandate and agenda.

J. Innovations: NRLM believes that successful innovations can reduce poverty. 5 percent of the Central allocation is, therefore, earmarked for innovations. Those innovations which have the potential for reaching out specifically to the poorest or for reaching out to the largest number of poor and having maximum impact with limited resources, would be preferred and supported.

K. Convergence: NRLM would place very high emphasis on convergence with other programmes of the Ministry of Rural Development and other Central Ministries and programmes of State Governments for developing synergies directly and through the institutions of the poor.

L. Partnerships with NGOs and other CSOs: NRLM would proactively seek partnerships with non-government organizations (NGOs) and other civil society organizations (CSOs), at two levels: strategic and implementation. The partnerships would be guided by core beliefs and values of NRLM, and mutual agreement on processes and outcomes. NRLM would develop a national framework for partnerships with NGOs and other CSOs. Further, NRLM would seek partnerships with various other stakeholders at various levels directly or through the institutions of the poor.

M. Linkages with PRIs: In view of the eminent roles of Panchayat Raj Institutions (PRIs) that include governance, commercial and political, it is necessary to consciously structure and facilitate a mutually beneficial working relationship between panchayats and institutions of the poor, particularly at the level of village panchayats. Formal platforms would be established for regular consultations between such institutions and PRIs for exchange of mutual advice, support and sharing of resources. However, care would be taken to protect their autonomy. Where there are no PRIs, the linkages would be with traditional local village institutions.

N. Sensitive Support Structures: Process-intensive effort of NRLM would require dedicated human resources. Realizing this, NRLM would be setting up sensitive and dedicated support structures at the national, state, district and sub-district levels. NRLM Advisory, Coordination and Empowered Committees and National Mission Management Unit at the national level, State Rural Livelihood Missions (SRLMs) as autonomous bodies and State Mission Management Units at state level, District Mission Management Units at district level, and sub-district units at block and/or cluster levels would constitute these support structures. The institutions of the poor, their staff and other social capital would also provide support. These support structures would be staffed with professionally competent and dedicated human resources through appropriate arrangements including partnerships and outsourcing of services.

O. Technical Support: NRLM would provide technical assistance to the states and all other partners for creating and strengthening their institutional capacities for its effective implementation. It would build national knowledge management and learning forums/systems. It would facilitate partnerships between institutions of the poor and banking sectors, public and private sectors, for ensuring last mile service delivery to reach the poor. It would build a national pool of experts, practitioners and advisers in all the relevant disciplines for providing handholding support to SRLMs for developing and executing state poverty reduction strategies.

7.5.2 Funding Pattern, Transition and Implementation: NRLM is a Centrally-sponsored scheme and financing of the programme would be shared between the Centre and the States in the ratio of 75:25 (90:10 in case of North Eastern States including Sikkim; completely from the Centre in case of UTs). The Central allocation earmarked for the States would broadly be distributed in relation to the incidence of poverty in the States.

All States/UTs would have to transit to NRLM within a period of one year from the date of formal launch of NRLM.

NRLM would fund states against appraised and approved annual action plans and state perspective and implementation plans that outline the results and the processes towards these results. It would review the performance against these plans half-yearly and annually and funds flow to the states would be based on the revised annual plans.

7.5.3 Monitoring, Evaluation and Learning: NRLM is process-intensive and therefore, it would constantly review, assess and learn from the qualitative and quantitative progress achieved at various levels. A robust IT-based monitoring, evaluation and learning system would be in place to facilitate learning and continuous improvement and support informed decision making at all levels.

NRLM would put in place various mechanisms for monitoring:

1. Accountability in institutions of the poor includes institutional self-monitoring, peer internal audit of processes and local social audit.
2. Management Information System (MIS) based input-output monitoring includes results framework-based MIS; milestones linked to investments/inputs; web-based MIS; real time input-output monitoring at various levels; and MIS with data of partners.
3. IT-framework for dedicated digital grid includes national database of poor, their institutions, and skill development (jobs/self-employment), national livelihood portal, communication/knowledge dissemination channels, thematic e-groups etc.
4. Internal review mechanisms at various levels.
5. External social audit, public expenditure tracking and community score cards.
6. Impact Assessment - state level baseline assessments and external interim impact evaluation studies of progress on key result indicators; independent national assessment of household level well-being through panel studies at periodic intervals and periodic thematic national assessments.
7. SRLM Annual Reports and NRLM Annual Report.
8. NRLM would put in place a comprehensive financial management system at SRLM to ensure transparency, efficiency and accountability. NRLM would position an IT-based fund tracking system and promote e-book keeping in institutions of the poor and in support structures.

7.5.4 Mahila Kisan Shasaktikaran Pariyojana (MKSP): In order to improve the present status of women in agriculture, and to enhance the opportunities for their empowerment, Government of India has announced Mahila Kisan Sashaktikaran Pariyojana (MKSP) as a sub-component of NRLM. MKSP recognizes the centrality of women in agriculture and therefore aims to provide direct and indirect support to enable them to achieve sustainable agriculture production. It will initiate a learning cycle by which women are enabled to learn and adopt appropriate technologies and farming systems. MKSP will be implemented as a sub-component of NRLM through specially formulated projects.

The salient features of MKSP are as follows:

1. Primary objective of MKSP is to empower women in agriculture by making systematic investments to enhance their participation and productivity in agriculture-based livelihood.
2. Through this scheme, it is proposed to create sustainable agricultural livelihood opportunities for women in agriculture and in the process ensure food and nutrition security at the household and the community levels.

3. Under MKSP, community-based women institutions in the rural area will be strengthened in order to enable them to manage their agriculture-based livelihood activities.
4. Under MKSP, use of locally-adopted resource conserving, farmer-led and environmentally-friendly technologies has been emphasized.
5. Ministry of Rural Development, Government of India would provide funding support or up to 75 percent (90 percent for North East and hill states) to the project submitted by the State Government/Project Implementing Agencies (PIAs) under MKSP. Balance is to be contributed by the respective State Governments or any other donor agencies.

The expected outcomes of MKSP are as follows:

1. Net increase in the income of women in agriculture on a sustainable basis.
2. Improvement in food and nutritional security of women in agriculture and their families.
3. Increase in area under cultivation, cropping intensity and food production by women.
4. Increased levels of skill and performance by women in agriculture.
5. Increased access of women in agriculture to productive land, inputs, credit, technology and information.
6. Drudgery reduction for women in agriculture through use or gender friendly tools/technologies.
7. Increased access to market and market information for better marketing of their product.
8. Increased soil health and fertility to sustain agriculture based livelihoods.
9. Increased visibility of women in agriculture as an interest group.

7.5.5 Twelfth Five Year Plan (2012-17) on NRLM: Pointing out the focus of NRLM, the Approach to the Twelfth Plan observed, "The experience with MGNREGA has clearly highlighted the problems that are often encountered when a programme is universalised without sufficient preparatory work and support systems being in place. This has been a problem with the SGSY scheme also. While the fast growth of the SHG-Bank Linkage (SBL) model is heartening, there are also many concerns. A large part of the problem derives from the top-down, target-driven approach that has undermined the demand-driven thrust, which was the original mandate. There are also reports of high rates of mortality in many SHGs, which has had an adverse impact on the credibility of the SBL model in the eyes of key stakeholders, including potential women members, as also bankers.

The real power of the SBL model lies in the economies of scale created by Self Help Group (SHG) Federations (comprising 150–200 SHGs each). This is evident, for example, in bulk purchase of inputs (seeds, fertilisers etc.) and marketing of outputs (crops, vegetables, milk, NTFPs etc). They can also provide larger loans for housing and health facilities to their members by tying up with large service or loan providers. A variety of insurance services can also be made available, including life, health, livestock and weather insurance. It has also been shown how doing business with SHG Federations can help public sector bank branches in remote rural areas become viable entities.

Taking a cue from the lessons of the SGSY experience, the Government of India has launched the National Rural Livelihoods Mission in 2011. There is a clear understanding that the SBL programme can only be successful if it is tied up with livelihood programmes such as improved agriculture, dairying, marketing, etc. Thus, the SBL and livelihood programmes are complementary to each other and their simultaneous implementation is the key to poverty alleviation. Incomes earned through livelihood initiatives need to be saved. Of these savings, women are the best custodians. These savings must, in turn, be reinvested in livelihood options that raise incomes, setting up a virtuous cycle. The distinctive focus of the NRLM is on Federations of SHGs that become powerful units of economic empowerment, enabling the poor to radically alter the balance of power in the markets they participate in as both producers and consumers. [3]

7.6 Indira Awaas Yojana (IAY)

Fulfilling the need for rural housing and tackling housing shortage, particularly for the poorest, is an important task to be undertaken as part of the poverty alleviation efforts of the Government. IAY is the flagship scheme of the Ministry of Rural Development (MoRD), Government of India to provide houses to the below-poverty-line (BPL) families in the rural areas. It has been in operation since 1985-86.

IAY is one of the very popular schemes of MoRD and has caught the imagination of the rural people. Funds are released in instalments directly to the beneficiaries and there is no credit portion as part of the assistance which enables timely release of funds. The beneficiaries construct the houses as per their own choice of design, technology and requirement.

7.6.1 Salient Features of IAY:

1. The funding of IAY is shared between the Centre and States in the ratio of 75:25. In the case of Union Territories, the entire funds of IAY are provided by the Centre. However, in the case of North-East States, the funding pattern is in the ratio of 90:10.
2. Under IAY, a BPL family is given grant of ₹ 45,000 for new construction in

plain areas and ₹ 48,500 for construction in hilly/difficult areas w.e.f. April, 2010. Besides, IAY funds (up to a maximum of 20 percent of the allocation) can be made available for upgradation or/and credit-cum-subsidy scheme at the rate of ₹ 15,000 for each dwelling unit. In addition, IAY houses have been included under the Different Rate of Interest (DRI) scheme for lending up to ₹ 20,000 per unit at an interest rate of 4 percent. As a special dispensation, the higher unit assistance of ₹ 48,500 applicable in the case of hilly/difficult areas has also been made available in focused 35 Left Wing Extremism (LWE districts).

3. Since reduction of shelterlessness is the primary objective, 75 percent weightage is given to housing shortage and 25 percent to the poverty ratios prescribed by Planning Commission for State level allocation. For district level allocation, 75 percent weightage is given again to housing shortage and 25 percent to SC/ST population of the concerned districts. On the basis of allocations made and targets fixed, District Rural Development Agency (DRDAs) Zila Parishads (ZPs) decide Panchayat-wise number of houses to be constructed under IAY and intimate the same to the concerned Gram Panchayat.
4. Thereafter, the beneficiaries are selected from the Permanent IAY waitlists prepared with the approval of respective Gram Sabha. Such waitlists are prepared out of the BPL List 2002.
5. At least 60 percent of the total IAY funds and physical targets should be utilized for construction/upgradation of dwelling units for SC/ST BPL households. A maximum 40 percent for non-SC/ST BPL rural households. IAY funds and physical targets are earmarked for BPL minorities in each State as indicated by the Ministry. 3 percent of the above categories are for physically and mentally challenged persons. From 2006-07 onwards, funds and physical targets under IAY are also being earmarked for BPL minorities in each State.
6. Further, the dwelling units are invariably allotted in the name of a female member of the beneficiary household. Alternatively, the same can be allotted in the name of both husband and wife. Only in case there is no eligible female member in the family the house is allotted in the name of an eligible male member.
7. Construction of the houses is the sole responsibility of the beneficiary. Engagement of contractors is strictly prohibited. Sanitary latrine and smokeless chullah are required to be constructed along with each IAY house.
8. 5 percent of the total allocated funds under IAY is kept apart to meet the exigencies arising out of natural calamities and other emergent situations like

riot, arson, fire, rehabilitation under exceptional circumstances with a district-wise ceiling of 10 percent of annual allocation (including State share) or ₹ 70 lakh whichever is higher. Proposals for this purpose have to be forwarded by State Governments/UTs showing the extent of damage and the estimated fund requirement. In order to facilitate timely relief to victims in the case of fire, riots and arson and enable immediate reconstruction of damaged houses, District Collectors/District Magistrates/ Deputy Commissioners at the district level are authorized to first incur the expenditure and extend assistance to victims of such calamities. The central share of the expenditure so incurred is reimbursed to them.

9. Instructions have been issued to all the DRDAs for convergence of various Centrally-sponsored schemes (CSS) with IAY. IAY beneficiaries need to get benefits available under Rajiv Gandhi Grameen Vidyutikaran Yojana (RGGVY), Total Sanitation Campaign (TSC), Janshree and Aam Aadmi Bima Yojana and Differential Rate of Interest (DRI) Scheme etc.
10. IAY is continuously reviewed through Monthly and Annual Reports received from the States/UTs. Senior officers at the level of Deputy Secretaries and above in the Ministry are appointed as Area Officers for different States/UTs. These Area Officers visit the allotted States/UTs from time to time and inspect the actual implementation of the programme in the field. They also participate in the State Level Co-ordination Committee Meetings providing thereby, a source of effective link between the policy makers, i.e. Government of India and the implementing agencies (States/UT Governments). The programme is also reviewed at the meetings with the State Secretaries of Rural Development and with the Project Directors of DRDAs in the workshops held every year.

7.6.2 Monitoring Mechanism: All the State Governments and UTs are required to send monthly and annual progress reports in respect of the physical and financial achievements under the IAY scheme. The performa of these reports is such that all critical details like SC/ST component, coverage of women beneficiaries, provision of smokeless chulhas and sanitary latrines, coverage of physically handicapped beneficiaries etc. are indicated. Financial monitoring is an automatic, concurrent process carried out through examination of utilization certificates, audit reports etc. which form the basis for release of funds.

Field inspections are carried out by officers of MoRD who are nominated as Area Officers. Third party inspections are also carried out by the National Level Monitors (NLMs) and District Level Monitors (DLMs). In addition, periodic review meetings are organized by MoRD, the most important being the quarterly meetings of the Performance Review Committee.

7.6.3 Allotment of Homestead Plot: A scheme was launched, w.e.f. August 2009 as part of IAY, for providing homestead sites to those rural BPL households whose names are included in the permanent IAY waitlists but who have neither agricultural land nor a house site.

₹ 10,000 per homestead site is being provided under the Scheme, the funding of which is shared by the Centre and the States in the ratio of 50:50. The States are also incentivized by allocating additional physical targets equal to the number of homestead sites provided by regularization of existing occupied land, allotment of Government land or purchase/acquisition of land as the case may be.

7.6.4 Critical Evaluation of IAY: Providing houses to the poorest has a positive impact on people's physical and mental health. Once the basic need of housing is fulfilled, citizens develop a sense of opportunity for livelihood, for improving living conditions and for continuing children's education. Undoubtedly, there is a direct link between a safe and secure housing and better standards of living and reduction in vulnerability.

The popularity of IAY can be attributed to the fact that the scheme enables beneficiaries to participate and involve themselves in construction of their homes. The role of the State Government is limited to releases and to facilitating use of appropriate technology. In spite of criticism from certain quarters about IAY being a full subsidy scheme, experience reveals that houses get completed more or less on time which may not be the case if credit is part of the assistance. Not surprisingly, evaluation studies reveal high levels of occupancy and satisfaction.

However, it is important to note the following remarks of the Eleventh Five Year Plan (2007-12) on IAY, "Studies have revealed that only about 50 percent of IAY houses have sanitary latrines and even a lesser percentage have installed smokeless chullas. This is a serious problem. Over a million women and children not only suffer from upper respiratory tract infections due to inhaling of indoor smoke but many die as a result. In addition, India is one of the countries in the world with much of its population not having access to sanitary means of excreta disposal (despite the existence of Total Sanitation Campaign, another Centrally Sponsored Scheme, which is part of the Bharat Nirman set of programmes). Houses built as part of the Central Government's own programmes, like IAY, need to succeed in building of smokeless chulhas and of sanitary latrines." [4]

Pointing out the drawbacks of the IAY scheme, the Approach Paper to the Twelfth Five Year Plan (2012-17) remarked, "A major weakness of the Indira Awaas Yojana (IAY) has been the quality of housing. There have been complaints about weak foundations, poor roofing materials and incomplete constructions. There is a clear need for developing and popularising innovative, location-specific technologies, materials, designs and methods through a network of institutions, which could result in low-cost, environment friendly and disaster resistant houses as per local cultural preferences. Better systems for monitoring of the programme are also required.

Part of the problem is linked to the available assistance under the IAY programme. This has been recently enhanced but it is widely felt that this enhancement may be inadequate. It is necessary to examine whether increasing the permissible loan amount even if at a slightly higher interest rate could solve the problem. This could be best achieved through the NRLM route by making it a loan product offered by SHGs. Finally, to transform IAY into a larger habitat development programme, we need to ensure domestic water, sanitation, clean fuel and electricity with housing. This calls for deeper convergence across various flagship programmes." [5]

7.7 Total Sanitation Campaign (TSC)

TSC under the restructured Central Rural Sanitation Programme (CRSP) was launched with effect from April 1, 1999 following a community-led and people-cantered approach. Thus, TSC moved away from the principle of State-wise allocation primarily based on poverty criterion to a demand-driven approach. TSC envisages a synergised interaction between the government, people and active NGO participation, provision of an alternative delivery system and more flexible, demand-oriented construction norms. The revised Tenth Five Year Plan strategy envisaged a shift from allocation-based programme to a demand-based project mode. Besides the paradigm shift envisages a greater household involvement, stress on software and emphasis on school sanitation.

TSC gives emphasis on Information, Education and Communication (IEC) for demand generation of sanitation facilities, providing for stronger back up systems such as trained masons and the basic construction and maintenance material through rural sanitary marts and production centres and including a thrust on school and anganwadi sanitation as an entry point for encouraging wider acceptance of sanitation by rural masses as key strategies. It also laid emphasis on hygiene education in schools for bringing about attitudinal and behavioural changes for relevant sanitation and hygiene practices from a young age and seeks to attain Goal 9 of the MDG by 2010 and *Sanitation for All* by 2012. TSC is a community-led and people-oriented programme.

7.7.1 Objectives: The main objectives of the TSC are the following:

1. Bring about an improvement in the general quality of life in rural areas.
2. Accelerate sanitation coverage.
3. Generate demand through awareness and health education.
4. Cover all schools and anganwadis in rural areas with sanitation facilities and

promote hygiene behaviour among students and teachers.
5. Encourage cost effective and appropriate technology development and application.
6. Endeavour to reduce water and sanitation related diseases.

7.7.2 Components: The components of TSC include start-up activities, IEC, individual household latrines, community sanitary complex, school sanitation and hygiene education and anganwadi toilets. Alternate delivery mechanism, in the form of Rural Sanitary marts and Production centres and administrative changes are also components of TSC.

7.7.3 Revised Guidelines: TSC guidelines were modified following approval by the Cabinet Committee on Economic Affairs on March 9, 2006. The modifications came into effect on April 1, 2006. Following are the revised TSC guidelines:

1. Unit cost of both models of household toilets was revised to take into consideration price escalation due to inflation. As a result, the cost of the two models was revised from the existing ₹ 625 to ₹ 1,500 and from ₹ 1,000 to ₹ 2,000. The objective is to make it a demand-driven campaign through creation of awareness and generating demand for sanitation as a basic necessity.
2. In order to bring parity with Sarva Shiksha Abhiyan, community contribution for construction of school and *anganwadi* toilets has been removed. Henceforth, Government of India and State Government share would be in the ratio of 70:30 for construction of institutional toilets which include school and *anganwadi* toilets. For all the school toilets taken up for construction w.e.f April 1, 2006, this provision would be applicable.
3. Solid and liquid waste management was approved as a component of TSC. Up to 10 percent of the total project cost can be utilized for this component.
4. It was decided to grant a revolving fund of maximum of ₹ 50 lakh subject to the ceiling of 5 percent of total project cost under the *alternative delivery mechanism component* to each district, which could be used for giving loan to members of SHGs and Milk Cooperative Societies whose credit worthiness is beyond any doubt. A maximum loan of ₹ 2000 per individual member can be granted. Members belonging to APL category may also be extended such loans subject to the condition that the amount is recovered in 10-12 monthly instalments.

7.7.4 Revision of Unit Cost of School and Anganwadi Toilets: Children are more receptive to new ideas and schools/anganwadis are appropriate institutions for changing the behaviour, mindset and habits of children from open defecation to the use of lavatory through motivation and education. The experience gained by children through use of toilets in school and sanitation education imparted by teachers would reach home and would also influence parents to adopt good sanitary habits. school sanitation, therefore, forms an integral part of every TSC project. Accordingly, toilets in all types of Government schools i.e. primary, upper primary, secondary and higher secondary and anganwadis, which are identified as not having this facility, are provided assistance under TSC for construction of toilets. Unit cost of school toilet block has been increased from ₹ 20,000 to ₹ 35,000 (₹ 38,500) for hilly and difficult areas) also unit cost of anganwadi toilet has been increased from ₹ 5,000 to ₹ 8,000 (₹ 10,000 for hilly and difficult areas) with effect from April 1, 2010.

Convergence with Integrated Child Development Scheme (ICDS), National Rural Health Mission (NRHM) and School Sanitation and Hygiene Education (SSHE) has been identified as a crucial component for the success of TSC and vice-versa. For this purpose, all state governments have been requested to include a module on sanitation in all in-service trainings and refresher courses of school teachers, ICDS workers and ASHA and health workers. Many states are reported to have done this. Co-ordination meetings have been held at the Government of India level also.

7.7.5 Twelfth Five Year Plan (2012-17) on TSC: Commenting on the problems of TSC, the Approach to the Twelfth Plan observed, "Questions of sustainability have somewhat undermined the otherwise dramatic success in the Total Sanitation Campaign (TSC). The Nirmal Gram Puraskars (NGPs) spurred competition among PRIs to hasten toilet construction, but it does not appear to have ensured sustained use. A 2008 study covering 162 NGP Gram Panchayats in six States shows that only 4.0 percent of GPs were genuinely open defecation free. In 32.0 percent of the GPs, more than 40.0 percent of the people are not using the toilets built for them under TSC.

The problem arises because TSC is becoming increasingly state-led and target-driven and often implemented without any conscious effort to create required awareness at the community level. The programme is often driven by a desire to achieve fund utilisation and not as an exercise organically linked to awareness creation and demand generation processes. Top-down IEC strategies of posters and brochures with no individual contact have proven to be ineffective. Great effort is required to sustain the gains of the adoption phase to ensure that slip-backs do not occur. A phased approach needs to be developed for achieving universalization with quality, based on a process truly driven by demand from a community that is committed to improved sanitation.

One of the limitations of the TSC is the narrow range of technology options offered in a country with such immensely diverse geographic, hydrologic, climatic and socio-economic conditions (high water table, flood prone, rocky ground, desert/water scarce areas and extreme low temperatures). This has led to many problems, including non-acceptance by local communities, water pollution especially in shallow water table regions, and waste of public funds." [6]

7.8 Rural Water Supply

7.8.1 Accelerated Rural Water Supply Programme (ARWSP): To accelerate the pace of coverage of problem villages, the Government of India introduced ARWSP in 1972-73 to assist States and UTs with 100 percent grants-in-aid to implement drinking water supply schemes in such villages. To ensure that all aspects of rural water supply are adequately addressed to, there are different components of ARWSP. 10 percent of the overall amount allocated under ARWSP is earmarked for North-East States. Allocation of funds to the States is based on a number of criteria such as rural population, special category hill States and water quality problems.

Though ground water is less susceptible to pollution, the quality problem in ground water is inherent in the form of contamination caused by the very nature of geological formation, viz. excess fluoride, arsenic, brackishness, iron etc. The reasons for chemical and bacteriological contamination are: poor hygienic conditions around the water sources, improper disposal of sewage and industrial waste water, callous disposal of solid waste, indiscriminate use of chemical fertilizers having high quantity of Nitrates used in the agricultural sector, pollution from industrial effluents (untreated), over-exploitation leading to quality degradation, pollution of the source due to ignorance of the people, overpopulation and lack of public awareness. The ground water level has depleted resulting in surfacing of quality problems due to higher concentration of the contaminants in the depleted sources of water. Inadequate recharging also aggravates the problem of chemical contamination.

In order to provide focused attention on tackling water quality problems, 20 percent of the ARWSP funds are retained at the Centre, to be released to water quality affected States. Tackling fluoride, arsenic and salinity are taken as priority areas.

7.8.2 Swajaldhara: The Government of India has been emphasizing the need for taking up community-based rural water supply programmes and with this end in view a beginning was made in 1999 by sanctioning Sector Reform Pilot Projects on an experimental basis. With the experience gained, the reform initiatives in the rural drinking water supply sector were opened up throughout the country by launching the Swajaldhara programme on December 25, 2002.

Swajaldhara programme, started as a part of Accelerated Rural Water Supply

Programme (ARWSP), aims to promote decentralized, demand-driven, community-managed rural water supply programme to bring in sustainability in the sector. The programme involves a community contribution of 10 percent of the project cost to instil a sense of ownership among the people and also to take over the O&M of the schemes constructed under the programme. The Centre provides 90 percent of the project cost as grant. Under other components of ARWSP, there is no such mandatory community contribution. Many States reported difficulty in implementation of the scheme. In this backdrop, the Swajaldhara provisions were modified. The salient features are as under:

1. For coverage, there is only one rural water supply programme, i.e. ARWSP with 50:50 sharing pattern between Centre and the States.
2. No separate allocation is made for Swajaldhara for new schemes/projects at the Government of India level.
3. Issue of enlisting community contribution has been left to the discretion of the State Government depending upon the local prevailing conditions.
4. For all on-going and approved schemes taken-up under Swajaldhara till March 31, 2007, funds will be provided to complete these ongoing schemes by the Government of India on old funding pattern.
5. Implementation of new rural water supply schemes under ARWSP on Swajaldhara principles is to be decided by the State Government and quantum of funds to be allocated for this purpose out of ARWSP fund, is left to the discretion of the State.

Swjaldhara principles are to be adopted by the State Governments as per local conditions and adequate flexibility has been provided to incorporate such principles under ongoing Accelerated Rural Water Supply Programme itself.

7.8.3 Online Monitoring: Online monitoring system, i.e. Integrated Management Information System (IMIS) has been introduced to strengthen monitoring mechanism and transparency whereby State Governments have been urged to report the physical and financial progress online on monthly basis and update the habitation wise data on yearly basis. System of on-line data entry has been introduced and State officials responsible for online data entry have been imparted training to undertake this job. Besides, periodic review meetings are conducted to review the physical and financial progress in the implementation of schemes in all the states.

7.8.4 National Rural Drinking Water Quality Monitoring and Surveillance Programme (NRDWQM&SP): The community-based NRDWQM&SP was launched in February 2006 which aims at testing of all drinking water sources by the grassroots level workers in each Panchayat by simple-to-use field test kits and joint sanitary surveys. One field test kit is provided to every Gram Panchayat in the country for this purpose. The positively tested samples are then tested at the District/State level laboratories for confirmation. National Institute of Communicable Diseases (NICD), under the Ministry of Health and Family Welfare is the National Referral Institute to act as Consultants for the implementation of the programme. Training of State Government officials.

7.8.5 National Rural Drinking Water Programme (NRDWP): Ensuring equity in availability of safe drinking water—with regard to gender, socially and economically weaker sections of the society, school children, socially vulnerable groups such as pregnant and lactating mothers, especially disabled and senior citizens, etc.—has been one of the prime concerns of Eleventh Plan. It was also decided that the major issues which need tackling during the Plan are problems of sustainability, water availability and supply, poor water quality, centralized versus decentralized approaches. In order to give effect to these issues, the Rural Water Supply Guidelines were revised w.e.f. April 1, 2009. The revised guidelines are known as National Rural Drinking Water Programme (NRDWP) which focuses on the following:

1. Moving from habitation coverage towards household level drinking water coverage.
2. Provision of NRDWP funds for support activities.
3. Increasing allocation for sustainability component.
4. Ensuring household level drinking water security through water budgeting and preparation of Village Water Security Plans.

A. Fund Allocation Criteria: NRDWP funds are allocated to States on the following criteria with percentage weightage in parentheses: rural population (40), rural SC and ST population (10), areas under Desert Development Programme, Drought Prone Areas Programme, Hill Area Development Programme, Special Category Hill States (40) and population managing their own water supply schemes (10).

B. Components of NRDWP and Sharing Pattern: NRDWP has 5 components with the percentage allocations shown in parentheses: coverage (45), quality (20), sustainability (20), operation and maintenance (10), support (5). The sharing pattern is 50:50 between the Centre and States for Coverage, Quality and O&M for all States except for the North East States and Jammu and Kashmir for which it is 90:10. The components of Sustainability and Support are funded on 100 percent Central share basis.

7.8.6 Role of Panchayati Raj Institutions (PRIs): With a view to promote involvement of user groups/panchayats in the selection and implementation of drinking water schemes and for subsequent operation and maintenance (O&M),

the State Governments are being encouraged to sign an MOU with Government of India Governments will need to draw up an Action Plan framework for involving the community and PRIs and transfer the drinking water assets in a phased manner. The MOU will commit the States to meet the Bharat Nirman targets, provide sufficient funds for the sector; set up suitable mechanism for convergence of programmes for conservation of water, ground water recharge etc. and empower PRIs to levy user charges for O&M.

7.8.7 Gender Budgeting: Any effort to improve service delivery in the core sector of rural water supply helps to reduce the drudgery of women in fetching water from long distances for domestic purposes.

Financial assistance to the States/UTs is given through ARWSP for creating and augmenting drinking water supply infrastructure in the rural areas. The primary unit of this intervention is a habitation. Therefore, all the households irrespective of caste, creed and gender acquire benefit of this programme. The allocations are based on the basis of inter-State allocation criteria, which take into account numerous factors such as number of uncovered habitations, rural population, geographical locations etc.

Therefore, since ARWSP is infrastructure related programme with habitation as unit of coverage, it is not possible to quantify separate allocation for women.

However, the ARWSP guidelines do take into account the importance of involvement of women as the major user group. Efforts have been made to involve women groups/Self-help Groups (SHGs) in planning, implementation and operation and maintenance of water supply schemes through representation in the Village Water and Sanitation Committees (VWSCs). Since collection of drinking water in villages is primarily done by women, they need to be actively involved in planning, choice of technologies, location of systems, implementation, operation and maintenance of water supply schemes. Towards this end, at least 1/3rd members of VWSCs are women and they get preference in training for repair of hand pumps etc.

7.9 Rajiv Gandhi Scheme for Empowerment of Adolescent Girls (RGSEAG), 2010

This scheme was launched on 19 November 2010 with the objective of empowering adolescent girls in the age group 11-18 years by bringing improvement in their nutritional and health status and upgrading various skills like home skills, life skills, and vocational skills. To start with, it will be implemented in 200 selected districts across the country on a pilot basis. RGSEAG would be implemented through State Governments/UT Administrations with 100 percent financial assistance from the Central Government for all inputs other than nutrition provision for which 50 percent

Central assistance to states/UTs would be provided. Anganwadi centres will be the focal points for delivery of services. Nearly 100 lakh adolescent girls in 200 districts are expected to be benefited per annum under the scheme. In these 200 districts, Kishori Shakti Yojna (KSY) and the Nutrition Programme for Adolescent Girls (NPAG) have been merged in the RGSEAG. In the remaining districts, the KSY will continue as before.

7.10 Gender-Sensitive Resettlement and Rehabilitation Policy

The process of involuntary resettlement as a result of large development projects often leads to loss of land, wage employment, and housing and shelter, calling for gender-sensitive plans toward land-based re-settlement, re-employment and re-construction of houses. For instance, women should also get legal rights to land allocated as part of a resettlement package. Women's livelihood and economic activities—be they gathering forest produce, working in the fields or selling agricultural, animal husbandry, forestry or fishery produce—need to be enumerated so that the resettlement and rehabilitation plan also makes provision for the restoration of their livelihood and income. Women's views need to be solicited regarding houses, toilets, water and sanitation.

The process of displacement and involuntary resettlement also leads to increased stress, psychological trauma, increasing exposure to parasitic and vector-borne diseases and to social evils and violence. Endemic infections may lead to the death of children and the elderly in the care of women. Alcoholism, gambling and prostitution and increase in the incidence of sexual abuse and violence as a result of large-scale dislocation of peoples adversely affect women in ways different from that of men. Involuntary resettlement also increases the risk that the affected household may fall into chronic food insecurity. Loss of common property resources (CPRs) like access to forests, water bodies and grazing lands are often disregarded by planners and are not compensated for. Loss of CPRs leads to women spending more time and energy accessing fuel, fodder and potable water. Involuntary resettlement also leads to loss of social status as a result of loss of community networks and social marginalisation. Women are affected, more deeply and differently than men, because they generally have lower levels of skills and education and have a limited social exposure. Women rely on community networks for emotional and practical support, for example, taking care of the children, and thus the dislocation of community networks can be traumatic for them. Community services and assets need to be restored and social networks and communities need to be rebuilt in consultation and with the active participation of women.

The fact that the impact of dislocation is different for women needs to be understood and mitigated. Also, in drawing up resettlement and rehabilitation plans, care should be taken to see that widows, elderly persons, divorced women and women-headed households do not suffer a loss of their rights as a result of patriarchal biases. Detailed studies of the impact of development projects, say large dams, on women's lives, especially regarding resettlement and rehabilitation need to be sponsored, which can then be used to formulate a gender-sensitive resettlement and rehabilitation policy. The issue of a gender-sensitive resettlement and rehabilitation policy has not been addressed and this deserves immediate public attention.

7.11 Gender Budgeting in India

Gender responsive budgeting or gender analysis of budgets is a very useful tool being used in India to promote gender mainstreaming. Gender budgeting refers to presentation of budgetary data in a manner such that the gender sensitivities of budgetary allocations are clearly highlighted. Gender budgeting includes carrying out an impact analysis of government programmes and its budgetary allocations on the overall socio-economic status of women in the country. A special reference by the Union Finance Minister in his budget speech for 2000-01 pertaining to the access of women to national resources marked the dawn of gender-sensitive budgeting in India.

7.11.1 Ministry of Women and Child Development (MWCD): In 2004-05, MWCD adopted the mission statement of Budgeting for Gender Equity. Since then, several initiatives have been taken by MWCD to operationalize gender budgeting. A strategic framework of activities to implement Budgeting for Gender Equity was disseminated to all relevant agencies. It identified the following areas for gender mainstreaming:

1. Quantification of allocation of resources for women in Union/State/Local Budgets.
2. Gender audit of policies of governments.
3. Impact assessment of various schemes.
4. Analyzing programmes and strategies.
5. Institutionalizing generation and collection of gender disaggregated data.
6. Consultations and capacity building.

Further, guidelines for gender-sensitive review of public expenditure and policy were framed in the form of checklists both for beneficiary-oriented sectors (such as health, rural development, human resource development, labour, drinking water, textiles, agriculture etc.) and for mainstream sectors that may appear "gender neutral" like defence, power, telecom, transport etc.

The Ministry has conducted several workshops and training programmes to disseminate the tools of gender budgeting and has advocated that a review may be undertaken with respect to the following:

1. Gender-based profile of public expenditure.
2. Beneficiary needs assessment.
3. Impact analysis.
4. Participative budgeting.
5. Spatial mapping.

The MWCD has also requested various Ministries of the Government of India to set up Gender Budgeting Cells to (a) undertake review of the public expenditure and policy, (b) collect gender disaggregated data, (c) conduct gender-based impact analysis, beneficiary needs assessment and beneficiary incidence analysis. As a result of these efforts 43 Ministries/Departments have set up Gender Budget Cells as a nodal agency for all gender responsive budgeting initiatives.

It is noteworthy that the National Policy for Empowerment of Women, 2001 had envisaged introduction of a gender perspective in the budgeting process as an operational strategy. A task force was set up at the national level in 2001 to examine this issue. On its recommendation, a sub-group was set up to suggest a framework for introduction of gender budgeting in the Government. The sub-group recommended that Gender Budgeting Units be set up in identified Departments, as well as an Interdepartmental Steering Committee to identify issues for gender budgeting that cut across departments. While initial gender budgeting efforts were limited to education, health, nutrition, access to resources and public services etc, the Department of Women and Child prepared in 2004 checklists to assist all departments in gender budget exercises and in using these to develop a gender perspective in planning. These check lists are not only for the conventional social sector Ministries/Departments but also seek to involve so called gender-neutral Departments like transport, power, home etc.

Through a consensus approach the Department has also advocated broad framework within the ambit of which the gender budgeting initiatives could be undertaken by all stake-holders including Government Departments (Centre and States), voluntary organizations, researchers and international bodies like United Nations Development Programme (UNDP). The intention is to synergise the activities taking place in realm of gender budgeting and help collage the information base on the subject.

7.11.2 Women's Component Plan (WCP) in Five Year Plans: WCP was the first major initiative taken by the Government to address women-related issues and requirements on a systematic basis involving the inputs from major Ministries/Departments. WCP involved efforts to ensure that not less than 30 percent of funds/benefits were earmarked for women under the various schemes.

Plan documents have, over the years, reflected the evolving trends in gender matters. Seventh Five Year Plan (1985-90) introduced the concept of monitoring of 27 beneficiary-oriented schemes for women by DWCD. The exercise continues and number of schemes covered is being expanded.

The Eighth Five Year Plan (1992-97) highlighted for the first time a gender perspective and the need to ensure a definite flow of funds from the general developmental sectors to women. The Plan document made an express statement that the benefits to development from different sectors should not by pass women and special programmes on women should complement the general development programmes. The later, in turn, should reflect great gender sensitivity.

In October 1996, the Planning Commission specifically directed Central ministries and departments, and the state governments to identify a 'women's component' in the various schemes and programmes with which they are concerned to facilitate achieving the objective of empowering women during the Ninth Plan.

On February 19, 1999, the National Development Council, one of the highest policy making bodies in the country, adopted the empowerment of women and socially disadvantaged groups as agents of socio-economic change and development as a specific objective of the Ninth Five Year Plan (1997-02). One of the strategies adopted for achieving this objective was to identify a 'women's component plan' to ensure that not less than 30 percent of funds and benefits from developmental sectors flow to women.

Ninth Five Year Plan (1997-02) adopted Women Component Plan as one of the major strategies and directed both the Central and State Governments to ensure "not less than 30 percent" of the funds/benefits are earmarked in all the women related sectors. Special vigil advocated on the flow of the earmarked funds/benefits through an effective mechanism to ensure that the proposed strategy brings forth a holistic approach towards empowering women.

Tenth Five Year Plan (2002-07) reinforced commitment to gender budgeting to establish its gender-differential impact and to translate gender commitments into budgetary commitments. It continued the process of dissecting the Government budget to establish its gender-differential impact and to translate gender commitments into budgetary commitments.

In the Eleventh Five Year Plan (2007-12), for the first time, women were recognized not just as equal citizens but as agents of economic and social growth. The Plan Document observed, "The approach to gender equity is based on the recognition that interventions in favour of women must be multi-pronged and they must: (i) provide women with basic entitlements, (ii) address the reality of globalization and its impact on women by prioritizing economic empowerment, (iii) ensure an environment free from all forms of violence against women (VAW)—physical, economic, social, psychological etc., (iv) ensure the participation and adequate representation of women at the highest policy levels, particularly in Parliament and State assemblies, and (v) strengthen existing institutional mechanisms and create new ones for gender main-streaming and effective policy implementation." [7]

7.11.3 Gender Budgeting in Union Budgets: The Finance Minister in his budget speech for 2004-05 highlighted the perceived need for budgetary data to be presented in a manner that highlight the gender sensitiveness of the budgetary allocations. He observed, "Women's groups have met me and urged me to consider gender budgeting. This means that the budget data should be presented in a manner that the gender sensitivities of the budgetary allocations are clearly highlighted. An expert group on Classification System of Government Transactions has submitted its report on July 6, 2004. It has recommended appropriate systems for data collection and representation in the budget. The group has also recommended introduction of periodic benefit-incidence analysis. Government will examine the recommendations, and I hope it will be possible for me to implement some of them in the Budget for 2005-06." [8]

This was followed by a more emphatic commitment in the budget speech of 2005-06, wherein the budgetary allocations under 10 demands for grants estimated at ₹ 14,379 crore were highlighted in a separate statement as a part of the Gender Budgeting exercise. The 2006-07 budget speech revealed an estimated allocation of ₹ 28,737 crore for the benefit of women under 24 demands for grants in 18 Ministries and Departments. [9]

Gender outcome assessment and evaluation is of utmost importance for ensuring the success of gender budgeting. For this it is necessary that the gender funds flowing into schemes are properly and correctly assessed. The Finance Ministry has made it mandatory that Gender Outcomes form a part of the Outcome Budget prepared by every Ministry/Department as part of the Budget documents.

7.11.4 Gender Budgeting at the Level of States: In the meeting of the National Development Council held on June 27-28, 2005, the Prime Minister emphasized upon the need for State Governments to join hands in the area of gender budgeting. He observed, "The issue of gender bias is another area which needs focused attention. In the Union Budget for 2005-06, we have made a beginning in gender budgeting by incorporating a separate statement highlighting gender sensitivities of budgetary allocations under 10 Demands for Grants, to be extended to all Central Ministries. But this task will remain incomplete unless all the States join hands in ensuring development justice to women. This is one of the important instruments to tackle the growing violence against women, which begins even before their birth and continues through their entire life span. It cuts across caste, class community and prevails in all parts, rural and urban. This is the right forum to pledge our wholehearted and unequivocal support for ensuring a violence-free world for our women and girl children."

The above position only reinforces the importance of extending gender budgeting initiatives to the State Governments. Further, implementation of all important schemes of the Government of India is with State Governments. Thus, any exercise in Gender Budgeting is incomplete without State Government initiatives States could consider setting up Gender Budget Cells in key Departments.

It is noteworthy that State Governments collectively reflect a higher amount of women-related expenditure than Government of India.

For conceptual framework of gender budgeting, see section 1.5 of chapter 1 of this book.

To sum up, The overall picture that emerges is one of greater disadvantage for women workers in general and those belonging to rural as well as SCs/STs in particular. Apart from such inherited disadvantages as lower social position, a number of other factors also contribute to such a picture. These are their limited asset position, access to resources, and low level of education and skill. Education, and consequently some ability to acquire formal skills, could be a moderating force but this aspect presents a dismal picture. The overall situation of women workers calls for interventions of a promotional nature from different entry points but with a strong emphasis on education.

In spite of promises and commitments and focus on women's development and empowerment, the present status of women continues to be quite dismal in terms of important human development parameters like health, nutrition, literacy, educational attainments, skill levels, occupational status etc. There are a number of gender-specific barriers which prevent women for gaining access to their rightful share in the flow of public goods and services. Unless the felt needs of women are incorporated and mainstreamed in the planning and development process it is apprehended that the fruits of economic growth are likely to completely bypass a significant section of the country's population which does not augur well for the future growth of the economy. This calls for a focused priority the strengthening, expansion and universalisation of gender budgeting in all its aspects.

End Notes

1. Government of India, Planning Commission, *An Approach to the Twelfth Five Year Plan*, October 2011, p. 5.
2. Ibid., pp. 60-61.
3. Ibid., pp. 61-62.
4. Government of India, Planning Commission, *Eleventh Five Year Plan* (2007-12), Volume III, p. 96.
5. Government of India, Planning Commission, *An Approach to the Twelfth Five Year Plan*, October 2011, p. 62.
6. Ibid., pp. 62-63.
7. Government of India, Planning Commission, *Eleventh Five Year Plan* (2007-12), Volume II, pp. 184-185.
8. Government of India, Ministry of Finance, Budget Papers 2004-05, *Speech of the Finance Minister*, pp. 17-18.
9. Government of India, Ministry of Finance, Budget Papers 2006-07, *Speech of the Finance Minister*, p. 6.

8

Social Empowerment of Women

8.1 Women and Health

Discrimination against women and girls impinges upon their right to health and manifests itself in the form of worsening health and nutrition indices. Thus, India continues to grapple with unacceptably high Maternal Mortality Rate (MMR), Infant Mortality Rate (IMR) and increasing rates of anaemia, malnutrition, HIV/AIDS among women.

Women also disproportionately lack access to health services. Inaccessibility of health centres and poverty prevent them from getting timely medical aid. Absence of toilets and drinking water adversely impacts their health.

Inadequacies of clean cooking fuels adversely impacts women and children's work burden, health and nutrition.

Women and girls spend a great deal of time gathering fuel, adversely affecting their productivity and education. Use of firewood and inferior fuels such as weeds or crop wastes leads to smoke-related ailments including respiratory diseases, cancer and cataracts resulting in blindness.

8.1.1 Health Needs of Women: Women and girls in India face a crisis of growing health needs. From the moment of conception to the end of life, the challenges to the female sex are enormous, especially those who are poor; suffer from multiple exclusions, including caste, class, geographic isolation and tribal status. Health policies have few specific strategies for improving access to marginalized groups.

Malnutrition begins during infancy and sets in motion a life long cycle of poor health. Over half of all Indian women suffer from anaemia, which acerbates maternal morbidity. More women die of maternal death related causes in India than in any other country in the world. Women as a whole are especially susceptible to many diseases because of their poor nutritional standards and discriminatory practices in health inputs right from their birth.

Furthermore, every form of violence against women has steadily increased including rapes, dowry murder and domestic violence. Despite the alarming health crisis of women and girls, the national policy focus prioritizes family planning and reproductive health without addressing underlying issues such as women's low participation in decision-making, which adversely affects their health status. It is noteworthy that the leading killer of women in India is tuberculosis. Yet due to the focus on maternal and reproductive health this fact is little known and there are no gender-specific policies or programmes in place with regard to this disease.

8.1.2 HIV/AIDS: HIV in India is spreading from high-risk groups to the general population in many areas, and from urban to rural areas. Women are increasingly becoming the face of the HIV epidemic and there are biological, social, legal, cultural, political and economic factors that make them more vulnerable to HIV/AIDS. These factors, in turn, have an impact on women's access to services, resources, and information. Women have limited ability to negotiate safer sex and the risk and reality of sexual violence also means an increased risk of HIV transmission through unprotected non-consensual sex. In India, testing for the HIV virus is rare until symptoms set in. The numbers suffering from HIV/AIDS are therefore likely to be far higher than estimated. Once HIV/AIDS enters the home, family budgets are reversed forever because of loss of income earning opportunities and expenditure on medical care. Women are the major caregivers in most cases.

A multi-sectoral, decentralized, gender-sensitive and community-based health policy is needed. Effective strategies that address the relationships between gender and HIV/AIDS require a focus on gender within health care in general. There is perhaps an urgent need that the response to the HIV/AIDS epidemic be made multi-sectoral and be integrated into comprehensive, decentralized, participatory community-based health services. A focus on increasing women's ability to access preventive and treatment and care services is crucial.

8.1.3 Reproductive Health: The human rights of women include their right to have control over and decide freely and responsibly on matters related to their sexuality, including sexual and reproductive health, free of coercion, discrimination and violence. Equal relationships between women and men in matters of sexual relations and reproduction—including full respect for the integrity of the person—require mutual respect, consent and shared responsibility for sexual behaviour and its consequences.

Reproductive health is a state of complete physical, mental and social well-being—and not merely the absence of disease or infirmity—in all matters relating to the reproductive system and to its functions and processes. Reproductive health therefore implies that people are able to have a satisfying and safe sex life and that they have the capability to reproduce and the freedom to decide if, when and how often to do so. Implicit in this last condition is the right of men and women to be informed and to have access to safe, effective, affordable and acceptable methods of family planning of their choice, as well as other methods of their choice. In line with the above definition of reproductive health, reproductive health care is defined as the constellation of methods, techniques and services that contribute to reproductive health and well-being by preventing and solving reproductive health problems. It also includes sexual health, the purpose of which is the enhancement of life and personal relations, and not merely counselling and care related to reproduction and sexually transmitted diseases.

Bearing in mind the above definition, reproductive rights embrace certain human rights that are already recognized in national laws, international human rights documents and other consensus documents. These rights rest on the recognition of the basic right of all couples and individuals to decide freely and responsibly the number, spacing and timing of their children and to have the information and means to do so, and the right to attain the highest standard of sexual and reproductive health. It also includes their right to make decisions concerning reproduction free of discrimination, coercion and violence, as expressed in human rights documents. In the exercise of this right, they should take into account the needs of their living and future children and their responsibilities towards the community. The promotion of the responsible exercise of these rights for all people should be the fundamental basis for government- and community-supported policies and programmes in the area of reproductive health, including family planning.

Reproductive health eludes many of the world's women because of (a) inadequate levels of knowledge about human sexuality and poor-quality reproductive health information and services, (b) prevalence of high-risk sexual behaviour (c) discriminatory social practices, (d) negative attitudes towards women and girls and (e) limited power many women and girls have over their sexual and reproductive lives. Adolescents are particularly vulnerable because of their lack of information and access to relevant services in most countries. Older women and men have distinct reproductive and sexual health issues which are often inadequately addressed.

8.1.4 Changing Pattern of Lifestyle Illness: India has made rapid strides in the health sector since Independence. With increased coverage and better access to health facilities, life expectancy in India has risen over the past 60 years. As per the Census 2001, the life expectancy for women was 65.3. As the life span increases, the incidence of chronic diseases is set to overtake infectious diseases. As many studies have pointed out, there are signs that India is entering the epidemiological transition with a change in disease patterns from infectious to chronic, degenerative and non-communicable diseases. This is attributed to improved nutrition, immunisation, and improved access to primary health care. In urban areas, more women are succumbing to newer lifestyle-related illnesses like diabetes, hypertension, cardiovascular and cancer.

A related issue is the fact that women in urban areas are often confined to the house and participate in the economy as home-based workers. To improve their conditions, more visibility is needed on the nature of the work and production system and the implications these might have for appropriate interventions.

8.1.5 Women and Ageing: Demographic ageing is a global phenomenon. With a comparatively young population, India is still poised to become home to the second largest number of older persons in the world. The asymmetry in the population pyramid with males outnumbering females as a whole and females outnumbering males at the upper end of the age spectrum is a peculiar feature of the Indian population.

There is lack of disaggregated data to assess the number of services availed of by aged women and their impact. The Government has committed itself to providing social security for the aged woman. The discrimination and subordination that the old women suffer, the glaring difference in education and literacy, income differentials between men and women are being looked into by Government for state intervention.

8.1.6 Specific Micronutrient Deficiencies in India: Some of the specific micronutrient deficiencies in the country which are of a magnitude that causes public health concerns are described below.

A. Iron Deficiency Anaemia (IDA): IDA is the most widespread micronutrient deficiency in the world affecting more than a billion people. It affects all age groups irrespective of gender, race, caste, creed and religion with higher incidence among vulnerable groups in developing world. Anaemia is associated with increased susceptibility to infections, reduction in work capacity and poor concentration. In India, this silent emergency is rampant among women belonging to reproductive age group, children and low socio-economic strata of the population. IDA reduces the capacity to learn and work, resulting in lower productivity and loss of wages, limiting economic and social development. Anaemia in pregnant women leads to adverse pregnancy outcomes such as high maternal and neonatal mortality, low birth weight, increased risk of obstetrical complications, increased morbidity and serious impairment of the physical and mental development of the child. Anaemia remains one of the major indirect causes of maternal mortality in India. In children, anaemia causes low scholastic skills leading many of them to be below average in classes or premature dropping out from schools. It also triggers increased morbidity from infectious diseases.

It is also seen that children born to mothers who were illiterate or who belonged to scheduled castes/tribes were more likely to be anaemic than their counterparts. Further, children born to moderately and severely anaemic mothers were also anaemic, reflecting the consequences of poor maternal health status on the health of the children. Research studies have suggested that severe iron deficiency anaemia during the first two years of life, when the brain is still developing, may cause permanent neurological damage adding further sense of urgency to the current efforts to prevent iron deficiency anaemia in children.

The current strategy, included as part of Reproductive and Child Health Programme (RCH) under National Rural Health Mission, recommends that pregnant and lactating women, infants, school children and adolescents should be targeted in the Nutritional Anaemia Prophylaxis Programme as per the recommended dosage.

B. Iodine Deficiency Disorders (IDDs): IDDs are a major public health problem for populations throughout the world, particularly for pregnant women and young children. They are a threat to the social and economic development of countries. The most devastating outcomes of iodine deficiency are increased pre-natal mortality and mental retardation. Iodine deficiency is the greatest cause of preventable brain damage in childhood which is the primary motivation behind the current worldwide drive to eliminate it. The main factor responsible for iodine deficiency is a low dietary supply of iodine. It occurs in populations living in areas where the soil has low iodine content as a result of past glaciations or the repeated leaching effects of snow, water and heavy rainfall. Crops grown in this soil, therefore, do not provide adequate amounts of iodine when consumed.

Goitre is the most visible manifestation of IDDs. In severely endemic areas, cretinism may affect up to 5-15 percent of the population. While cretinism is the most extreme manifestation, of considerably greater significance are the more subtle degrees of mental impairment leading to poor school performance, reduced intellectual ability and impaired work capacity.

IDDs have been recognized as a public health problem in India since the 1920s. No State in India is completely free from IDDs. A third of all children in the world that are born with IDD-related mental damage live in India.

Indian National Goitre Control Programme (NGCP) was started in 1962 with a focus on the goitre belt in the country. However, the programme of universal iodization was introduced only in 1984, when all edible salt in the market was required to offer 30 ppm (parts per million) iodine at the production level. This was legalized through the PFA (Prevention of Food Adulteration) Act, 1988 that also banned the availability of crystalline salt (non-iodized) as an edible product. It was accepted variably by the different States, some putting only a partial ban and others none at all. Based on the recommendations of the Central Council of Health, the Government took a policy decision to iodise the entire edible salt in the country by 1992. Since 1992, the National Iodine Deficiency Disorders

Control Programme (NIDDCP) is the new name given to the erstwhile National Goitre Control Programme. This change has been effected with a view to cover the wide spectrum of iodine deficiency, such as mental and physical retardation, deaf-mutism and cretinism, under the programme. Due to various research reports, the Central Government lifted the ban on the sale of non-iodized salt in 2000. The States chose to retain or revoke the ban depending upon their own assessment. In 2005, a country-wide universal ban on sale of non-iodized salt for human consumption was again been promulgated by the Central Government.

C. Vitamin A Deficiency (VAD): Vitamin A is an important micronutrient for maintaining normal growth, regulating cellular proliferation and differentiation, controlling development, and maintaining visual and reproductive functions. Vitamin A Deficiency is one of the major deficiencies among lower income strata population in India. Human beings cannot produce this micronutrient in the body itself. Hence it has to be externally provided. This deficiency is seen greater in pre-school children and pregnant and lactating women due to higher need for this micronutrient. In severe cases it can even lead to total blindness.

VAD has been recognized as a major controllable public health and nutritional problem. An estimated 5.7 percent children in India suffer from eye signs of vitamin A deficiency. Recent evidence suggests that even mild vitamin A deficiency probably increases morbidity and mortality in children, emphasizing the public health importance of this disorder.

Way back in 1970, a National Programme for Prevention of Nutritional Blindness was initiated to fight this deficiency. The beneficiaries of this programme were pre-school children (1-5 years). Further, the programme was modified in 1992 to cover children in the age group of 9 months to 3 years only. Presently, Vitamin A supplementation exists as an integral component of RCH programme which is a part of National Rural Health Mission. Ministry of Health and Family Welfare, Government of India, issued guidelines to the States in November 2006 extending the programme to cover children up to 5 years.

8.1.7 National Health Policy, 2002: The Department of Health has formulated the National Health Policy (NHP), 2002 which was approved by the Cabinet in 2002. The National Health Policy, 2002 aims at achieving an acceptable standard of good health amongst the general population of the country and has set the goals for the next two decades.

Areas of attention in the Tenth Five Year Plan (2002-07) included the reorganization and restructuring of existing health care infrastructure at primary, secondary and tertiary levels so that they have the capacity to render health care services to the population residing in well defined geographical areas and have appropriate referral linkages with each other. Appropriate delegation of powers to Panchayati Raj institutions to ensure local accountability of public health care providers, horizontal integration of all aspects of the current vertical disease control programme, including supp-lies monitoring, IEC, training and administrative arrangements, development of appropriate two-way referral system utilizing information technology, exploring alternative systems of health care financing, and defining the role of various stakeholders—government, private and voluntary sectors—are the other focus areas.

8.1.8 Sarva Swasthya Abhiyan (SSA): The Tenth Five Year Plan (2002-07) indicated the dismal picture of the health services infrastructure and emphasized the need to invest more on building good primary-level care and referral services. The plan emphasized on restructuring and developing the health infrastructure, especially at the primary level. The plan highlighted the importance of the role of decentralization but did not state how this would be achieved. Programme-driven health care was in focus. Verticality and technical solutions were given more importance than the comprehensive primary health care. The multi-sectoral approach that is much needed for a vibrant health system had not been well thought out.

Eleventh Five Year Plan (2007-12) envisages inclusive growth by introducing National Urban Health Mission (NUHM) which along with National Rural Health Mission (NRHM) will form Sarva Swasthya Abhiyan (SSA). NRHM was launched for meeting health needs of all age groups and reduce disease burden across rural India. NUHM will be launched to meet the unmet needs of the urban population. NUHM based on health insurance and public-private partnership will provide integrated health service delivery to the urban poor. Initially, the focus will be on urban slums. NUHM will be aligned with NRHM and existing urban schemes. Besides, Sarva Swasthya Abhiyan aims for inclusive growth by finding solutions for strengthening health services and focusing on neglected areas and groups.

8.1.9 National Rural Health Mission (NRHM): NRHM was launched on April 12, 2005, to provide accessible, affordable and accountable quality health services to the poorest households in the remotest rural regions. The thrust of the Mission was on establishing a fully functional, community owned, decentralized health delivery system with inter-sectoral convergence at all levels, to ensure simultaneous action on a wide range of determinants of health like water, sanitation, education, nutrition, social and gender equality. Under the NRHM, the focus was on a functional health system at all levels, from the village to the district.

The Mission aims to provide universal access to equitable, affordable and quality health care which is accountable and at the same time responsive to the needs of the people. The Mission is expected to achieve the goals set under the National Health Policy and the Millennium Development Goals.

To achieve these goals, NRHM facilitates increased access and utilization of quality health services by all, forge a partnership between the Central, State and the local governments, set up a platform for involving the PRIs and the community in the management of primary health programmes and infrastructure and provides an opportunity for promoting equity and social justice. The NRHM establishes a mechanism to provide flexibility to the States and the community to promote local initiatives and develop a framework for promoting inter-sectoral convergence for promotive and preventive health care. The Mission has also defined core and supplementary strategies.

A. Strategies of NRHM:

(a) Core Strategies: These are the following:

1. Train and enhance capacity of Panchayati Raj Institutions (PRIs) to supervise and manage public health services.
2. Promote access to improved health care at household level through the Accredited Social Health Activist (ASHA).
3. Health Plan for each village through Village Health Committee of the Panchayat.
4. Strengthen sub-centre through an untied fund to enable local planning and action and more Multi Purpose Workers (MPWs).
5. Strengthen existing PHCs and CHCs and provision of 30-50 bedded CHC per Lakh population for improved curative care to a normative standard (Indian Public Health Service Standards defining personnel, equipment and management standards).
6. Prepare and implement an inter-sectoral District Health Plan prepared by the District Health Mission, including drinking water, sanitation, hygiene and nutrition.
7. Integrate vertical health and family welfare programmes at National, State and District levels.
8. Technical Support to National, State and District Health Missions for Public Health Management.
9. Strengthen capacities for data collection, assessment and review for evidence-based planning, monitoring and supervision.
10. Formulate transparent policies for deployment and career development of Human Resources for health.
11. Develop capacities for preventive health care at all levels for promoting

healthy life styles, reduction in consumption of tobacco and alcohol, etc.

12. Promote non-profit sector particularly in underserved areas.

(b) Supplementary Strategies: These include the following:

1. Regulation of Private Sector including the informal rural practitioners to ensure availability of quality service to citizens at reasonable cost.
2. Promotion of Public Private Partnerships (PPP) for achieving public health goals.
3. Reorienting medical education to support health issues including regulation of Medical Care and Medical Ethics.
4. Effective and viable risk-pooling and social health insurance to provide health security to the poor by ensuring accessible, affordable, accountable and good quality health care.

B. Five Planks of the National Rural Health Mission:

1. The Mission is expected to address the gaps in the provision of effective health care to rural population with special focus on 18 States, which have weak public health indicators and/or weak infrastructure.
2. The Mission is a shift away from the vertical health and family welfare programmes to a new architecture of all inclusive health development in which societies under different programmes will be merged and resources pooled at the district level.
3. The Mission aims at effective integration of health concerns with determinants of health like safe drinking water, sanitation and nutrition through integrated District Plans for Health. There is a provision for flexible funds so that the States can utilise them in the areas they feel are important.
4. The Mission provides for appointment of Accredited Social Health Activist (ASHA) in each village and strengthening public health infrastructure, including outreach through mobile clinics. It emphasizes involvement of the non-profit sector, especially in the under served areas. It also aims at flexibility at the local level by providing for untied funds.
5. The Mission, in its supplementary strategies, aims at fostering public-private partnerships; improving equity and reducing out of pocket expenses; introducing effective risk-pooling mechanisms and social health insurance; and taking advantage of local health traditions.

In the Eleventh Five Year Plan, the emphasis under NRHM will not be on numerical achievements only but also on Indian Public Health Service Standards and enforcement of guidelines for improving the functioning of infrastructure being strengthened and created. It has been felt that the Mission Directors, both at the Centre and the States, should be officials with public health background, supported by the Civil Service cadres.

NRHM has successfully provided a platform for community health action at all levels. Besides merger of Departments of Health and Family Welfare in all States, NRHM has successfully moved towards a single State and District level Health Society for effective integration and convergence. Through a concerted effort at decentralized planning through preparation of District Health Action Plans, NRHM has managed to bring about intra-health sector and inter-sectoral convergence for effectiveness and efficiency. In all the States, specific health needs of people have been articulated for local action. With the establishment of public institutions like the Village Health and Sanitation Committees (VH&SCs), Hospital Development Committees and PRI-led Committees, it is the civil society to which the health system is being made increasingly accountable. Through untied and flexible financing, NRHM is trying to drive reforms that empower local communities to make their own decisions. It is thus a serious effort at putting people's health in people's hands.

8.1.10 Janani Suraksha Yojana (JSY): To change the behaviour of the community towards institutional delivery, the Government of India, under NRHM in 2005, modified the National Maternity Benefit Scheme (NMBS), [1] from that of a nutrition-improving initiative to the JSY. The scheme has the dual objectives of reducing maternal and infant mortality by promoting institutional deliveries. Though the JSY is implemented in all States and UTs, its focus is on States having low institutional delivery rate. The scheme is 100 percent centrally sponsored and integrates cash assistance with maternal care. It is funded through the flexi-pool mechanism.

While the JSY scheme is meant to promote institutional delivery, it has to take two critical factors into account, one being that India does not have the institutional capacity to receive the 26 million women giving birth each year, and the other being that around half of all maternal deaths occur outside of delivery, during pregnancy, abortions and postpartum complications. If institutions are preoccupied with handling the huge numbers of normal childbirths, there will be inevitable neglect of life-threatening complications faced by women. They will be compelled to vacate beds in the shortest time. Consequently, complications during pregnancy and after childbirth will not be given attention. Second, JSY money sometimes does not reach hospitals on time, and as a result, poor women and their families do not receive the promised money.

8.2 Family Planning and Welfare

As per the Census of India, 2011, the population of India as on March 1, 2011 stood at 1210 million, with males at 624 million and females at 586 million. Viewed globally, India constitutes 17 percent of the world population. India is following the demographic transition pattern of all developing countries from initial levels of *high birth rate–high death rate* to the intermediate transition stage of *high birth rate–low death rate* which manifests in high rates of population growth, before graduating to *low birth rate–low death rate* stage.

The current high population growth rate is due to (a) the large size of the population in the reproductive age-group, (b) higher fertility due to unmet need for contraception and (c) high wanted fertility due to prevailing high IMR.

The goal of population stabilization can be achieved only when child survival, maternal health and contraception issues are addressed simultaneously and effectively. Actual success in containing the growth of population would, however, depend upon: (a) publicly-related support from community leaders, (b) resources available for the family welfare programmes, (c) efficiency and accountability in the States health system for ensuring effective delivery of services to citizens and (d) women's education and status in the family. All these inputs have so far not been uniformly available to the required extent for the family welfare programmes, thereby not allowing the optimal benefits to be reaped from the same.

8.2.1 Family Welfare in the National Population Policy (NPP), 2000: NPP adopted in February 2000 affirmed the commitment of the Government towards stabilizing the population of the country by providing for its citizens voluntary and informed decisions about their family size. The policy envisaged certain National Socio-Demographic goals to be achieved by 2010 for paving the way for a stable population in the country by 2045, at a level consistent with the requirements of sustainable economic growth and social development. It also provided a policy for advancing goals and prioritizing strategies during the next decade, to meet the reproductive and child health needs of the people of India, and to achieve net replacement levels of fertility (Total Fertility Rate = 2:1) by 2010.

It was decided to relocate the National Population Stabilization Fund (NPSF) from the National Commission on Population to the Department of Family Welfare. The NPSF was created with core funding of ₹ 100 crore from Government of India and will invite funds from the voluntary and corporate sectors.

An Empowered Action Group (EAG) was constituted in the Ministry of Health and Family Welfare with Union Minister for Health and Family Welfare as Chairman on March 20, 2001. The EAG aims at assisting States with weak socio-demographic indicators to attain the goals listed in the National Population Policy, 2000. In the first instance, the States of Bihar, Uttar Pradesh, Madhya Pradesh, Rajasthan, Orissa, Jharkhand, Uttaranchal and Chhattisgarh were chosen for focussed attention.

Population Census 2011 showed a decline in the sex ratio in the age group 0-6 years in several States. For the country as a whole the child sex ratio is 914 girls per 1,000 boys which is much less than 927 recorded in the 2001 Census. The Government is keen to strengthen the implementation mechanism of Pre-Natal Diagnostic Techniques (Regulation and Prevention of Misuse) Act, 1994.

The Reproductive and Child Health Programme (RCH) was launched on October 10, 1997 which combines fertility regulation, safe motherhood, child survival and Reproductive Tract Infections (RTI)/Sexually Transmitted Infections (STI). This programme is primarily implemented through the primary health care infrastructure.

Vitamin A deficiency, which can lead to blindness, has been prevalent in the country, especially among the pre-school children. Under the programme for prevention and control of vitamin A deficiency among children, five doses of vitamin A are administered to all children less than 3 years of age.

Iron deficiency (anaemia) is widely prevalent not only in women of child-bearing age but also in young children. The National Family Health Survey-II (1998-99) revealed that 74.3 percent children under the age of 3 years were anaemic. There is a marginal difference in the prevalence in the rural and urban areas. While 75.3 percent of rural children were found to be anaemic, the prevalence in urban children was 70.8 percent. Iron folic acid tablets containing 20 mg of elemental iron and 0.1 mg of folic acid are provided at the sub-centre level.

The agenda for population stabilization is multi-sectoral which necessitates decentralization and convergence across sectors. In cooperation with State Governments, the Department of Family Welfare is bringing about a convergence between the NGOs, the Self-help Groups, Zila Saksharta Samitis and Panchayati Raj Institutions, to improve integrated service delivery at community and household levels.

8.3 Nutrition Support

Although the country has been able to eliminate nutritional deficiency syndrome like pellagra, beriberi, scurvy etc. yet chronic energy deficiency among adults, under-nutrition among children and micronutrient deficiencies are still prevalent across all section of the population. The country has adopted a multi-sectoral and multi-pronged strategy to combat these problems and to improve the nutritional status of the population.

One half of the children under the age of 5 years in India are moderately or severely malnourished, 30 percent of newborn children are significantly under weight and nearly 60 percent of women are anaemic. Under the Integrated Child Development Scheme (ICDS), the Department of Women and Child Development implements the food supplementation programme for improving nutritional status of mothers and children. Ministry of Health and Family Welfare implements programmes for tackling major micronutrient deficiencies such as vitamin A and iodine deficiency etc.

To address the needs of under-nourished infants and children below 3 years, 15 percent of the total Additional Central Assistance (ACA) is earmarked for the nutrition component under the Pradhan Mantri Gramodaya Yojana (PMGY). ACA under the nutrition component of PMGY is an additionality for providing nutrition to children in 0-3 years. States are required to ensure that all below poverty line (BPL) children in 0-3 years are registered for PMGY and provided requisite nutrition.

The programme of Nutritional Support to Primary Education, popularly known as Mid-day Meal Scheme, was launched in 1995 as a fully-funded Centrally Sponsored Scheme. Under this scheme, all children in primary schools in government and government-aided schools are covered. Ideally, a hot meal is provided to the children at school for 10 months in a year. The foodgrains are delivered directly at the district level by the Food Corporation of India, under instructions from the Department of Education in the Government of India.

8.3.1 National Nutrition Mission (NNM): The Prime Minister, in his Independence Day speech on August 15, 2001 announced the setting up of NNM. Under this Mission, subsidized foodgrains are made available to adolescent girls and expectant and nursing mothers, belonging to below-poverty-line families. NNM is headed by the Prime Minister and its Executive Committee is under the Human Resource Development Minister.

8.3.2 Time-bound Goals of the Eleventh Five Year Plan

1. To reduce Maternal Mortality Ratio (MMR) to 1 per 1000 live births.
2. To reduce Infant Mortality Rate (IMR) to 28 per 1000 live births.
3. To reduce Total Fertility Rate to 2.1.
4. To provide clean drinking water for all by 2009 and ensuring no slip-backs.
5. To reduce malnutrition among children of age group 0-3 to half its present level.
6. To reduce anaemia among women and girls by 50 percent.
7. To raise the sex ratio for age group 0-6 to 935 by 2011-12 and 950 by 2016-17.

Considerable achievements have been made over the last 65 years to improve health standards; such as in life expectancy, child mortality, infant mortality and maternal mortality. Small pox and guinea worm have been eradicated and there is hope that poliomyelitis will be contained in the near future. Nevertheless, problems abound. Malnutrition affects a large proportion of children. An unacceptably high proportion of the population continues to suffer and die from new diseases which are emerging apart from continuing and new threats posed by the existing ones. Pregnancy and childbirth related complications also contribute to the suffering and mortality.

India has to deal with rising costs of health care and growing expectations of the people. The challenge of quality health services in remote rural regions has to be urgently met. Given the magnitude of the problem, there is the need to transform public health care into an accountable, accessible and affordable system of quality services.

Special attention needs to be given to the health of vulnerable groups like adolescent girls, women, children, older persons, disabled and primitive tribal groups. The contribution of the private sector in providing primary, secondary and tertiary services should be enhanced through various measures including partnership with the Government. Good governance, transparency and accountability in the delivery of health services should be ensured through involvement of Panchayati Raj Institutions (PRIs), Community and Civil Society Groups.

8.4 Women and Education

There is an increased awareness that education is one of the most valuable means of achieving gender equality and the empowerment of women. Education is seen as a critical factor in breaking the inter-generational cycle of transmission of poverty. The power of education lies not just in imparting formal literacy, but rather in the acquisition of skills that enable access to multiple literacy—economic, legal, health, political and media etc.

Education is a key intervention in initiating and sustaining processes of empowerment. Good quality education can help women and marginalized communities to (a) improve their status, (b) enable them to have greater access to information and resources and (c) challenge various forms of discrimination. Education helps strengthen democratic processes as it allows for greater and more equitable participation. Being educated leads to greater self-confidence and self-esteem. It enables engagement with development processes and institutions of governance from a position of strength. Poor women from socially disadvantaged communities are invariably not literate and therefore find themselves at a disadvantage when participating in development processes.

It is, however, important to recognise that while being literate or educated is necessary for empowerment, it does not automatically ensure it. For that a society needs an education system which is of good quality and promotes critical thinking. From the perspective of gender this means that education and literacy should enable women and girls to critically analyse their situations, raise questions about their subordination and help them make informed choices. It is well-known that the institution of schooling is an important site for socialisation that actually reinforces rather than challenges patriarchy and gender discrimination. It is in this context that the content and pedagogy of education become critical considerations.

The focus of educational planning is generally on formal education but this is only one dimension of the educational provisioning, especially when needs of deprived women are under consideration and empowerment of women is the main objective.

8.4.1 Education for All: The 86th Constitutional Amendment Act, 2002 made free and compulsory education a justiciable fundamental right for all children in the 6-14 year age group. The Government of India is committed to realising the goal of elementary education for all and bridging of gender and social gaps by 2010. The *Sarva Shiksha Abhiyan* (SSA), launched in 2001-02, is the national umbrella programme that is spearheading the universalisation of elementary education through a community-owned approach, with a specific focus on the provision of quality education. SSA has relied on the Education Guarantee Scheme (EGS) and Alternative and Innovative Education (AIE) which are specially designed to provide access to school-less habitations. The scheme provides flexible strategies for out-of-school children through bridge courses, residential camps, drop-in-centres, summer camps, remedial coaching etc. to bring these children to school.

Though the content of education and classroom pedagogy are critical to altering gender and other social relations it has not been paid the attention it deserves. Efforts to make curricula gender-sensitive have been undertaken but can be considered initial attempts as they have remained largely at the level of removing stereotypes or increasing visibility and have not looked at gender in terms of social relations.

Problems related to the representation of marginalized communities continue to exist and contribute to the deep sense of alienation of these communities from the mainstream education system and a reason for children dropping out. Sexuality is addressed in a problematic manner in educational materials. It is either related to population or reproductive health or seen as a problem associated with promiscuity and shame. Classrooms need to be transformed into spaces that can help girls think critically. Discriminatory practices based on identity-based prejudices need to be monitored and stopped. Corporal punishment, which is wide spread, needs to be checked. The role of the teacher is naturally crucial in this context.

8.4.2 Sexual Harassment, Violence and Women's Education: Sexual harassment and violence against girls and young women within educational institutions is widespread but under-reported. There are systematic mechanisms to gather data that indicate the extent of the problem. While some universities have formulated guidelines and established mechanisms to deal with sexual harassment, many educational institutions still do not have policies. Though technically the guidelines should cover schools, no efforts have been made to implement the guidelines in schools where sexual harassment is fairly common but is rarely reported. One only has the media (print and electronic) to rely on for such information. Another area that has not received much attention is the impact of conflict and communal and sectarian violence on education. Communal and sectarian violence and long-term conflicts severely impact opportunities for girls and women's education. In volatile situations girls are kept away from schools.

In parts of India, like the North East and Kashmir, that have been experiencing conflict for several years, the ground level situation reveals that prolonged violence has negatively impacted the education systems there and the education opportunities for women and girls in various ways. Dropout rate of girls is high because of fear, insecurity, restricted mobility, displacement, migration etc. School participation and quality of education for girls is impacted by measures to control women's sexuality and mobility, like diktats imposing a dress code by religious bodies, militants or separatist groups.

In such situations schooling and other educational interventions can bring about a semblance of normalcy and prevent alienation from the mainstream. No systematic efforts have been made to understand and monitor the impact of conflict on education, especially women and girls. There are no policy guidelines on how to respond to the impact of violence and conflict. There are no mandated special provisions to deal with the particular problems arising out of such situations. Education provisioning, from gender perspective, should find a place in any policy on internal displacements and associated relief and rehabilitation measures.

8.4.3 Elementary Education: Within the education sector, elementary education has been given the highest priority in terms of sub-sectoral allocations and a number of schemes launched by the Central Government to meet the needs of the educationally disadvantaged. A brief description of select programmes for elementary education is as follows.

A. Sarva Shiksha Abhiyan (SSA): Launched in November 2000, SSA is a comprehensive programme and the main vehicle for providing elementary education to all children. The goals of SSA are the following:

1. All children in School, Education Guarantee Centre, Alternate School, Back-to-School camp by 2005.
2. Bridge all gender and social category gaps at the primary stage by 2007 and at elementary education level by 2010.
3. Universal retention by 2010.
4. Focus on elementary education of satisfactory quality with emphasis on education for life.

SSA, implemented in partnership with the States, addresses the needs of 209 million children in the age group of 6-14 years. It covers 9.72 lakh existing primary and upper primary schools and 36.95 lakh teachers.

SSA is the culmination of all previous endeavours and experiences in implementing various education programmes. SSA has been the single largest holistic programme addressing all aspects of elementary education covering over one million elementary schools SSA has brought primary education to the doorstep of millions of children and enrolled them, including first generation learners, through successive fast track initiatives in hitherto unserved and underserved habitations.

B. Kasturba Gandhi Balika Vidyalaya Scheme (KGBVS): KGBVS was launched in July 2004 to set up 750 residential schools at elementary level for girls belonging predominantly to the SC, ST, OBC and minorities in Educationally Backward Blocks (EBBs). All 750 KGBVs have now been sanctioned by the Government of India, with 117 KGBVs (15.6 percent) allocated to blocks with substantial minority population. A minimum of 75 percent of the enrolment in KGBVs is reserved for girls from the target groups and the remaining 25 percent is open for girls belonging to the BPL category. The Tenth Plan allocation for the scheme was ₹ 427 crore.

C. District Primary Education Programme (DPEP): Started in 1994, DPEP, an externally aided project, aimed at the holistic development of primary education covering Classes I to V. It had specific objectives of reducing the dropout rate to less than 10 percent, reducing disparities among gender and social groups in the enrolment to less than 5 percent and improving the level of learning achievement compared to the baseline surveys. However, these ambitious targets could not be achieved. Still, DPEP has brought a sea change in the implementation of school education programme with its decentralized approach and focus on community participation. At its peak, DPEP covered 273 districts in 17 States. Now it continues in only 17 districts of Orissa and Rajasthan where it would be completed in 2008.

D. National Programme of Nutritional Support to Primary Education: Launched on August 15, 1995 with the objective to boost the Universalisation of

Primary Education by impacting upon enrolment, attendance, retention and nutritional needs of children studying in class I–V. Under this programme more than 10 crore children are being targeted for coverage. At present, Gujarat, Kerala, Tamil Nadu, Madhya Pradesh, Chattisgarh, Orissa, Karnataka and Delhi are providing cooked meals. The remaining States and UTs are distributing foodgrains (wheat/rice).

E. Pradhan Mantri Gramodaya Yojana: This programme was launched during 2000-01 and envisages Additional Central Assistance for basic minimum services in certain priority areas. The scheme has six components covering elementary education, primary health, rural shelter, rural drinking water, nutrition and rural electrification. A minimum of 10 percent of ACA for all components except nutrition (for which it is 15 percent) has been fixed. The allocation for the remaining 35 percent of ACA would be decided by the States and UTs among the components of the Scheme, as per their priorities. Funds for elementary education sector under PMGY are utilized to further the goal of Universalisation of Elementary Education.

F. National Programme for Education of Girls at Elementary Level (NPEGEL): It is an important component of SSA. NPEGEL provides additional support by way of girl-child friendly schools, stationery, uniforms, etc. for girls' education in educationally backward blocks (EBB), and in other areas for elementary education of under privileged and disadvantaged sections. EBBs are blocks with female literacy below, and gender gap above, the national average. Apart from EBBs, NPEGEL is also implemented in blocks of districts which are not covered under EBBs but have at least 5 percent SC/ST population and where SC/ST female literacy is below 10 percent, and also in select urban slums. In the Tenth Five Year Plan, an amount of ₹ 1064.80 crore was earmarked for this programme.

Launched in July, 2003 as a focused intervention aimed at enhancing girls' education, NPEGEL provides for development of a "model school" in every cluster with more intense community mobilisation and supervision of girls' enrolment in schools. Gender-sensitisation of teachers, development of gender-sensitive learning materials and provision of need-based incentives like stationery, workbooks and uniforms are some of the objectives under NPEGEL. It is being implemented in about 3,164 educationally backward blocks in 25 States.

Under NPEGEL, around 31,450 model schools have been developed and 1.97 lakh teachers gender-sensitised. Over 51,345 Early Childhood Care and Education (ECCE) centres are being supported in areas not covered by Integrated Child Development Services (ICDS) scheme to help free girls from sibling care responsibilities and attend schools. Free uniforms have been given as a direct educational incentive to about 2 crore girls in educationally backward blocks. 1.84 crore girls have been benefited under NPEGEL till October 31, 2006.

G. Education Guarantee Scheme and Alternative and Innovative Education (EGS&AIE): Another important component of SSA is the EGS&AIE. It is specially designed to provide access to elementary education to children in school-less habitations and out-of-school children. It supports flexible strategies for out-of-school children through bridge courses, residential camps, drop-in centres, summer camps, remedial coaching, etc., and helped to provide elementary education to 85.67 lakh children in 2004-05.

H. Mahila Samakhya (MS): MS, an externally aided project for women's empowerment, was started with Dutch assistance in 1989. Since 2005-06 it is being funded by GOI. The programme endeavours to create an environment for women to learn at their own pace, set their own priorities and seek knowledge and information to make informed choices. It has strengthened women's abilities to effectively participate in village level education programmes. The programme is implemented in 9 states covering 83 districts. The States of M.P. and Chhattisgarh have registered MS societies through which the programme is initiated. It provides for vocational and skill development as well as educational development of adolescent girls and women in rural areas.

I. Prarambhik Shiksha Kosh (PSK): Department of Elementary Education and Literacy issued orders on November 14, 2005 constituting Prarambhik Shiksha Kosh (PSK) to receive the proceeds of the education cess imposed through Finance (No. 2) Act, 2004. PSK is a separate, dedicated, non-lapsable fund to be maintained by the Ministry of Human Resource Development.

J. Problem Areas: In education, the elementary sector is besieged by numerous systemic problems such as inadequate school infrastructure, presence of single-teacher schools, high teacher absenteeism (especially in rural areas), large-scale teacher vacancies, inadequate equipment, etc. This brings into focus the role of decentralization and people's participation in the provision of basic services. It is essential that control over schools and teachers should be transferred to local bodies, having a direct interest in teacher performance. This has also been highlighted as an area of emphasis in the Tenth Plan.

The National Policy on Education (NPE), 1986, as modified in 1992, emphasised three aspects in relation to elementary education:

1. Universal access and enrolment.
2. Universal retention of children up to 14 years of age.
3. A substantial improvement in the quality of education to enable all children to achieve essential levels of learning.

NPE emphasised that education must play a positive and interventionist role in correcting social and regional imbalance, empowering women, and in securing a rightful place for the disadvantaged and the minorities. Government is firmly committed to providing education for all, the priority areas being free and compulsory elementary education, covering children with special needs, eradication of illiteracy, education for women's equality, and special focus on the education of SCs/STs and minorities.

8.4.4 Adult Education: Literacy is the most essential prerequisite for individual empowerment. A new thrust was given to adult literacy in the National Policy on Education (NPE), 1986 and the Plan of Action 1992, which advocated a three-pronged strategy of adult education, elementary education and non-formal education to eradicate illiteracy. The National Literacy Mission (NLM) was launched on May 5, 1988 as a Technology Mission to impart functional literacy to non-literates in the country in the age group of 15-35 years in a time-bound manner. This age-group is the focus of attention because it is in the productive and reproductive period of life. NLM was set up with an initial target to make 80 million persons literate by 1995, which was later enhanced to 100 million by 1997 and the revised target was to achieve a threshold level of 75 percent literacy by 2007.

The Total Literacy Campaign (TLC) has been the principal strategy of NLM for eradication of illiteracy in the target group. These campaigns are area-specific, time-bound, volunteer-based, cost effective and outcome-oriented. They are implemented by Zila Saksharata Samities and district level literacy societies.

Keeping pace with its endeavours, campaigns and programmes, the NLM has strengthened and revitalized the States Literacy Missions which have been imparted greater autonomy. They now have the authority to plan, implement and monitor literacy programmes and sanction continuing education programmes at the State level. The NLM has also come to recognize the great potential that NGOs have in furthering its programmes and schemes. Given the major role, NGOs are now allowed to receive funds from *Zila Sakshara Samities* and actually run continuing education centres. The *Jan Shikshan Sansthans* have expanded their outreach and are also catering to the rural segment by offering vocational training courses. At present, 137 districts are implementing TLCs, 165 districts Post-Literacy Programmes and 295 districts Continuing Education Programmes. In addition, 157 Jan Shikshan Sansthan have been set up to provide vocational training to the neo-literates and backward sections of the society, and 25 State Resource Centres established for providing academic and technical resource support for the literacy programmes.

NLM has accorded priority for the promotion of female literacy. According to

2001 Census, 47 districts in the country have female literacy rate below 30 percent. Most of these districts are concentrated in Bihar, Jharkhand, Uttar Pradesh and Orissa. Special innovative projects have been taken up to raise the level of female literacy in these areas. Special efforts have been made to target female Panchayati Raj functionaries and make them literate.

A. Jan Shikshan Sansthan (JSS): The objective of JSS Scheme is educational, vocational and occupational development of socio-economically backward and educationally disadvantaged groups of urban/rural population, particularly neo-literates, semi-literates, SCs, STs, women and girls, slum dwellers, migrant workers etc. By linking literacy with vocational training, JSSs seek to improve the quality of life of the beneficiaries. JSSs offer around 284 different types of vocational courses—from candle and agarbatti making, to computer training and hospital/health care. The total number of JSS is 198.

B. Weaknesses of Adult Education Programmes: The constraints in the implementation of adult education programmes include inadequate participation of the State Governments, low motivation and training of voluntary teachers/preraks, lack of convergence of programmes, and weak management and supervision structure for implementation of NLM. Besides, the funding for various components of NLM schemes is inadequate and the level of community participation is also low.

8.5 Women and Media

Media plays a critical role in changing gender stereotypes. The approach to media strategy in India has been to use it as an instrument of change and to control its possible misuse. Media is encouraged to develop a code of conduct, professional guidelines, other self-regulatory mechanisms to remove gender stereotypes and promote a balanced portrayal of women and men.

The existing law on regulating content in the media is contained in different sources. Thus, Article 51A of the Constitution states that it shall be the duty of every citizen of India to renounce practices derogatory to the dignity of women. Similarly, Section 294 of the IPC provides for penalties for obscene acts or conduct. The Indecent Representation of Women (Prohibition) Act, 1986 prohibits indecent representation of women through advertisement or in publications, writings, paintings, figures or in any other manner. The Act was enacted in the year 1986 and since then the issue of what is *obscene* has been a subject of great debate. The Act itself mostly revolves around how the object will affect society and the public morality rather than how it offends women.

The Indian Information Technology Act, 2000 has declared online pornography a punishable offence.

The role of the media in portraying women and the female gender as a whole leaves much to be desired. Press and the print media are generally found to unduly sensationalize traumatic events such as rape etc thereby invading the privacy of the victim. Very few positive stories of girls/women are published who have stood up for their rights or are achievers. Similarly, the electronic media and films portray serial/films highly derogatory to women, glorifying subservience of the woman to her husband/in laws, celebrating the birth of the boy child and portraying the disappointments of the family at the birth of the girl child. Eve teasing/sexual harassment is often a *fun* item in Indian films. As a result the general populace is fed on a regular diet of stories/news that are highly gender abusive, thus reinforcing traditional views that the women are an inferior race and can be freely exploited.

The media has perforce to become gender sensitive and more responsible when portraying women and thus play a significant role in bringing about attitudinal changes in the society. A gender-friendly media policy needs to be formulated for this purpose.

Negative, violent and/or degrading images of women including pornography, stereotyped portrayals, have increased in different forms using new communication technologies in some instances, and bias against women remains in the media. Poverty, the lack of access and opportunities, illiteracy, lack of computer literacy and language barriers, prevent women from using the information and communication technologies, including the internet. Development of and access to internet infrastructure is limited especially in developing countries and particularly for women.

The lack of gender sensitivity in the media is evidenced by the failure to eliminate the gender-based stereotyping and the reinforcement of women's traditional role that can be found in public and private media. The continued projection of negative and degrading images of women in media communications is evident. The world- wide trend towards consumerism has created a climate in which advertisements and commercial messages often portray women primarily as consumers and target girls and women of all ages inappropriately. Advertisements of beauty products, magazines and beauty pageants mushrooming all over have led to the creation of an image of an *ideal woman.*

Media policy needs to be gender proactive. There is a need to encourage media to project positive images and balanced portrayal of women and girls to enable attitudinal changes. The media policy should also help in generating awareness on gender issues and concerns so that the process of societal reorientation towards creating a gender just society gets widely disseminated.

8.6 Women and Migration

The movement and mobility of people generally has increased in recent years. While the rights of people to free movement need to be respected, issues of health, sanitation and water supply have emerged as critical constraints in expansion of urban areas and in particular in providing reasonable living conditions to all residents.

Public policy with respect to *migration* is another area for consideration. Due to extreme poverty or seasonal farm work, women are forced to migrate to semi-urban/urban areas. There are many social and economic consequences which these women face such as exploitation in work place, wage differentials, low paid work etc. Also their access to safe housing, food, sanitation and health remain precarious. A very alarming feature of unregulated migration is the trafficking of young girls and women by duping, luring or kidnapping them. Such women are forced into prostitution, bonded labour or slavery. These social aspects need to be looked into in greater detail while reviewing the migration policy.

8.7 Vulnerability of Widows

Among women, widows are the most vulnerable sections of the society. Several studies have pointed out that female widowhood in India tends to be associated with economic deprivation. The amelioration of the socio-economic conditions of widows in India has not been given due consideration at the level of the Central Government. Some State Governments have introduced special pension schemes for widows, but the rates of pension are low and the actual coverage is also low. The eligibility criteria are restrictive and the bureaucratic hurdles are difficult to overcome. It is doubtful whether the pension schemes, as they exist today, can be said to be an effective instrument of social security to women.

8.8 Task Force on Women and Children

In order to address the developmental issues relating to women, a Task Force on Women and Children (Chairman: K.C. Pant) was constituted by the Government in August 2000. In its report submitted in April 2002, the Task Force, inter alia, recommended the setting up of an Inter-Ministerial Standing Committee in the Department of Women and Child Development, composed of officials and non-official experts to review and monitor gender mainstreaming in government. The Task Force also reviewed the whole gamut of legislations concerning women and recommended amendment of 22 laws to make them more effective.

End Note

1. **National Maternity Benefit Scheme (NMBS):** Under it there is a provision for payment of ₹ 500 per pregnancy to women belonging to poor households for pre-natal and post-natal maternity care up to the first two live births. This benefit is provided to eligible women of 19 years and above. The objective of the scheme is to extend financial assistance to pregnant women from BPL households, for the first two live births. To ensure better linkage with nutrition and national population control programmes, NMBS was transferred to Department of Family Welfare and was renamed as *Janani Suraksha Yojana* in 2001-02. It is now part of the National Rural Health Mission.

9

Political Empowerment of Women

In the early years of the Independence of India in 1947, much of the country's governance was in the hands of elected representatives and the official machinery. Such a centralized approach did not produce desired results, especially in terms of the inclusion of marginalized groups within the governance processes. Constitutional, legislative and policy reforms since then and the continued administrative decentralization have increased the political participation of marginalized groups, especially poor women. Women's increased political participation has yielded positive results. Issues central to development—including health, nutrition, family income and education—have taken centre-stage as women participate in Panchayati Raj Institutions (PRI), village development boards and other governance structures.

9.1 Women in Decision-making

There has been growing acceptance of the importance to society of the full participation of women in decision-making and power at all levels and in all fora, including inter-governmental, governmental, and non-governmental sectors. In some countries, women have also attained higher positions in these spheres. An increasing number of countries applied affirmative and positive action policies, including quota systems or voluntary agreements in some countries, measurable goals and targets, developed training programmes for women's leadership and introduced measures to reconcile family and work responsibilities of both women and men. National mechanisms and machineries for the advancement of women as well as national and international networks of women politicians, parliamentarians, activists and professionals in various fields have been established or upgraded and strengthened.

Despite general acceptance of the need for a gender balance in decision-making bodies at all levels, a gap between *de jure* and *de facto* equality has persisted. Notwithstanding substantial improvements of *de jure* equality between women and men, the actual participation of women at the highest levels of national and international decision-making has not significantly changed and gross under-representation of women in decision-making bodies in all areas, including *inter alia* politics, conflict prevention and resolution mechanisms, the economy, the environment and the media hinders the inclusion of a gender perspective in these critical spheres of influence. Women continue to be underrepresented at the legislative, ministerial and sub-ministerial levels, as well as at the highest levels of the corporate sector and other social and economic institutions. Traditionally assigned gender roles limit women's choices in education and careers and compel women to assume the burden for household responsibilities.

Initiatives and programmes aimed at women's increased participation in decision-making are hindered by a host of factors, among which the following are prominent:

1. Lack of human and financial resources for training and advocacy for political careers.
2. Gender-sensitive attitudes towards women in society.
3. Lack of accountability of elected officials and political parties for promoting gender equality and women's participation in public life.
4. Lack of social awareness of the importance of balanced participation of women and men in decision-making.
5. Lack of willingness on the part of men to share power; sufficient dialogue and co-operation with women's non-governmental organizations, along with organizational and political structures, which enable all women to participate in all spheres of political decision-making.

9.2 Women in Local Bodies: Panchayats and Municipalities

Towns and cities contribute substantially to the economic development of the country. These urban centres also play an important support role in the development of rural hinterland. To keep this economic transformation in line with needs and realities at the grassroots level, it is necessary that the people and their representatives are fully involved in the planning and implementation of the programmes at local level. If democracy in Parliament and State Legislatures is to remain strong and stable, its roots must reach towns and villages and the cities where the people live.

9.2.1 Constitutional Provisions Regarding Local Bodies: The Constitution of India has made detailed provisions for ensuring protection of democracy in Parliament and in State Legislatures. Hence, democracy in these institutions has survived and flourished. However, the Constitution did not make local self-government in urban areas a clear-cut Constitutional obligation. While Article 40 of the Constitution requires the strengthening of the units of local self-government in the States, particularly *panchayati raj* Institutions, there is no specific reference to municipalities except implicitly in Entry 5 of List II (State List) in the Seventh Schedule of the Constitution, which places the subject of local self-government as a responsibility of the State. Entry 5 reads as under:

"Local Government, that is to say, the constitution and powers of municipal corporations, improvement trusts, district boards, mining settlement authorities and other local authorities for the purpose of local self-government or village administration."

As a consequence of inadequate Constitutional provision for local self-government, democracy in municipal governance was not stable. Though the respective municipal acts of the States provided for regular elections to municipal bodies, they were frequently suspended and superseded for indefinite periods of time. Frequent and indefinite suspensions or supersessions eroded the very basis of local self-government and had a negative effect on democracy at the grassroots level. The general position with regard to financial resources of the municipal bodies was also not satisfactory. Over the years, there was a steady encroachment on the assigned functions and revenues of Urban Local Bodies (ULBs) by specialized agencies of the State Governments.

In short, local bodies could not function effectively because of (a) inadequate devolution of functions and financial powers (b) failure to hold regular elections and prolonged supersession and (c) lack of participation from weaker sections of society. Consequently, local bodies in many States had become weak and ineffective as units of self-government in the democratic set up of India.

The weakened status of ULBs crystallized public opinion in favour of a Constitutional guarantee to safeguard the interests of urban local bodies in order to provide for the following:

1. Regular and fair conduct of elections to these bodies.
2. Holding of elections within a specified time limit in case of supersession.
3. Adequate representation of SC/ST and women in the elected bodies.
4. Placing on firm footing the relationship between the State Governments and the urban local bodies with respect to (a) functions and taxation powers of the urban local bodies and (b) arrangement for revenue sharing between the State Government and the urban local bodies.
5. Involvement of elected representatives at grassroots level in planning at the district and metropolitan levels.

9.3 Decentralisation Initiative, 1992 and Reservation of Seats for Women

The Seventy-third and Seventy-fourth Amendment Bills relating to *panchayats* and municipalities respectively were introduced in the Parliament in September 1991 to provide constitutional remedy for the inadequacies plaguing these bodies which were unable to perform effectively as vibrant democratic units of self-government. The Bills were referred to two joint bodies of Parliament and after necessary revision were reintroduced in July 1992, and passed by Parliament in December 1992. Both the Bills were ratified by the required number of States [Article 368(ii)] and the President gave his assent in April 1993. The Seventy-third Amendment Act relating to *panchayats* came into force from April 24, 1993. The Seventy-fourth Amendment Act relating to municipalities came into force from June 1, 1993. The changes made by the Seventy-third and Seventy-fourth Amendment Acts to the Constitution were of historical importance and are summarised in Table 9.1.

In short, *panchayats* and municipalities are now constitutional bodies forming third tier to the federal polity of India. India's decentralisation initiative in the form of Seventy-third and Seventy-fourth Amendments poses challenges and offers opportunities.

Table 9.1: Seventy-third and Seventy-fourth Constitutional Amendment Acts

Act	Date on which came into force	Amendments made
Constitution (Seventy-third Amendment) Act 1992	24. 4. 1993	A new Part IX relating to Panchayats was inserted. In clause (3) of Article 280, sub-clause (bb) was inserted which provides for measures to supplement the resources of the Panchayats. Eleventh Schedule added to the Constitution which provides an illustrative list for the devolution of functions to Panchayats.
Constitution (Seventy-fourth Amendment) Act, 1992	1. 6. 1993	A new Part IXA relating to Municipalities was inserted. In clause (3) of Article 280, sub-clause (c) was re-lettered as sub-clause (d) and before sub-clause (d) as so re-lettered, sub-clause (c) was inserted which provides for measures to supplement the resources of the Municipalities. Twelfth Schedule added to the Constitution which provides an illustrative list for the devolution of functions to Municipalities.

Source: Government of India, Ministry of Law, Justice and Company Affairs, *The Constitution of India (Supplement to the Third Edition)*, 1994.

9.4 Constitution (Seventy-third Amendment) Act, 1992

The passage of the Constitution (Seventy-third Amendment) Act, 1992 marked a watershed in the history of modern India. With this amendment, a uniform structure of *panchayats* emerged throughout the country.

Article 243 G read with Eleventh Schedule of the Constitution explicitly requires the States to devolve powers and authority on *panchayats* which may be necessary to enable them to function as institutions of self-government. The Eleventh Schedule of the Constitution is reproduced in Table 9.2.

Table 9.2: Eleventh Schedule of the Constitution (Article 243 G)

1.	Agriculture, including agricultural extension.
2.	Land improvement, land reforms, land consolidation and soil conservation.
3.	Minor irrigation, water management and watershed development.
4.	Animal husbandry, dairying and poultry.
5.	Fisheries.
6.	Social forestry and farm forestry.
7.	Minor forest produce.
8.	Small-scale industries, including food processing industries.
9.	Khadi, village and cottage industries.
10.	Rural housing.
11.	Drinking water
12.	Fuel and fodder.
13.	Roads, culverts, bridges, ferries, waterways and other means of communication.
14.	Rural electrification, including distribution of electricity.
15.	Non-conventional energy sources.
16.	Poverty alleviation programmes.
17.	Education, including primary and secondary schools.
18.	Technical training and vocational education.
19.	Adult and non-formal education.
20.	Libraries.
21.	Cultural activities.
22.	Markets and fairs.
23.	Health and sanitation, including hospitals, primary health centres and dispensaries.
24.	Family welfare.
25.	Women and child development.
26.	Social welfare, including welfare of the handicapped and mentally retarded.
27.	Welfare of the weaker sections, and in particular, of the Scheduled Castes and the Scheduled Tribes.
28.	Public distribution system.
29.	Maintenance of community assets.

9.5 Constitution (Seventy-fourth Amendment) Act, 1992

The passage of the Constitution (Seventy-fourth Amendment) Act, 1992 was a landmark in the history of municipal administration in India. Article 243W read with Twelfth Schedule of the Constitution provides the illustrative list for the devolution of functions to the municipalities. The Twelfth Schedule of the Constitution is reproduced in Table 9.3. Many States have amended their municipal laws to ensure conformity with the new constitutional provisions.

Table 9.3: Twelfth Schedule of the Constitution (Article 243 W)

1.	Urban planning including town planning.
2.	Regulation of land-use and construction of buildings.
3.	Planning for economic and social development.
4.	Roads and bridges.
5.	Water supply for domestic, industrial and commercial purposes.
6.	Public health, sanitation conservancy and solid waste management.
7.	Fire services.
8.	Urban forestry, protection of the environment and promotion of ecological aspects.
9.	Safeguarding the interests of weaker sections of society, including the handicapped and mentally retarded.
10.	Slum improvement and upgradation.
11.	Urban poverty alleviation.
12.	Provision of urban amenities and facilities such as parks, gardens, play-grounds.
13.	Promotion of cultural, educational and aesthetic aspects.
14.	Burials and burial grounds; cremations, cremation grounds and electric crematoriums.
15.	Cattle ponds; prevention of cruelty to animals.
16.	Vital statistics including registration of births and deaths.
17.	Public amenities including street lighting, parking lots, bus stops and public conveniences.
18.	Regulation of slaughter houses and tanneries.

Through this amendment a new Part IX-A relating to municipalities was incorporated in the Constitution to provide for, *inter alia,* the constitution of three types of municipalities, viz. *Nagar Panchayat* for a transitional area, i.e. an area in transition from a rural to urban area [1]; Municipal Council for smaller urban area, and Municipal Corporation for larger urban area (Article 243 Q).

The Constitution (Seventy-fourth Amendment) Act, 1992 conferred constitutional status to the structure and mandate of municipalities so as to enable them to function as vibrant democratic and self-governing institutions at the grassroots level. [2]

The objectives of the Seventy-fourth Amendment included decentralisation of power and popular participation in the planning, management, and delivery of civic services.

The main provisions introduced by the Seventy-fourth Amendment are as under:

9.5.1 Constitution of Municipalities: It provides for constitution of 3 types of municipalities depending upon the size and area namely (a) Nagar Panchayat for an area in transition from rural to urban area, (b) Municipal Council for smaller urban area and (c) Municipal Corporation for larger urban area. Demographic and other conditions—which are determining factors for constituting a particular type of municipality—differ a great deal from one State to another. It has, therefore, been left to the State Legislatures to decide which specific type of municipality will be constituted for particular urban area.

9.5.2 Composition of Municipalities: The seats shall be filled by direct elections. Besides the seats filled by direct elections, some seats may be filled by nomination of persons having special knowledge and experience in municipal administration. Persons so nominated shall not have the right to vote in the meetings of the municipality. The Legislature of a State may, by law, also provide for the representation in a municipality of members of the House of the People and the members of the Legislative Assembly of the State representing constituencies which comprise wholly or partly the Municipal area and also the Members of the Council of States and the members of the Legislative Council of the State registered as electors within the municipal area. The manner of election of Chairpersons of municipalities has been left to be specified by the State Legislature.

9.5.3 Constitution of Wards Committees: This provides for constitution of Ward Committees in all municipalities with a population of 3 lakh or more.

9.5.4 Reservation of Seats: In order to provide for adequate representation of SC/ST and of women in the municipal bodies, provisions have been made for reservation of seats. The proportion of seats to be reserved for SC/ST to the total number of seats shall be same as the proportion of the population of SC/ST in the municipal area. The reservation would be made in respect of seats to be filled by direct elections only. Not less than one-third of the total number of seats reserved for SC/ST shall be reserved for women belonging to SC/ST. This is a mandatory provision.

In respect of women, the seats shall be reserved to the extent of not less than one-third of the total number of seats. This includes seats reserved for women belonging to SC/ST. These reservations will apply for direct elections only. This is also a mandatory provision. There will be no bar on State Legislatures from making provisions for reservation of seats in any municipality or office of Chairperson in the municipalities in favour of backward class of citizens. This is an optional provision.

9.5.5 Duration of Municipalities: The municipality has a fixed term of 5 years from the date appointed for its first meeting. Elections to constitute a municipality are required to be completed before the expiration of the duration of the municipality. If the municipality is dissolved before the expiry of 5 years, the elections for constituting a new municipality are required to be completed within a period of 6 months from the date of its dissolution.

9.5.6 Powers and Functions of the Municipalities: All municipalities would be empowered with such powers and responsibilities as may be necessary to enable them to function as effective institutions of self-government. The State Legislature may, by law, specify what powers and responsibilities would be given to the municipalities in respect of preparation of plans for economic development and social justice and for implementation of schemes as may be entrusted to them. An illustrative list of functions that may be entrusted to the municipalities has been incorporated as the Twelfth Schedule of the Constitution.

9.5.7 Finances of Municipalities: It has been left to the Legislature of a State to specify by law matters relating to imposition of taxes. Such law may specify the following:

1. Taxes, duties, fees, etc. which could be levied and collected by the municipalities, as per the procedure to be laid down in the State law.
2. Taxes, duties, fees, etc. which would be levied and collected by the State Government and a share passed on to the municipalities.
3. Grant-in-aid that would be given to the municipalities from the State.
4. Constitution of funds for crediting and withdrawal of moneys by the municipalities.

9.5.8 Finance Commission: The Finance Commission constituted under Article 243-I to review the financial positions of Panchayati Raj Institutions shall also review the financial position of the municipalities and will make recommendations to the Governor.

The recommendations of the Finance Commission will cover the following:

1. Distribution between the State Government and Municipalities of the net proceeds of the taxes, duties, tolls and fees leviable by the State.
2. Allocation of share of such proceeds between the Municipalities at all levels in the State.

3. Determination of taxes, duties, tolls and fees to be assigned or appropriated by the Municipalities.
4. Grants-in-aid to Municipalities from the Consolidated Fund of the State.
5. Measures needed to improve the financial position of the Municipalities.

9.5.9 Elections to Municipalities: The superintendence, direction and control of the preparation of the electoral rolls for, and the conduct of, all elections to the panchayats and municipalities shall be vested in the State Election Commissions.

9.5.10 Audit and Accounts: The maintenance of the accounts of the municipalities and other audit shall be done in accordance with the provisions in the State law. The State Legislatures will be free to make appropriate provisions in this regard depending upon the local needs and institutional framework available for this purpose.

9.5.11 Committee for District Planning: Planning and allocation of resources at the district level for the Panchayati Raj Institutions are normally to be done by the Zilla Parishad. With regard to urban areas, municipal bodies discharge these functions within their respective jurisdictions. However, some important questions may arise, which would concern the urban-rural interface, and it may be necessary to take an overall view with regard to development of the district as a whole and decide on allocation of investments between the rural and urban institutions. Provision has, therefore, been made for the constitution of a Planning Committee at the district level with a view to consolidating the plans prepared by the Panchayats and the Municipalities and preparing a development plan for the district as a whole. The District Planning Committee in preparing the Draft Development Plan shall have regard to the following:

1. Matter of common interest between the Panchayats and the Municipalities including spatial planning.
2. Sharing of water and other physical and natural resources.
3. Integrated development of infrastructure and environment conservation.
4. Extent and type of available resources, whether financial or otherwise.

The Draft District Development Plan so prepared and recommended by the District Planning Committee shall be forwarded by the Chairperson of the Committee to the State Government.

9.5.12 Metropolitan Planning Committees: It is provided in the Act that in every Metropolitan area (with a population of 10 lakhs or more), a Metropolitan Planning Committee shall be constituted for preparing a draft development plan for the metropolitan area as a whole.

The Metropolitan Planning Committee shall take into account the following for preparation of the Draft Development Plan:

1. Plan prepared by the Municipalities and the Panchayats in the metropolitan

area.

2. Matter of common interest between the Municipalities and Panchayats including coordinated spatial plans of the area.
3. Sharing of water and other physical and natural resources.
4. Integrated development of infrastructure and environmental conservation.
5. Overall objectives and priorities set by the Government of India and the State Government.
6. Extent and nature of investments likely to be made in the metropolitan area by agencies of the Government.
7. Other available resources, financial and otherwise.

In short, the salient features of the Seventy-fourth Amendment are the following:

1. It provides a framework for the assignment of appropriate governmental functions to municipalities through the Twelfth Schedule of the Constitution read with Article 243 W. The Twelfth Schedule defines the functional domain of municipalities. Many of the functions included in this Schedule have distributional and developmental attributes. The Twelfth Schedule generally contains traditional functions of municipalities. However, some non-traditional functions are also discernible from the list. These are: (a) protection of the environment and promotion of ecological aspects, (b) safeguarding the interests of weaker sections of society including the handicapped and mentally retarded, (c) urban poverty alleviation, and (d) promotion of cultural and aesthetic aspects.
2. States are statutorily required to constitute a finance commission (Article 243-I and 243-Y), once in every 5 years, to recommend to their legislatures measures to improve municipal finances including (i) assignment of taxes, duties, tolls, and fees, (ii) sharing of state taxes, and (iii) provision of grants-in-aid.
3. Finance Commission constituted by the Government of India is obligated to recommend measures to augment the Consolidated Fund of State Governments to supplement the resources of the municipalities on the basis of the recommendations made by the State Finance Commissions [Article 280(3)(c)].
4. It is mandatory to constitute in every State at the district level a District Planning Committee to consolidate and prepare development plan for the district as a whole (Article 243 ZD). Similarly, it is mandatory to constitute in every metropolitan area a Metropolitan Planning Committee to prepare a development plan for the metropolitan area as a whole (Article 243 ZE).
5. It mandates that a municipality if dissolved by a State Government, must be

reconstituted within six months [Article 243 U(3)]. This is meant to ensure the continuity of civic affairs by elected representatives of the people.

6. It ensures reservation of seats for women and other disadvantaged categories (Article 243 T).

In terms of Article 243ZC of the Constitution, nothing in Part IXA shall apply to Scheduled areas and Tribal areas as referred to in Article 244 of the Constitution. However, Parliament may by law, extend the provisions of Part IXA to these areas subject to such exceptions and modifications as may be specified in that law.

In order to provide time to allow changes to be made in the then existing laws which were inconsistent with the provisions of the Constitution (Seventy-fourth Amendment) Act, a transition period of 1 year was provided for.

The amended State municipal laws provide for detailed provisions for constitution and composition of municipalities, reservation of seats for SC/ST and women, fixed term of 5 years and re-election of municipalities within a period of 6 months in case of dissolution, functions and financial powers of municipalities, setting up of State Finance Commission etc.

9.6 Amendment to Article 243T of the Constitution to Provide for 50 percent Reservation for Women in Urban Local Bodies

The Constitution (112th Amendment) Bill 2009 to provide for 50 percent reservation of women in Urban Local Bodies (ULBs) was introduced in Lok Sabha on November 24, 2009. Through this Bill the Government of India seeks to increase the representation of women in ULBs from the present level of one-third to 50 percent which would also include enhancement of reservation for women up to 50 percent in seats reserved for Scheduled Castes (SCs), Scheduled Tribes (STs), and 50 percent reservations for women in the posts of Chairpersons. This would result in increased representation of women in ULBs and is likely to yield significant benefits in terms of higher priority to women's issues in critical areas of urban Governance and service delivery such as water supply, sanitation, solid waste management, education and health, etc. Presently the bill is under the consideration of the Parliamentary Standing Committee on Urban Development.

9.7 New Status of Municipalities: An Assessment

The Seventy-fourth amendment was made with the intention to make municipalities self-governing units. The situation existing before and after the Seventy-fourth amendment is summarised in Table 9.4.

Table 9.4: Status of Municipalities in India

Before the 74th Amendment	After the 74th Amendment
No all-India framework for devolution of functions.	12th Schedule read with Article 243 W of the Constitution provides guide points for assignment of functions to municipalities.
High degree of arbitrariness in the system of fiscal transfers from the State Governments to municipalities. No periodic assessment of financial needs of municipalities.	State Finance Commission (SFC) to be constituted statutorily in every State every Fifth year (Article 243-I and 243-Y) to review the financial position of municipalities and suggest measures to improve the same.
No role for the National Finance Commission as regards the finances of urban local bodies.	National Finance Commission is required to augment the Consolidated Fund of State Governments to supplement the resources of the municipalities on the basis of the recommendations made by the SFCs [Article 280(3)(c)].
Absence of constitutional bodies to prepare development plans for local areas.	Mandatory constitution of District Planning Committees (Article 243ZD) and Metropolitan Planning Committees (Article 243ZE) for consolidation and preparation of development plans.
Failure to hold regular elections and prolonged supersessions.	A municipality if dissolved by a State Government must be reconstituted within six months [Article 243 U(3)].
Lack of participation from weaker sections of society.	Reservation of seats for women and other disadvantaged categories (Article 243 T).

In the federal polity of India, local bodies are institutions created by the State Governments (entry 5 of List II of the Seventh Schedule). They enjoy only those powers and responsibilities which are assigned to them. Twelfth Schedule of the Constitution lists the functions and responsibilities that may be transferred to municipalities. The permissive nature of Seventy-fourth Amendment is clear and the State Governments enjoy full discretion as regards the transfer of functions to municipalities.

No doubt, municipalities have acquired constitutional status after the said Amendment, they are completely dependent on respective State Governments in terms of self-governance.

9.7.1 Desirability and Feasibility of Uniformity in Municipal Functions: A careful reading of the Twelfth Schedule shows that many of the functions listed in it found place in the Municipal Acts of various States even before the enactment of the conformity legislations by them. Hence, the Twelfth Schedule has been generally accepted as a guiding list of municipal functions.

Should there be all-India uniformity in delegating functions and financial powers to local bodies? There is a weak case for all-India uniformity as regards functional domain of local bodies. State Governments and their local bodies have diverse economic and social conditions. It is by no means rational to expect uniformity in the functions and powers of the Greater Bombay Municipal Corporation and the municipality of a small township of a backward State. Similarly, it is debatable if local bodies should have uniform taxation powers.

Though it will be useful to prepare a reference list regarding functions (Eleventh and Twelfth Schedules), assigned taxes, shareable taxes, user charges, fees etc., all-India uniformity in these matters would be too much to expect.

Even at the level of a State, uniformity is not desirable in view of diverse city conditions and intra-State disparities. This fact has been recognised by the Constitution while providing for the constitution of 3 types of municipal bodies: Nagar Panchayats, Municipal Councils, and Municipal Corporations (Article 243 Q). However, it does not distinguish between the functional domains of the 3 types of municipal bodies. The determination of the functions of municipalities of different sizes is left to the wisdom of the State Governments.

However, there exists a·case for uniformity of functions among similar municipalities in a State. If a State chooses to allocate dissimilar functions and powers to similar municipalities (say Municipal Councils), there can be genuine resentment among the municipalities discriminated against. It is here that objective criteria based on population size, geographical area, or constitutional categorisation (Article 243 Q) are needed to prevent misuse of political authority.

The Constitution should provide, at least, a list of minimum functions to be transferred to municipalities of various types by the State Governments.

9.7.2 Role of State Finance Commissions: The State Finance Commission is set up under Article 243-I read with Article 243-Y of the Constitution. It is required to review the financial position of the municipalities and make recommendations as to:

(a) the principles which should govern –

i. the distribution between the State and the Municipalities of the net proceeds of taxes, duties, tolls and fees leviable by the State, which may be divided between them, and the allocations between the Municipalities of their respective shares of such proceeds.

ii. the determination of the taxes, duties, tolls and fees which may be assigned to, or appropriated by, the Municipalities.

iii. the grants-in-aid to Municipalities from the Consolidated Fund of the State.

(b) the measures needed to improve the financial position of the Municipalities.

(c) any other matter referred to the Finance Commission in the interest of sound finance of the Municipalities.

As required under the Constitution, all State Governments set up Finance Commissions. These State Finance Commissions (SFCs) are expected to strengthen local bodies so that they may function as democratic units for the socio-economic development of urban and rural areas of our country.

The task of the First Finance Commission of a State was difficult and arduous in the absence of precedence and it was expected to make suo moto all such studies in areas which never existed before. Nevertheless, the work of the First Finance Commission was crucial because it paved the way for subsequent commissions. The following observations may be made in this regard.

1. New Constitutional arrangement (Seventy-fourth Amendment) implies that the whole range of a State's tax revenue is open to sharing with municipalities. SFCs are expected to evolve principles of tax assignment, tax sharing, and grants to municipalities with a view to mitigate their weak financial position. They are also required to evolve criteria with regard to adequacy and objectivity of grants.
2. Sharing of State tax revenue with municipalities depends wholly on the discretion of State Government.
3. In determining devolution of funds, the SFCs would do well to keep in mind, *inter alia*, the following factors.

(a) Resource position of the State.

(b) Normative deficits of municipalities. Any system which underestimates the gap between revenue and expenditure should be discouraged.

(c) Degree of dependence of municipalities for funds on the State Government.

(d) Capacity of a municipality to utilise devolved resources.

(e) A State Finance Commission may consider introduction of a system of incentives and disincentives into the entire governmental grants on objective lines. Municipalities which are able to raise resources through levy of user charges and benefit taxes should be considered for incentive grants from the State Government.

A. Determination and Filling of Budgetary Gaps: A State Finance Commission has to determine the budgetary gaps of municipalities for the period of its award. Thereafter, it has to devise formulae for filling the gaps so determined.

(a) Determination of the Budgetary Gaps: Two approaches may be followed for this purpose: (a) trend growth rate and (b) normative approach.

Under the first approach, average annual growth rate in a variable during a reference period (say 1994-95 through 2006-07) is worked out and the same is projected for a future period (say 2007-08 through 2011-12). It is assumed that past behaviour of the variable will be repeated in future. Thus, *actuals* or *accounts* of revenue and expenditure of a government may be used to compute the average annual growth rate of the two aggregates over a stated period. Applying the computed average to a future period, one can work out estimated revenue, expenditure and budgetary gap for any future year.

Under the second method, revenue of a government is assessed normatively and certain norms are applied to assess expenditure. In other words, *needs* and *capacities* of different governments are assessed normatively and such normative assessments are used to meet budgetary gaps of the governments. More specifically, fiscal performance of a government is judged on the basis of *what ought to be* rather than *what it actually is*.

In the context of the work of a State Finance Commission, normative approach should apply to both the State Government and municipalities and that the assessment of revenue and expenditure should be done in a manner so as to maintain incentives for greater revenue efforts and economy in spending.

(b) Filling the Gap: Once budgetary gaps of municipalities are determined, the next task of a State Finance Commission is to devise formulae for filling these gaps. For this purpose, it has to work out a judicious mix of tax devolution and grants.

It is noteworthy that the term *gap-filling* in the context of State-municipal fiscal relations has a different connotation than at the national level.

At the national level, even after the transfer to the States of a share of divisible taxes, the resources of some of the States may remain inadequate to meet their needs. Thus, a Finance Commission determines the grants equal to deficit of each State so that the non-Plan revenue accounts of the States are balanced or left with a surplus every year. In other words, deficits of non-Plan revenue account which remain after tax devolution are covered through grants. This is called the gap-filling approach (or more appropriately net gap-filling approach).

It is possible that even before tax devolution from the Centre, some high-income States have surplus in their non-Plan revenue account. Thus, while a State cannot be denied a part of a shared Central tax even if it has no demonstrated financial need, grants are given upon genuine financial needs of the States.

However, the working of a State Finance Commission is different. Like the National Finance Commission, it is not bound by any constitutional restrictions regarding the type of taxes to be shared with municipalities. In fact, the whole field of State taxation is open to it for determining tax devolution. In other words, tax devolution and grants are to be used simultaneously to cover the budgetary gaps of municipalities. In this case, gap-filling means how to cover the projected budgetary gaps of municipalities through a judicious mix of tax devolution and grants with due regard to the underlying principles of the two methods to effect transfers from a higher to a lower level government.

9.8 Tenth Finance Commission (FC-X) on Local Bodies

FC-X did not have any mandate, in its terms of reference, to make recommendations for the local bodies. However, the Seventy-third and Seventy-fourth Constitutional amendments had become effective before the Commission had finalised its report and, therefore, it took the view that in terms of the sub-clauses (bb) and (c) of the article 280(3), it was obliged to make recommendations regarding measures needed to augment the Consolidated Fund of the States for supplementation of the resources of the panchayats and the municipalities. FC-X analysed the scope of such duty cast on it and made the following observations:

1. The need for augmentation of the Consolidated Fund of the States should first be ascertained and only thereafter the measures for such augmentation be recommended.
2. Such measures need not necessarily involve transfer of resources from the Centre.
3. Once the SFCs complete their task, the Finance Commission becomes duly bound to assess and build into the expenditure stream of the States the funding requirements for supplementing the resources of the panchayats and the municipalities. Measures needed for augmentation of the Consolidated Funds of the States may be determined accordingly.
4. The responsibility for sharing and assigning taxes and providing grants to the local bodies rests with the States and does not stand transferred to the Centre.
5. The transfer of duties and functions listed in the Eleventh and Twelfth Schedules of the Constitution would also involve concomitant transfer of staff and resources. Transfers of duties and functions to the local bodies should, therefore, not entail any extra financial burden.

Since the recommendations of the State Finance Commissions were not available to the FC-X, the latter was in doubt whether it could recommend measures for augmenting State resources for the purpose of supplementing the resources of panchayats and municipalities. To resolve the dilemma, it decided to make *ad hoc* provision of specific grants to States in the following manner.

1. An *ad hoc* provision of ₹ 100 per capita of rural population in each State to be

distributed amongst panchayats over and above their due by way of their share of the assigned taxes, duties, tolls, fees etc.

2. A provision of ₹ 1,000 crore for the 5 year period (1995-2000) covered by its recommendations for urban local bodies.

While making these provisions for grants to panchayats/municipalities, the FC-X made it clear that this need not necessarily be a precedent for future Commissions.

9.9 Eleventh Finance Commission (FC-XI) on Local Bodies

FC-XI was the first to be required by the President, in terms of the Seventy-third and Seventy-fourth Amendments to the Constitution, to recommend the measures needed to augment the Consolidated Fund of a State to supplement the resources of the panchayats and municipalities in the State on the basis of the recommendations of the State Finance Commissions.

The FC-XI recommended grants totalling ₹ 10,000 crore for local bodies during 2000-2005, to be utilised mainly for maintenance of civic services. Of this, ₹ 1,600 crore per annum was for rural local bodies and ₹ 400 crore per annum was for urban local bodies. FC-XI recommended that the amounts of ₹ 1,600 crore and ₹ 400 crore provided for the panchayats and municipalities respectively, for each of the five years (2000-05) be distributed among the States on the following criteria and weights.

1. Population 40 percent.
2. Index of decentralisation 20 percent.
3. Distance from highest per capita income 20 percent.
4. Revenue effort 10 percent.
5. Geographical area 10 percent.

The grants given to local bodies were primarily meant for maintenance of civil services including primary health and family welfare, education as well as other public utility services.

9.10 Twelfth Finance Commission (FC-XII) on Local Bodies

FC-XII made the following recommendations regarding local bodies.

1. A total grant of ₹ 20,000 crore for the panchayati raj institutions and ₹ 5,000 crore for the urban local bodies may be given to the states for the period 2005-10.
2. PRIs should be encouraged to take over the assets relating to water supply and sanitation and utilize the grants for repairs/rejuvenation as also the O&M costs. The PRIs should, however, recover at least 50 percent of the recurring costs in the form of user charges.

3. Out of the grants allocated for the panchayats, priority should be given to expenditure on the O&M costs of water supply and sanitation. This will facilitate panchayats to take over the schemes and operate them.
4. At least 50 percent of the grants provided to each state for the urban local bodies should be earmarked for the scheme of solid waste management through public-private partnership. The municipalities should concentrate on collection, segregation and transportation of solid waste. The cost of these activities, whether carried out in house or out sourced, could be met from the grants.
5. Besides expenditure on the O&M costs of water supply and sanitation in rural areas and on the schemes of solid waste management in urban areas, PRIs and ULBs should, out of the grants allocated, give high priority to expenditure on creation of data base and maintenance of accounts through the use of modern technology and management systems, wherever possible. Some of the modern methods like Geographic Information Systems (GIS) for mapping of properties in urban areas and computerization for switching over to a modern system of financial management would go a long way in creating strong local governments, fulfilling the spirit of the Seventy-third and Seventy-fourth Constitutional amendments.
6. States may assess the requirement of each local body on the basis of the principles stated by us and earmark funds accordingly out of the total allocation re-commended by us.
7. Grants have not been recommended separately for the normal and the excluded areas under the Fifth and Sixth Schedule of the Constitution. The states having such areas may distribute the grants recommended by us to all local bodies, including those in the excluded areas, in a fair and just manner.
8. Central Government should not impose any condition other than those prescribed by us, for release or utilization of these grants, which are largely in the nature of a correction of vertical imbalance between the centre and the states.
9. Normal practice of insisting on the utilization of amounts already released before further releases are considered, may continue and the grants may be released to a state only after it certifies that the previous releases have been passed on to the local bodies. The amounts due to the states in the first year of our award period i.e. 2005-06 may be released without such an insistence.
10. State Governments should not take more than 15 days in transferring the grants to local bodies after these are released by the central government. The centre should take a serious view of any undue delay on the part of the state.
11. Central Government should take note of our views on the issues, while

formulating or revising various policy measures. In particular, action may be taken to raise the ceiling on profession tax.

12. States should adopt the best practices to improve the resources of the panchayats.
13. Suggestions made by us in respect of state finance commissions should be acted upon with a view to strengthening the institution of SFCs, so that it may play an effective role in the system of fiscal transfers to the third tier of government.

9.11 Thirteenth Finance Commission (FC-XIII) on Local Bodies

Regarding the functioning of local bodies, the FC-XIII observed, "There has been considerable progress in the empowerment of Panchayati Raj Institutions (PRIs) and municipalities since the Tenth Finance Commission (FC-X) first made a provision for explicitly supporting local bodies through grants, subsequent to the passage of the 73rd and 74th amendments to the Constitution in 1993. Approximately 30 lakh representatives are regularly elected to about 2.5 lakh local institutions all over the country. Providing basic services at the grassroots level makes them the primary interface of the citizens' interaction with the government. The principle of subsidiarity implies that matters are best handled by the least centralised competent authority. Following this, these institutions need to be adequately empowered—both functionally and financially—to enable them to fulfil the role envisaged for them in the Constitution. The State Finance Commissions (SFCs), which buttress the functioning of local bodies, also need to be strengthened so as to make their functioning more predictable and the process of implementing their recommendations more transparent. A number of recommendations were made by FC-XI and FC-XII towards this end. Some of these recommendations, though important, have not been implemented so far. More needs to be done to promote effective decentralisation." [3]

9.12 Women in Local Bodies: An Appraisal

Legislative enactments have dramatically increased women's access to decision-making structures in recent years. The Seventy-third and Seventy-fourth Constitutional Amendments passed in 1993 provide for reservation of 33 percent of elected seats for women at different levels of local governance in both rural and urban local bodies. Also there would be one-third reservation for women to posts of chairperson of these bodies. One-third of the seats are further reserved for women belonging to the SC/ST community. The Panchayats (Extension to Schedule Areas) Act 1996 (PESA) made this amendment applicable to Schedule V areas. This has dramatically increased women's participation in local bodies.

For every 5 year tenure of local governments, about 1 million women get elected to panchayats and local bodies. In some states, the number of elected women exceeds the reserved one-third quota.

The Constitution provides for rotation of seats reserved for women but does not prescribe the number of terms for which seats may be served for rotation. Seats are reserved for one term, two terms or more depending upon the provisions made by the State Legislature in the State law. The option to reserve seats for more than one terms is open, but it is for the State Legislature to decide the number of terms for which seats will remain reserved. Tamil Nadu has taken a positive step by freezing the reserved seats for women for two terms.

Local government institutions have not been given full financial and political powers to function independently but 29 subjects ranging from agriculture to poverty eradication have been devolved to these institutions. In theory, the presidents of the gram panchayats, block panchayats and district panchayats are responsible for prioritising the developmental needs of the villagers and allocating the grants accordingly. In practice, the level of responsiveness and manner of functioning of the panchayats varies considerably across states. As far as women's participation is concerned, the legislative enactments have ensured that they are represented in all states.

9.12.1 Lack of Confidence: Many of the elected women entering the public arena for the first time lack confidence, feel isolated, and have no previous political experience. They need to develop their innate leadership skills. Studies conducted in different parts of the country show that 95 percent of the elected women representatives (EWRs) are first-timers in politics and join politics because that is what their male family/village members want. As first timers without previous exposure to politics, many of the elected women lack the capacity to function properly in the panchayats and municipalities, and consequently are not taken seriously by their colleagues. Sustained training and networking efforts are being undertaken both by government and non-government agencies to ensure that women's capacity to participate improves. With just a few years of experience, women have emerged as articulate, motivated leaders all over the country.

Gender budgeting involving grassroots elected women representatives is being used for advocacy in several places. Increased networking and formation of confederations of elected women representatives has helped to strengthen women's leadership. This approach has been especially successful in southern and western India. The formation of these networks promotes solidarity among the elected women representatives, otherwise divided by caste, religion and geographical boundaries. Thus, formation of these networks is the first step in the direction of empowering women. Their position as panchayat members adds to their ability to intervene and negotiate with the community. The presence of EWRs in the dispute resolution process lends support and confidence to other women. The networks have also been able to promote capacity building.

9.12.2 Proxy Politics: Constitutional provisions apart, there are complaints from various parts of the country regarding effective participation of women in local governance structures. Proxy politics, power brokering and gender discrimination continue, and many women sarpanches have to face violence for challenging existing societal power centres. In other cases, women are in PRI only in name. In reality, it is the male family members who hold the power. In spite of the affirmative action in panchayati raj in favour of marginalized communities, exclusion of caste, poverty, tribal status, gender and caste sharply demarcate those who have political power from those who do not. Central and State Governments should not delay any further the devolution and decentralization of powers from higher bodies (Government of India or State Governments) to the panchayati raj structures. This devolution right now is lagging in almost all the States. The three Fs—funds, functions and functionaries—in most States are still in the same position prior to 1993. In the absence of this basic requirement, the Constitutional provisions are not only being violated, but there is lack of clarity at the field level which leads to dysfunctional situations.

India has primarily relied upon the method of reservation to ensure women's presence in decision-making bodies. This has increased *de jure*, but not necessarily *de facto*, participation. There is need to encourage women's participation in other kinds of groups and associations which contribute to an atmosphere of leadership by women, as well as supporting training and networking for elected women.

9.13 Gender Mainstreaming in Legislatures, Judiciary and Police

While the planning process and public expenditure in terms of programmes and schemes are sought to be included in gender budgeting, yet without gender sensitivity of important organs such as police and judiciary, the implementation will not be successful. This is especially true of schemes which have a strong element of protection or are rights based. For example, if a woman is not given her due share of property or other assets as per law, it is essential that these agencies help and support her in getting her share without much delay or harassment. This can happen only if gender sensitivity is inculcated in such bodies and they are made aware of the laws, policies, programmes and other initiatives for women. It is also important that justice delivery is quick with the enforcement machinery being responsive and gender sensitive to women's needs especially in cases of domestic violence and personal assault.

It is, therefore, necessary to induct a larger number of women in these bodies at different levels. This will encourage women to actively participate in power sharing and active participation in decision-making. Efforts should be made to provide coaching facilities and support services so that women can compete along with men both at entry and to facilitate upward mobility of women in these institutions.

The setting up of women police stations, women's help desk in every police station, and increasing the strength of women police to 30 percent of the total force has been reiterated a number of times by the Ministry of Women and Child Development in a number of forums. The Ministry of Home Affairs should take requisite steps to fulfil their obligations towards gender budgeting by engendering the police force.

True, efforts have been made to empower women socially, economically and politically, but as a result of the lack of synergy or coordination between these activities, the outcomes are not satisfactory. For example the increasing induction of women representatives into the PRIs should have meant automatic improvement in the lives of rural women, but if it has not happened, it is because the elected women were not educated or literate or even made aware of their rights. Also there are many groups of women who on account of tradition, culture, ethnic, social or religious background are more vulnerable compared to the women in the mainstream sector.

It is imperative that an integrated policy and strategy be formulated that addresses economic, social, and political empowerment simultaneously and holistically along with the requisite programmes and schemes. Once such a comprehensive policy and programs flowing from it are put in place, it will be possible to enable an all round development of women, which will usher in true empowerment.

To sum up, notable constitutional, legislative and policy reforms, and continued administrative decentralization have demonstrated the commitment of Governments (Centre and States) to increase political participation of women at grassroots level. Although only one-third of seats were reserved for women by the Seventy-third and Seventy-fourth constitutional amendments, the actual representation is higher at all levels. Increased political participation of women has yielded a range of positive results, not only for women but also for their families and communities. Central issues in development such as health, nutrition, family income and education are finding their way to the top of the agenda for action. Women's participation brings about more inclusive governance and effective community-cantered development. Yet in many places, especially in states like UP, Bihar and Rajasthan, women continue to serve as proxies.

Over the years, efforts towards gender sensitisation of a traditionally male-dominated society have been intensified. These have included the following: (a) gender sensitisation of the law enforcement agencies—especially the police and the judiciary—through periodic training given by Government agencies and NGOs, (b) gender sensitisation of the training given by the National Judicial Academy, (c) gender sensitisation module of State level training institutions for the orientation of officials, (d) sensitisation of medical officers who are responsible for implementing the Prenatal Diagnostic Techniques (Prevention of Misuse and Regulation) Act and (e) National Research and Training Centre set up at the country's premier institution, the Lal Bahadur Shastri National Academy of Administration, for the training of administrators seeks to impart training in gender concerns.

End Notes

1. Here, 'a transitional area', 'a smaller urban area', or 'a larger urban area' means such area as the Governor may specify by public notification having regard to the population of the area, the density of the population, the revenue generated for local administration, the percentage of employment in non-agricultural activities and such other factors.
2. Following is the Statement of Objects and Reasons appended to the Constitution Seventy-third Amendment) Bill, 1991 which was enacted as the Constitution (Seventy-fourth Amendment) Act, 1992.
   In many States local bodies have become weak and ineffective on account of a variety of reasons, including the failure to hold regular elections, prolonged supersessions and inadequate devolution of powers and functions. As a result, Urban Local Bodies are not able to perform effectively as vibrant democratic units of self-government.
   Having regard to these inadequacies, it is considered necessary that provisions relating to Urban Local Bodies are incorporated in the Constitution particularly for (i) putting on a firmer footing the relationship between the State Government and the Urban Local Bodies with respect to (a) the functions and taxation powers; and (b) arrangements for revenue sharing; (ii) Ensuring regular conduct of elections; (iii) ensuring timely elections in the case of supersession; and (iv) providing adequate representation for the weaker sections like Scheduled Castes, Scheduled Tribes and women.
3. *Report of the Thirteenth Finance Commission*, December 2009, p. 149.

10

Welfare, Development and Empowerment of Women in India's Five Year Plans

The planning process has evolved over the years from purely welfare-oriented approach where women were regarded as objects of charity to the development programmes and currently to their empowerment. In the earlier phase of economic planning, women's development concerns had a low profile.

There were, however, some significant beginnings. A major initiative was the establishment of the Central Social Welfare Board in 1953 to promote and assist voluntary organisations in the field of women welfare, child welfare and welfare of the handicapped. Some legislative measures were also undertaken to protect the interests of women as, for instance, the Suppression of Immoral Traffic in Women and Girls Act, 1956, the Hindu Succession Act, 1956, the Dowry Prohibition Act, 1961 and the Maternity Benefit Act, 1961.

10.1 First Five Year Plan to Ninth Five Year Plan

Development of women received attention of the Government right from the First Five Year Plan (1951-56), but the same was treated as a subject of welfare and clubbed together with the welfare of the disadvantaged groups like destitute, disabled, aged, etc. The Central Social Welfare Board (CSWB) was set up in 1953 as an Apex Body at national level to promote voluntary action at various levels, especially at the grassroots, to take up welfare-related activities for women and children.

Under the community development programme, Mahila Mandals were promoted and supported since the Second Five Year Plan (1956-61). The Plan continued to reflect the same welfare approach, besides giving priority to women's education, and launching measures to improve maternal and child health services, supplementary feeding for children and expectant and nursing mothers.

The Third Five Year Plan (1961-66) and the Fourth Five Year Plan (1969-74) accorded a high priority to education of women. Measures to improve maternal and child health services, supplementary feeding for children and nursing and expectant mothers were introduced. The Fifth Five Year Plan (1974-79) supported economic development, employment and training for women as the principal focus for their socio-economic development. The main approach in these Plans was generally to view women as the beneficiaries of social services rather than as contributors to development.

The shift in the approach from *welfare* to *development* of women could take place only in the Sixth Five Year Plan (1980-85). Accordingly, the Sixth Plan adopted a multi-disciplinary approach with a special thrust on the three core sectors of health, education and employment. It was only from the Sixth Plan onwards that women secured a special niche and space in the national plans and planning process primarily with thrusts on health, education and employment of women.

In the Seventh Five Year Plan (1985-90), the developmental programmes for women continued with the major objective of raising their economic and social status and bringing them into the mainstream of national development. A significant step in this direction was to identify/promote the Beneficiary-oriented Schemes (BOS) in various developmental sectors which extended direct benefits to women. The thrust on generation of both skilled and unskilled employment through proper education and vocational training continued.

The Eighth Five Year Plan (1992-97), with human development as its major focus, played a very important role in the development of women. It promised to ensure that benefits of development from different sectors did not by-pass women. It implemented special programmes to complement the general development programmes and monitored the flow of benefits to women from other development sectors to enable women to function as equal partners and participants in the development process.

The Ninth Five Year Plan (1997-02) made two significant changes in the conceptual strategy of planning for women. Firstly, *empowerment of women* became one of the nine primary objectives of the Ninth Plan. To this effect, the Approach of the Plan was to create an enabling environment where women could freely exercise their rights, both within and outside home, as equal partners along with men. Secondly, the Plan attempted *convergence of existing services* available in both women-specific and women-related sectors. To this effect, it directed both the Centre and the States to adopt a special strategy of Women's Component Plan (WCP) through which not less than 30 percent of funds/benefits flow to women from all the general development sectors. It also suggested that a special vigil be kept on the flow of the earmarked funds/benefits through an effective mechanism to ensure that the proposed strategy resulted in a holistic approach towards empowering women.

The 1970s brought women to the forefront of development concerns with the publication of the Report of the Committee on Status of Women in India, the observance of the International Women's Year in 1975 and the preparation of a National Plan of Action for Women. This decade also saw the enactment of important specific legislations like the Equal Remuneration Act, 1976. The creation of a separate Bureau of Women's Development and the setting up of a national committee with the Prime Minister as President were intended to provide strong administrative support to women's development. During the Sixth Plan, a multi-sectoral approach was adopted for women's development and, for the first time, a coordinated picture was presented in the Plan. A separate Department of Women's Welfare was carved out at the Centre in 1985 from the then existing Ministry of Social and Women's Welfare to give a separate identity and to provide a nodal point on matters relating to women's development. Legislative measures were taken to provide protection to women against discrimination, exploitation, atrocities and violence. Various labour legislations were amended to safeguard the interests of women and provide for their welfare.

10.2 Tenth Five Year Plan (2002-07)

The promotion of gender equality and the empowerment of women was one of the central concerns of the Tenth Plan which spelt out a three-pronged strategy for empowering women:

1. **Social Empowerment:** Create an enabling environment through adopting various policies and programmes for development of women, besides providing them easy and equal access to all the basic minimum services so as to enable them to realise their full potential.
2. **Economic Empowerment:** Ensure provision of training, employment and income generation activities with both forward and backward linkages with the ultimate objective of making all women economically independent and self-reliant.
3. **Gender Justice:** Eliminate all forms of gender discrimination and thus enable women to enjoy not only *de jure* but also *de facto* rights and fundamental freedom on par with men in all spheres, viz. political, economic, social, civil, cultural etc.

The Tenth Plan categorized the developmental needs of the female population using the tool of age and classified them into five age-groups.

1. Girls in the age group of 0-14.
2. Adolescent girls in the age group of 15-19.
3. Women in the reproductive age group of 15 to 44.
4. Women in the economically active age group of 15 to 59.
5. Older women in the age group of 60+ and above.

The first two categories comprising infants, children and young girls represented roughly half of the country's female population. Within these two categories, there were certain defenceless sub-groups such as the girl children of tender years when discrimination—in matters such as food intake, health and medical care, schooling, recreational facilities—is entrenched within families, communities and larger social formations. Another group consisted of girls stepping from childhood to adolescence, facing a new grown-up world, with very little preparation of learning, knowledge or skills to come to terms with their own emerging sexuality in a patriarchal environment.

Due to the untiring efforts of the women's movement, the country amended and enacted various women-related legislations during the Tenth Plan. The Married Women's Property Act, 1874 and Hindu Succession Act, 1956 were amended and the Protection of Women from Domestic Violence Act, 2005 was passed. The Union Budget for 2005-06, for the first time, included a separate statement highlighting the gender sensitivities of the budgetary allocation under 10 demands for grants. Gender Budgeting Cells were set up in 52 Central Ministries/Departments to review public expenditure, collect gender disaggregated data and conduct gender-based impact analysis.

10.3 Gender-specific Concerns in the Mid-term Review of the Tenth Plan

The Tenth Plan goals of reduction of Maternal Mortality Rate (MMR) to 2 per 1,000 live births by 2007 and to 1 per 1,000 live births by 2012 and arresting the decline in the child sex ratio were reviewed in the Mid-term appraisal of the Plan and it was found that both these goals remained unfulfilled. The Mid-term Review also listed the major areas of gender concern which continued to persist over the years such as wide gender gaps in literacy and in wage rates, escalating violence against women and the rising incidence of female feticide and infanticide. Other important concerns expressed were the growing feminization of poverty and the exploitation of women in low-paid, hazardous and insecure jobs in the unorganized sector and in the export processing or special economic zones. The need to address problems relating to trafficking of young girls for sexual exploitation and domestic labour and prevention of child marriages was highlighted in the report.

The Mid-term Review also highlighted a number of focus areas which needed to be addressed if the objective of women empowerment was to become a reality. Some of the suggestions included (a) review of laws affecting women and children, (b) increasing women's participation in decision-making and the political processes including passing of the women's Reservation Bill and (c) empowering women representatives of the panchayati raj institutions (PRIs) to take independent decisions. The issue of displacement and its impact on women and children was discussed emphasizing the formulation of gender sensitive resettlement and rehabilitation policies.

Specific suggestions were made of the need to strengthen the women's component plan (WCP) as it was felt that there were a number of Ministries and Departments, which had the potential to go beyond 30 percent of funds under WCP programmes. It also called for assessing the gender impact of all programmes as the reality was that women still remained largely untouched by gender-just and gender-sensitive budgets.

10.4 Eleventh Five Year Plan (2007-12)

The vision of the Eleventh Plan is to end the multifaceted exclusions and discriminations faced by women and children and to ensure that every woman and child in the country is able to develop to her/his full potential and share the benefits of economic growth and prosperity.

The Eleventh Plan recognizes that women and children are not homogenous categories. They belong to diverse castes, classes, communities, economic groups, and are located within a range of geographic and development zones. Consequently, some groups are more vulnerable than others. Mapping and addressing the specific deprivations that arise from these multiple locations is essential for the success of planned interventions. Thus, apart from the general programme interventions, special targeted interventions, catering to the differential needs of these groups would be undertaken during the Eleventh Plan.

In the Eleventh Plan, for the first time, women are recognised not just as equal citizens but as agents of economic and social growth. The approach to gender equity is based on the recognition that interventions in favour of women must be multi-pronged and they must (i) provide women with basic entitlements (ii) address the reality of globalization and its impact on women by prioritizing economic empowerment (iii) ensure an environment free from all forms of violence against women—physical, economic, social, psychological and (iv) ensure the participation and adequate representation of women at the highest policy levels, particularly in Parliament and Assemblies (v) strengthen existing institutional mechanisms and create new ones for gender mainstreaming and effective policy implementation.

The child development approach in the Eleventh Plan is to ensure that children do not lose their childhood because of work, disease and despair. It is based on the understanding that the rights of all children, including those who do not face adverse circumstances, must be protected everywhere and at all times so that they do not fall out of the social security net. Successful integration of survival, development, protection and participation policies are important for the overall well being of the child.

Essence of the Approach: The essence of the Eleventh Plan strategy for Women Agency and Child Rights is as under.

1. Recognition of the right of every woman and child to develop to her/his full potential.
2. Recognition of the differential needs of different groups of women and children.
3. Need for inter-sectoral convergence as well as focused women and child specific measures through Ministry of Women and Child Development.
4. Partnership with civil society to create permanent institutional mechanisms that incorporate the experiences, capacities and knowledge of voluntary organizations and women's groups in the process of development planning.

Monitorable Targets for the Eleventh Plan: The Eleventh Plan lays down six monitorable targets.

1. Raise the sex ratio for age group 0-6 from 927 in 2001 to 935 by 2011-12 and to 950 by 2016-17.
2. Ensure that at least 33 percent of the direct and indirect beneficiaries of all government schemes are women and girl children.
3. Reduce infant mortality rate (IMR) from 57 to 28 and maternal mortality ratio (MMR) from 3.01 to 1 per 1000 live births.
4. Reduce malnutrition among children of age group 0-3 to half its present level
5. Reduce anaemia among women and girls by 50 percent by the end of the Eleventh Plan.
6. Reduce dropout rate for primary and secondary schooling by 10 percent for both girls as well as boys.

Eleventh Plan Strategies to Protect Rights of Children: The following strategies would be adopted during the Eleventh Plan to ensure that every child enjoys her childhood and all her rights without any fear and without the need to work:

1. Developing specific interventions to address malnutrition, neo-natal and infant mortality.
2. Creating child friendly protective services.
3. Identifying the most vulnerable and marginalized children and ensuring age and situation specific interventions.
4. Reviewing all legal provisions for children and undertaking necessary amendments based on international commitments.
5. Ensuring effective implementation of laws and polices by personnel trained to work with children.
6. Establishing child impact as a core indicator of Eleventh Plan interventions,

with special emphasis on the status of the girl child.

7. Creating a protective environment for children through implementation of schemes and programmes based on *the best interest of the child.* Some of the current initiatives only address the needs of children once they have fallen through the protective net. While these initiatives to identify such children and rehabilitate them are critical, there is an equal need for legislative changes and programmatic interventions, so that prevention is fore-grounded and children grow up in a protective environment.
8. Undertaking a child rights review of all existing developmental policies and plans to assess their impact on children and to ensure that children are not further marginalized.
9. Recognising that crèches and day care are important for child development, empowerment of women, and retention of girls in schools.
10. Ensuring survival of the girl child and her right to be born. Shift to *lifecycle and capability approach* where the girl child's contribution in economic and social terms is recognised.
11. Ensuring multi-pronged programme, focussing on preventing children from falling out of the protective net, ameliorative initiatives for children who are already out of the protective net and ensuring long-term and sustainable rehabilitation by upgrading quality of services and addressing regional imbalances.
12. Recognising that children are best cared for in their own families, strengthening family capabilities to care and protect the child.
13. Ensuring institutional care to those children who need the same.
14. Involving PRIs, VOs and urban local bodies in implementation, monitoring and evaluation by devolving powers and resources to the Panchayat level, and providing them with technical and administrative support.
15. Recognizing *Child Budgeting* as an important policy analysis tool to take stock of development investments for children and identify gaps in resource investment and utilisation.
16. Strengthening capacity of families and communities, police, judiciary, teachers, PRI representatives, bureaucrats and other implementation personnel who deal directly with children.

To sum up, the planning process has evolved over the years from a purely welfare-oriented approach to the development approach and currently to their empowerment. It was only from the Sixth Five year Plan onwards that women secured a special niche and space in the national plans and planning process primarily with thrusts on health, education and employment. A paradigm shift occurred in the Eighth Plan where empowerment of women was recognized and accepted as a distinct strategy. A further impetus for sectoral contribution to women's programmes was received with the introduction of the concept of Women's Component Plan in the Ninth Plan whereby identified ministries were required to indicate the flow of funds to the women's programmes and schemes. The Ninth Plan laid emphasis on the participation of people in the planning process, and the promotion of self-help groups. The approach was to access women living in poverty and to guide them to help themselves.

In the Tenth Plan, for the first time, monitorable targets were set for a few key indicators of human development which included reduction in gender gaps in literacy, wage rates and reduction in MMR. The Tenth Plan called for a three-pronged strategy of social empowerment, economic empowerment and providing gender justice to create an enabling environment of positive economic and social policies for women and eliminating all forms of discrimination against them and thus advance gender equality goals. During the Tenth Plan also, emphasis continued on empowerment of women through SHG movement.

The Eleventh Plan seeks to reduce disparities across regions and communities by ensuring access to basic physical infrastructure as well as health and educational services to all, recognize gender as a cross-cutting theme across all sectors and commits to respect and promote the rights of the common person.

11

Human Rights and Violence against Women

11.1 Meaning, Nature and Forms of Violence against Women

Violence against women (VAW) includes any act of gender-based violence that results in, or is likely to result in, physical, sexual or psychological harm or suffering to women, including threats of such acts, coercion or arbitrary deprivation of liberty, whether occurring in public or private life. Violence against women manifests itself in many ways and is one of the most pervasive forms of human rights abuse in the world today. While all women may experience violence, it intersects with other social and identity-based constructs like caste, religion, ethnicity, disability, and sexual orientation to make specific groups vulnerable to different and particular forms of violence. Thus, the nature of the violence and how it manifests itself may differ because of social location.

Forms of violence that take place at the community level include witch hunting, sati, child marriage, and incidents of public stripping. These unfortunately are increasing in prevalence. In recent years there have been disturbing reports of cases of sati and its subsequent glorification. There has been an alarming rise in reported cases of honour crimes committed in the name of protecting family or community honour. Equally worrying is the growing numbers of anti-women strictures being pronounced by community-based structures like caste and religious panchayats. The brunt of these so-called judgments—which in some cases have resulted in brutal punishments such as dismemberment and mutilation—are usually borne by women or the women's family.

Many such actions follow when women try and change age-old, narrow and regressive social norms like marrying outside one's caste or religion. Many of these so-called judgments are not only anti-women but go against the Constitution.

Experiences from the ground and various reports are now showing that women are specifically targeted in situations of communal and sectarian violence as they embody the so-called honour of the community. If a particular community or group is to be attacked and humiliated, women are targeted. In such situations women are victims of various forms of sexual violence including rape, molestation, mutilation, stripping etc.

Yet another form of violence relates to *acid attacks* on women. This is a heinous form of violence against women and has lasting impact on their autonomy and freedom of movement.

It is widely accepted that violence against women and girls, whether occurring in public or private life, is a human rights issue. It is also accepted that states have an obligation to exercise due diligence to prevent investigate and punish acts of violence whether those acts are perpetrated by the state or private persons and provide protection to victims. There is increased awareness and commitment to prevent and combat violence against women and girls, including domestic violence, which violates, impairs and nullifies the enjoyment of their human rights and fundamental freedoms.

Women continue to be victims of various forms of violence. Inadequate understanding of the root causes of all forms of violence against women and girls hinders efforts to eliminate violence against women and girls. Inadequate data on violence further impede informed policymaking and analysis. Socio-cultural attitudes which are discriminatory and economic inequalities reinforce women's subordinate place in society. This makes women and girls vulnerable to many forms of violence—physical, sexual and psychological—occurring in the family. This may include battering, sexual abuse of female children in the household, dowry-related violence, marital rape, female genital mutilation and other traditional practices harmful to women.

Domestic violence—including sexual violence in marriage—is still treated as a private matter in some countries. Insufficient awareness of the consequences of domestic violence, how to prevent it, and the rights of victims still exists. Although improving, the legal and legislative measures—especially in the criminal justice area to eliminate different forms of violence against women and children, including domestic violence and child pornography—are weak in many countries. It is also noted that in some countries problems have arisen from the use of new information and communication technologies for trafficking in women and children and for the purposes of all forms of economic and sexual exploitation.

Violence against women and girls is a major obstacle to the achievement of the objectives of gender equality, development and peace. Main forms of gender-based violence include the following:

1. Battering and other domestic violence.
2. Sexual abuse.
3. Sexual slavery and exploitation.
4. Trafficking in women and children.
5. Forced prostitution and sexual harassment.

The main reasons for gender-based violence are the following:

1. Cultural prejudice.
2. Racism and racial discrimination.
3. Xenophobia.
4. Pornography.
5. Ethnic cleansing.
6. Armed conflict.
7. Foreign occupation.
8. Religious and anti-religious extremism.
9. Terrorism.

Violence against women is incompatible with the dignity and worth of the human person and must be combated and eliminated.

11.2 Human Rights in India

After Independence in 1947, legal reforms have been undertaken in India to prohibit all forms of discrimination and discriminatory provisions have been eliminated in civil, penal and personal status law governing marriage and family relations, women's property and ownership rights and work and employment rights. Steps have been taken to realize women's enjoyment of their human rights through the creation of an enabling environment, including the adoption of policy measures, the improvement of enforcement and monitoring mechanisms and the implementation of legal literacy and awareness campaigns at all levels.

The Constitution of India prohibits discrimination between men and women on the grounds of religion, sex, caste or place of birth, and enables the State to allow affirmative discrimination in favour of women as a fundamental right. By this principle, human rights as fundamental rights have been put on an equal footing for all. India has ratified significant international human rights instruments, including the ratification of the Convention on Elimination of All Forms of Discrimination against Women (CEDAW), 1993.

Government has created independent national institutions for the protection and promotion of human rights of all citizens, especially women, religious minorities and caste-based communities.

1. National Human Rights Commission (NHRC), 1994.
2. National Commission for Minorities, 1992.
3. National Commission for Scheduled Castes and Scheduled Tribes, 1990.
4. National Commission for Women, 1990.

28 States Governments and Union Territories have set up State Commissions for Women to act as statutory ombudspersons. Human Rights Commissions have been set up in 9 states.

The Supreme Court of India through its activist role has infused dynamism into the constitutional and legal provisions and has issued directives to the State from time to time to further safeguard and strengthen the rights of women. Through a series of Public Interest Litigation (PIL), any person/persons who in the event of violation of rights and is unable to approach the Court (by reason of poverty, disability, social or economic advantage) can maintain an application for an appropriate direction, order or writ. This has further contributed to the cause of gender justice. Certain landmark judgements of the Supreme Court on matters such as the need for a Uniform Civil Code for all women irrespective of religion, the need for equal property rights for women, particularly in the case of inheritance, pronouncements on child prostitution, need for in-camera trial of rape victims etc. are evidence of an activist role of the Court.

To effectively deal with the problem of violence against women, and to bridge the gap between public and the private sphere, there have been numerous governmental and non-governmental interventions. The government is working in two steps. In the first step, it is working towards the strengthening of the existing legislation through review and amendments, wherever required, and developing institutional mechanisms, i.e. National and State Commissions for Women, women police cells in police stations and *all-women police stations*, etc. Its other course of action centres around running projects that provide support to vulnerable women, rehabilitation of victims of violence through schemes like *Swadhar*, and setting up of help lines for women in distress. Family courts have been set up in some States to adjudicate cases relating to maintenance, custody and divorce.

11.3 Sexual Harassment of Women

The National Commission for Women (NCW) prepared a Code of Conduct for the work place and circulated the same to all ministries, educational institutions, public and private sector undertakings and various NGOs for information and implementation. The University Grants Commission has formulated a code of conduct for students and staff of Universities. The Central Board of Secondary Education (CBSE) has taken action to ensure that all affiliated schools and educational institutions abide by these guidelines. All Ministries have set up Complaint Committees to look into such matters.

In a case of sexual harassment of a woman at the workplace, the inquiry conducted by the Complaints Committee should be deemed as inquiry conducted in a departmental inquiry under the disciplinary proceedings, drawn up against the delinquent official. The Department of Personnel and Training has informed all Ministries/Departments of Government of India that the findings of the

Complaints Committee regarding sexual harassment of the complainant/victim will be binding on the Disciplinary Authority to initiate disciplinary proceedings against the government servant(s). The report of the Complaints Committee should be treated as the preliminary report against the accused government servant.

11.4 Rape and Sexual abuse

The increased incidence of rape cases in recent times may be because more cases are being reported now. Currently, the crime of rape is dealt with in Sections 375-377 of the Indian Penal Code.

11.4.1 Relief and Rehabilitation of Rape victims: The Supreme Court in Delhi Domestic Working Women's Forum vs. Union of India and others writ petition (CRL) No. 362/93 had directed the National Commission for Women to evolve a "scheme so as to wipe out the tears of unfortunate victims of rape." It observed that given the Directive principles contained in Article 38(1) of the Constitution, it was necessary to set up a Criminal Injuries Compensation Board. Besides the mental anguish, rape victims frequently incur substantial financial loss and in some cases are too traumatized to continue in employment. The Court further directed that compensation for victims shall be awarded by the Court on conviction of the offender and by the Criminal Injuries Compensation Board irrespective of whether or not a conviction has taken place. The Board shall take into account pain, suffering and shock as well as loss of earnings due to pregnancy and the expenses of child birth if this occurs as a result of rape. Accordingly, NCW has drafted a scheme titled "Relief and Rehabilitation of Rape Victims".

The Supreme Court of India has ruled that delay by rape victims in filing complaints against the accused cannot be used as a defence to escape conviction. A division bench of the Supreme Court ruled in September 2004 that lower courts could not "disregard" the prosecution case because a First Information Report (FIR) had been filed late.

11.5 Other Crimes

In addition to the above, other gender-specific crimes that have been recognized under the IPC and special laws are Sati, Bigamy, Molestation, Obscenity, Indecent Representation of Women, Kidnapping, Abduction and Importation of Girls. Aspects of investigation, arrest and prosecution of these crimes are the responsibility of state governments. The criminal justice system has to pay particular attention to the needs of women who are subjected to these specific forms of violence.

11.6 Organized Crime: Trafficking in Women

Human trafficking, both forced and under false promises, is widespread, but no accurate data is available. Trafficking, however, is usually and wrongly, conflated with prostitution. The purposes of trafficking include, (besides prostitution), entertainment, industry, forced labour, domestic work, camel jockeys, illegal adoption of children, bonded labour, forced marriage, drug trafficking, begging etc.

Poverty, breakdown in livelihood options, food insecurity, unemployment, debts, occurrence of disasters, and conflicts leave the victims, particularly women, in miserable situations with practically no choices for survival. Girls are also trafficked in the name of marriage. Victims often find themselves unwillingly trapped in a life of physical and sexual abuse.

The situation of women who have been trafficked into sex work is particularly vulnerable. They have little control over their earnings and face the risk of pregnancies, abortions, maternal mortality, sexually transmitted diseases such as HIV and AIDS. The Immoral Trafficking (Prevention) Act, 1956 penalizes all persons involved in trafficking women for sex work and living off their income. Unfortunately, the law has been implemented in a highly moralistic manner resulting in the further victimization of trafficked women. The objective of the Act, i.e. the punishment of those involved in trafficking has not been met.

11.6.1 Ujjawala: The problem of cross border trafficking especially of young children and women from Bangladesh and Nepal into India, has been growing in recent years. Central Sector Scheme called Ujjawala was launched on December 4, 2007. The scheme consists of five components:

1. **Prevention:** Formation of community vigilance groups and adolescent groups. Awareness and sensitisation of functionaries like police, community leaders though preparation of IEC material and workshops.
2. **Rescue:** Safe withdrawal of the victim from the place of exploitation.
3. **Rehabilitation:** Provision of safe shelter for victims with fulfilment of basic needs such food, clothing, counselling, medical care, legal aid, and vocational training and income generation activities.
4. **Reintegration:** Restoration of the victim to the family/community (only if she desires) and covering costs of the same.
5. **Repatriation:** Support to cross-border victims for their safe repatriation to the country of their origin.

11.7 Sexual Harassment of Women at Workplace

In India, women are entering the labour workforce in unprecedented numbers. In the light of this development, there is, more than ever before, a pressing need for the rights of women to be respected and protected, particularly at the workplace. Further, with the greater representation of women in the unorganized sector, there is a need for institutions and a policy to be set up to empower women.

Women's rights at the workplace are important for many reasons. The obvious reason is the right of women to be free from unwanted sexual conduct and advances. The issue of sexual harassment at the workplace extends far beyond an individual woman. It impacts on workforce productivity, economic development, and the overall growth of the country.

The Supreme Court in the case of *Vishaka vs. State of Rajasthan* held that sexual harassment at the workplace is a violation of the rights guaranteed by Articles 14, 15 and 21 and that women have rights to gender equality, to work with dignity in a safe working environment and be protected from sexual harassment or abuse. The court in this case defined "*sexual harassment at the workplace*" and issued a set of guidelines for employers to redress and prevent this kind of violation of women's human rights at workplace.

Since then various government establishments have amended their respective statutes for the prevention and addressing complaints of sexual harassment. However, a large section of women in the private and the unorganized sector are still unprotected.

To sum up, gender discrimination and all other forms of discrimination—in particular racism, racial discrimination, xenophobia and related intolerance—continue to cause threat to the enjoyment of women of their human rights and fundamental freedoms. In situations of armed conflict and foreign occupation, human rights of women have been extensively violated.

In many countries, women have insufficient access to the law, resulting from illiteracy, lack of legal literacy, information and resources, insensitivity and gender bias, and lack of awareness of the human rights of women by law enforcement officials and the judiciary who in many cases fail to respect the human rights of women and the dignity and worth of the human person. There is insufficient recognition of women's and girls' reproductive rights, as well as barriers to their full enjoyment of those rights. Some women and girls continue to encounter barriers to justice and enjoyment of their human rights because of such factors as their race, language, ethnicity, culture, religion, disability or socio-economic class or because they are migrants, displaced women or refugees.

12

Protecting the Girl Child

The care and focus given to a child as a girl and as an adolescent—with focus on her health and nutrition, education and economic potential—determines her empowerment as a woman. A healthy, literate and empowered adolescent girl is able to contribute positively to the society.

The Constitution of India has laid special emphasis on the wellbeing and protection of the children. It not only grants equality and prohibits any kind of discrimination but also protects children against exploitation and abuse. It also empowers the State to adopt measures of positive discrimination in favour of children.

India ratified the UN Convention on the Rights of the Child in 1992 and formulated the National Plan of Action for Children in the same year. The period 1991–2000 was also observed as the SAARC Decade of the Girl Child. The commitments at the international and national levels have translated into a specific focus on the development of the girl child and adolescent girls, especially on their survival, health, education and protection. The Tenth Five-Year Plan (2002–07), viewed the development of children not merely as the most desirable investment for the country's future.

12.1 Campaign for the Girl Child's Right to Life

The Central Social Welfare Board and State Boards launched a year-long awareness drive on Human Rights Day (December 10, 2003) against female foeticide and celebrated this day as Manvi Sanrakshan Diwas (Protection of Women Day). The objective of the drive was to make people aware of the seriousness of the problem and to generate consciousness against sex selection through workshops, seminars, rallies, print and audiovisual campaigns. Key target groups identified were women's groups, self-help groups (SHGs), youth groups, medical practitioners, resident welfare associations in urban areas, and panchayats in rural areas.

Mass communication media are widely being used for disseminating messages condemning female foeticide. Government of India launched the 'Save the Girl Child Campaign' with a view to lessen son preference by highlighting achievements of young girls.

Responding to the declining sex ratio as a social problem, the *Akal Takth*—

the highest seat of spiritual and temporal authority amongst Sikhs—issued a *hukumnama* (diktat) on April 6, 2001, prohibiting prenatal sex determination to stop the practice of female foeticide.

The state of Goa has introduced a landmark legislation for the protection of children, particularly to ensure elimination of all forms of discrimination against the girl child and to prevent pre-natal sex selection and female foeticide and female infanticide and foeticide. The Goa Children Act, 2003 seeks to protect the rights of the child, and gives special attention to the needs of the girl child and the elimination of all gender biases. It bans child prostitution and all forms of trafficking of girl child and sexual abuse.

The *Janani Suraksha* Scheme (revamped National Maternity Benefit Scheme) is a package of services geared at reducing maternal mortality, neo-natal mortality, female foeticide and gender disparity. It also aims at improving registration of births and deaths, amongst most disadvantaged strata of population, by increasing access to institutional delivery.

Under the scheme, pregnant women get ₹ 500 after delivery of a male child and ₹ 1,000 after delivery of a female child. A National Commitment Campaign was launched on the occasion of World Population Day on July 11, 2003 focussing on two key elements—Safe Motherhood and Adolescence. It included a signature campaign by students, politicians, sports persons and film stars in favour of the slogan, *Beti ho ya beta, rakhein parivar chota* (whether boy or girl, keep family small).

In addition to legal action and awareness campaigns, *Balika Samriddhi Yojana* was launched in 1997 to help in raising the overall status of the girl child and bring about a positive change in family and community attitudes. A cash grant of ₹ 500 is made to the mother of a girl (up to 2 per mother) and a further amount is invested in a financial instrument for education of girl child and to make her economically independent. This is paid to the girl when she attains the age of 18 years and remains unmarried till then. In addition, the girl child is entitled to receive a scholarship for each class of study successfully completed.

12.2 Health and Malnutrition

Adolescent girls are highly susceptible to anaemia which is responsible for miscarriage, stillbirths, premature births, low birth weight babies and maternal mortality during child birth. Girls need 10 percent more iron than boys for biological reasons. Studies undertaken to develop National Strategy for Reducing Childhood Malnutrition under the Regional Technical Assistance programme of Asian Development Bank identified female illiteracy, age at marriage of girls and age at the first child birth as the critical determinants of malnutrition and low birth weight in newborns which directly and indirectly influence infant and maternal mortality rates.

The Government's Integrated Child Development Services (ICDS) programme, the world's largest early childcare and development programme, reaches 34 million children aged 0-6 years and 7 million pregnant and nursing mothers.

Interventions include training of *Anganwadi* (childcare) workers, improved communication strategies, improved monitoring and reporting systems, provision of essential supplies, and development of community-based early childcare interventions.

The *Pradhan Mantri Gramoday Yojana*, started in 2000-01, has nutrition as one of its components which caters to children in the age group of 6-36 months so as to prevent the onset of under-nutrition in that age group.

As part of the ICDS programme, the *Kishori Shakti Yojana*, an intervention for adolescent girls (11-18 years) was launched in 2000-01. The scheme is currently being implemented in 2,000 blocks across the country. This intervention seeks to address the needs of adolescents for self development, nutrition and health status, literacy and numerical skills, vocational skills etc.

12.3 Education and Schooling

Under the *Sarva Shiksha Abhiyan* (Education for All), specific strategies have been designed to enhance girls access, enrolment and schooling. The recently launched National Plan for Education at the Elementary Level (NPEGEL), an integral part of the SSA, provides a dynamic framework for accelerating progress in girls' education. Innovative approaches to encouraging and ensuring equality in access to education for girls include residential bridge courses Iron and folic acid supplementation of adolescent girls is being undertaken in the World Bank Assisted ICDS projects and also under the Reproductive and Child Health Programme of Department of Family Welfare on a pilot scale. Micro-nutrient supplements are provided to adolescent girls through ICDS in 4 States in collaboration with the Micro-nutrient Initiative.

12.4 Sexual Abuse and Trafficking

Young girls are especially vulnerable to sexual abuse and trafficking. The Supreme Court of India has issued fresh guidelines for the trial of child abuse cases, aimed at protecting victims from being harassed during trial. Expressing concern over increasing incidence of crimes against children, the court suggested the enactment of stricter legislation to punish child-sex offenders.

In-camera trials, previously permitted only in rape cases, are now available in cases of child abuse and violence. The revamped Juvenile Justice Act, 2000 assures that the child in need of care and protection as per the Act is defined to cover those found vulnerable and likely to be inducted into drug abuse or trafficking. Section 23 provides for punishment to a person having actual charge of or control over a child and who assaults, abandons or wilfully neglects the child or causes or procures him to be assaulted, abandoned, exposed or neglected in a manner likely to cause unnecessary mental or physical suffering. In addition Section 24 provides for punishment for employment or use of a child for begging. Section 25 provides for penalty for giving intoxicating liquor or narcotic drug or psychotropic substance to a child.

12.5 Measures to Protect the Girl Child

The persistence of poverty, discriminatory attitudes towards women and girls, negative cultural attitudes and practices against girls have contributed to a lack of opportunities for girls to become confident and self-reliant, and independent adults.

12.5.1 Dhanalakshmi: This is a Central Sector Scheme, fully funded by the centre, which attempts to tackle the acute problem of declining sex ratio. It was launched in 2008 to bring about a change in the mindset of the family towards the girl child. It provides cash transfers to the family of the girl child (preferably the mother) on fulfilment of certain conditionalities like birth registration, immunisation, enrolment and retention in school and marriage after attaining the age of 18 years. An amount of ₹ 5,000 is provided at registration of birth; ₹ 1,000 on enrolment for education; and ₹ 6,250 is provided in varying instalments as her education proceeds. The total amount provided to the beneficiary is ₹ 13,500, along with an insurance cover. The scheme is in operation on a pilot basis in 11 blocks across seven states; Andhra Pradesh, Bihar, Chhattisgarh, Orissa, Jharkhand, Punjab and Uttar Pradesh.

12.5.2 Prevention of Child Pornography: On January 30, 1997, the United Nations General Assembly adopted, through a Resolution, the Model Law on Electronic Commerce adopted by the United Nations Commission on International Trade Law. This is referred to as the UNCITRAL Model Law on E-Commerce.

Following the UN Resolution, Indian Parliament passed the Information Technology Act (ITA), 2000 in May 2000 and notified it for effectiveness on October 17, 2000.

ITA, 2000 was substantially amended through the Information Technology Amendment Act, 2008 which was passed by the two houses of the Indian Parliament on December 23 and 24, 2008. It got the Presidential assent on

February 5, 2009 and was notified for effectiveness on October 27, 2009.

Section 67B—a new section added in the ITA, 2008—deals with child pornography. It states: Whoever,

(a) publishes or transmits or causes to be published or transmitted material in any electronic form which depicts children engaged in sexually explicit act or conduct or;
(b) creates text or digital images, collects, seeks, browses, downloads, advertises, promotes, exchanges or distributes material in any electronic form depicting children in obscene or indecent or sexually explicit manner or;
(c) cultivates, entices or induces children to online relationship with one or more children for and on sexually explicit act or in a manner that may offend a reasonable adult on the computer resource or;
(d) facilitates abusing children online or;
(e) records in any electronic form own abuse or that of others pertaining to sexually explicit act with children.

shall be punished on first conviction with imprisonment of either description for a term which may extend to five years and with a fine which may extend to ten lakh rupees and in the event of second or subsequent conviction with imprisonment of either description for a term which may extend to seven years and also with fine which may extend to ₹ 10 lakh.

Provided that the provisions of this section do not extend to any book, pamphlet, paper, writing, drawing, painting, representation or figure in electronic form:

(i) the publication of which is proved to be justified as being for the public good on the ground that such book, pamphlet, paper writing, drawing, painting, representation or figure is in the interest of science, literature, art or learning or other objects of general concern; or
(ii) which is kept or used for bonafide heritage or religious purposes

Explanation: For the purposes of this section, "children" means a person who has not completed the age of 18 years.

13

Women and the Environment

With privatisation, liberalisation and globalisation of the Indian economy, environment and forest sectors are also undergoing signs of change. Also, with the looming dangers of global warming and climate change, environment has emerged as a matter of great concern both at the national and international levels. Environment and forests sectors are increasingly figuring as areas of interests in the bilateral, plurilateral and multilateral free trade agreements. India being a founder member of the World Trade Organisation (WTO) is governed by its basic binding principles and has been actively participating in such trade negotiations. The Doha Round of trade negotiations launched in November 2001 introduced negotiations in environmental goods and services. As a result, both the environmental goods and environmental services have emerged as areas of significance for India.

In recognition of the link between gender equality, poverty eradication, sustainable development and environmental protection, governments in many countries have included income-generating activities for women, training in natural resource management and environmental protection in their development strategies. Projects have been launched to preserve and utilize women's traditional ecological knowledge, in the management of natural resources, and preservation of bio-diversity.

There is still a lack of public awareness about environmental risks faced by women and of the benefits of gender equality for promoting environmental protection. Women's limited access to technical skills, resources and information in developing countries have impeded women's effective participation in decision-making regarding the sustainable environment

13.1 Women and Natural Resources

The linkage between women, natural resources and the domestic economies of poor rural households in India are fairly clear and they can be categorized into the following three patterns.

1. Natural resources are central to the livelihoods in India. Poor households are dependent on free bio-mass goods and common property resources than better off households.
2. Women are the primary gatherers and managers of biomass goods in poor

rural households. Women perform key roles not only in the gathering but also in the processing, storing, utilization and marketing of free biomass goods.

3. Women's roles and responsibilities are pivotal not only in the management of natural resources but also in the management of domestic economy.

Thus, natural resources provide both subsistence needs and cash incomes, particularly to poor rural households.

13.2 Effects of Degradation of Natural Resources on Women

In fragile ecological regions, the gradual degradation of natural resources has depleted the social resources of people such as nutrition, health (particularly of women and children), education, housing etc. With the migration of men to urban areas and increase in the responsibility and workload of women, the girl child of the family becomes victim of degradation. She has to discontinue her education in order to take care of her younger siblings and becomes their foster mother at a very young age. These girl children also attend to all domestic chores and feed the animals while the mother is miles away in the jungles to collect fuel wood and forest produces. In many rural and tribal communities, particularly among the resource poor, the following common social features/phenomena are observed:

1. Drop-out of girl from formal schools.
2. Early child marriage.
3. Early and frequent child births.
4. Malnutrition and poor health.
5. Maternal mortality.
6. Infant morbidity and mortality.
7. Large family size.
8. Poor sanitation.
9. Poverty and debts.

This social phenomenon is a clear picture of vulnerability of women to poverty. The root cause of these problems is poverty caused due to the degradation of soil, water resources and the scarcity of biomass resources to meet daily needs. In addition to this, ignorance of people also plays an important role in deteriorating the social conditions of the people leading to poor quality of life. The parents in resource poor families would like to shrug away with the responsibility of daughters by getting them married at a very young age with minimum expenses. However, they are ignorant of the fact that early child marriage would not only spoil the future of their daughter but also becomes a fragile basis for future generations.

Environmental concerns also warrant gender mainstreaming. Providing alternative sources of fuel for women especially in rural areas reduces both her drudgery with collection of firewood and exposure to pollutants. Thus, switching from fossil fuel to non-conventional fuel based systems such as green fuels (bio-mass), solar power, hydro power etc. should be stressed. Women's SHGs should be encouraged to be actively involved in Watershed Committees, Joint Forest Management Committees etc.

Disaster management *policy* should become gender sensitive as experience has shown that women are most affected by disasters whether manmade or natural. The tendency for trafficking, sale of women and children is quite common in these extenuating circumstances. The emergency response systems in the event of such disasters should have well thought out gender relief measures to cater to afflicted women and children without any delay.

Appendices

Appendix 1

Fourth World Conference on Women (Beijing, 1995) and the Beijing Platform for Action (PFA)

---

1. Introduction

The Fourth World Conference on Women, held in Beijing in 1995 was a landmark event that set the pace for women's empowerment. The Beijing Platform for Action (PFA) pegged on the pillars of human rights and gender equality, was accepted by India without reservation.

The governments which came together at the Twenty-third Special Session of the General Assembly entitled "Women 2000: Gender Equality, Development and Peace for the Twenty-first Century" reaffirmed their commitment to the goals and objectives contained in the Beijing Declaration and the Platform for Action adopted at the Fourth World Conference on Women in 1995 as contained in the report of the Conference.

2. Objectives and Critical Areas for Priority

The Beijing Declaration and Platform for Action set as goals gender equality, development and peace and constituted an agenda for the empowerment of women. The Governments reviewed and appraised progress and identified obstacles and current challenges in the implementation of the Platform for Action. They recognized that the goals and commitments made in the Platform for Action have not been fully implemented and achieved and agreed upon further actions and initiatives at local, national, regional, and international levels to accelerate its implementation and to ensure that commitments for gender equality, development and peace are fully realized.

The Beijing Platform for Action identified 12 critical areas for priority action to achieve the advancement and empowerment of women. The Commission on the Status of Women reviewed progress in each of the 12 critical areas of concern and since 1996 has adopted agreed conclusions and recommendations for accelerated implementation. The Platform for Action, together with these agreed conclusions and recommendations, forms the basis for further progress towards the achievement of gender equality, development and peace in the 21st century.

The objective of the Platform for Action, which is in full conformity with the purposes and principles of the Charter of the United Nations and international law, is the empowerment of all women. The full realization of all human rights and fundamental freedoms of all women is essential for the empowerment of women. While the significance of national and regional particularities and various historical, cultural and religious backgrounds must be borne in mind, it is the duty of States, regardless of their political, economic and cultural systems, to promote and protect all human rights and fundamental freedoms. The implementation of the Platform, as well as further actions and initiatives, including through national laws and the formulation of strategies, policies, programmes and development priorities, is the sovereign responsibility of each State, in conformity with all human rights and fundamental freedoms, and the significance of and full respect for various religious and ethical values, cultural backgrounds and philosophical convictions of individuals and their communities should contribute to the full enjoyment by women of their human rights in order to achieve equality, development and peace.

The Platform for Action emphasized that women share common concerns that can be addressed only by working together and in partnership with men towards the common goal of gender equality around the world. It respects and values the full diversity of women's situations and conditions and recognizes that some women face particular barriers to their empowerment.

The Platform for Action recognized that women face barriers to full equality and advancement because of such factors as their race, age, language, ethnicity, culture, religion or disability, because they are indigenous women or because of other status. Many women encounter specific obstacles related to their family status, particularly as single parents; and to their socio-economic status, including their living conditions in rural, isolated or impoverished areas. Additional barriers also exist for refugee women, other displaced women, including internally displaced women as well as for immigrant women and migrant women, including women migrant workers. Many women are also particularly affected by environmental disasters, serious and infectious diseases and various forms of violence against women.

3. Achievements and Obstacles in the Implementation of Platform for Action

Assessment of achievements and obstacles must be made in relation to the commitments made in the Beijing Platform for Action and its 12 critical areas, namely by looking into the actions taken and the results attained, as indicated in national reports as well as taking note of the reports of the Secretary-General and of the results, conclusions and agreements of the five regional meetings held in preparation for the special session of the General Assembly and other relevant sources. Such assessment shows that, even though significant positive developments can be identified, barriers remain and there is still the need to further implement the goals and commitments made in Beijing. The summary of achievements and of persistent or new obstacles can, therefore, constitute a global framework for the identification of further actions and initiatives to overcome obstacles and to achieve the full and accelerated implementation of the Platform for Action at all levels and in all areas.

4. Challenges in Implementing the Beijing Declaration and the Platform for Action

The review and appraisal of the implementation of the Beijing Declaration and the Platform for Action occurred in a rapidly changing global context. Since 1995, a number of issues have gained prominence and acquired new dimensions which pose additional challenges to the full and accelerated implementation of the Platform in order to realize gender equality, development and peace by Governments, intergovernmental bodies, international organizations, the private sector, and non-governmental organizations as appropriate. Continued political commitment to gender equality, at all levels, is needed for the full implementation of the Platform for Action.

Globalization has presented new challenges for the fulfilment of the commitments made and the realization of the goals of the Beijing Conference. The globalization process has in some countries, resulted in policy shifts in favour of more open trade and financial flows, privatization of state-owned enterprises and in many cases lower public spending particularly on social services. This change has transformed patterns of production and accelerated technological advances in information and communication and affected the lives of women, both as workers and consumers. In a large number of countries, particularly in developing and least developed countries, these changes have also adversely impacted on the lives of women and have increased inequality. The gender impact of these changes has not been systematically evaluated. Globalization also has cultural, political, and social impacts affecting cultural values, lifestyles and forms of communication as well as implications for the achievement of sustainable development. Benefits of the growing global economy have been unevenly distributed leading to wider economic disparities, the feminization of poverty, increased gender inequality, including through often deteriorating work conditions and unsafe working environments especially in the informal economy and rural areas. While globalization has brought greater economic opportunities and autonomy to some women, many others have been marginalized, due to deepening inequalities among and within countries, by depriving them from the benefits of this process. Although in many countries the level of participation of women in the labour force has risen, in other cases, the application of certain economic policies have had a negative impact such that increases in women's employment often have not been matched by improvements in wages, promotions and working conditions. In many cases, women continue to be employed in low paid, part-time, and contract jobs marked by insecurity and by safety and health hazards. In many countries women, especially new entrants into the labour market, continue to be among the first to lose jobs and the last to be rehired.

5. Actions and Initiatives to Overcome Obstacles in the Implementation of the Beijing Platform for Action

In view of the evaluation of progress made five years since the Beijing Conference in implementing the Beijing Declaration and Platform for Action, contained in chapter II, as well as the current challenges affecting its full realization, outlined in chapter III, Governments now recommit themselves to the Beijing Declaration and Platform for Action and also commit to further actions and initiatives to overcome the obstacles and address the challenges. Governments, in taking continued and additional steps to achieve the goals of the Platform, recognize that the full enjoyment of all human rights–civil, cultural, economic, political and social, including the right to development–are universal, indivisible, interdependent and interrelated, and are essential for realizing gender equality, development and peace in the twenty-first century.

Organizations of the United Nations system and the Bretton Woods institutions, as well as the World Trade Organization, other international and regional intergovernmental bodies, parliaments, civil society, including the private sector and NGOs, trade unions and other stakeholders are called upon to support government efforts and, where appropriate, develop complementary programmes of their own to achieve full and effective implementation of the Platform for Action.

Governments and intergovernmental organizations recognize the contribution and complementary role of NGOs, with full respect for their autonomy, in ensuring the effective implementation of the Platform for Action and should continue to strengthen partnerships with NGOs, particularly women's organizations in contributing to the effective implementation and follow-up of the Platform for Action.

Experience has shown that the goal of gender equality can be fully achieved only in the context of renewed relations among different stakeholders at all levels. The full effective participation of women on the basis of equality in all spheres of society is necessary to contribute to this goal.

Achieving gender equality and empowerment of women requires redressing inequalities between women and men and girls and boys and ensuring their equal rights, responsibilities, opportunities, and possibilities. Gender equality implies that women's as well as men's needs, interests, concerns, experiences and priorities are an integral dimension of the design, implementation, national monitoring, and follow-up and evaluation, including at the international level, of all actions in all areas.

By adopting the Platform for Action governments and the international community agreed to a common development agenda with gender equality and women's empowerment as underlying principles. The efforts towards ensuring women's participation in development have expanded and need to combine a focus on women's conditions and basic needs with an holistic approach based on equal rights and partnerships, promotion and protection of all human rights and fundamental freedoms. Policies and programmes should be formulated to achieve the goal of people-centred sustainable development, secure livelihoods and adequate social protection measures, including safety nets, strengthened support systems for families, equal access to and control over financial and economic resources, and eliminate increasing and disproportionate poverty among women. All economic policies, institutions and resource allocation should adopt a gender perspective to ensure that development dividends are shared on equal grounds.

Increased efforts are needed to provide equal access to education, health, and social services and to ensure women's and girls' rights to education and the enjoyment of the highest attainable standard of physical and mental health and well-being throughout the life cycle, as well as adequate, affordable and universally accessible health care and services including sexual and reproductive health, particularly in the face of the HIV/AIDS pandemic; they are also necessary with regard to the growing proportion of older women.

Given that a majority of the world's women are subsistence producers and users of environmental resources, there is a need to recognize and integrate women's knowledge and priorities in the conservation and management of such resources to ensure their sustainability. Programmes and infrastructures that are gender-sensitive are needed in order to effectively respond to disaster and emergency situations that threaten the environment, livelihood security, as well as the management of the basic requirements of daily life.

Sustaining the livelihoods of populations in States with limited or scarce resources, including Small Island Developing States is critically dependent on the preservation and protection of the environment. Women's customary knowledge, management and sustainable use of biodiversity should be recognized.

Political will and commitment at all levels are crucial to ensure mainstreaming of a gender perspective in the adoption and implementation of comprehensive and action oriented policies in all areas. Policy commitments are essential for further developing the necessary framework which ensures women's equal access to and control over economic and financial resources, training, services and institutions as well as their participation in decision making and management. Policy making processes require the partnership of women and men at all levels. Men and boys should also be actively involved and encouraged in all efforts to achieve the goals of the Platform for Action and its implementation.

5.1 Actions to be Taken at the National Level

5.1.1 Actions to be Taken by Governments

- Set and encourage the use of explicit short- and long-term time bound targets or measurable goals, including where appropriate, quotas, to promote progress towards gender balance, including women's equal access to and full participation on a basis of equality with men in all areas and at all levels of public life, especially in decision- and policy making positions, in political parties and political activities, in all government ministries and at key policy-making institutions, as well as in local development bodies and authorities;
- Address the barriers faced by women, particularly by indigenous and other marginalized women, in accessing and participating in politics and decision-making, including lack of training, women's double burden of paid and unpaid work, negative societal attitudes and stereotypes;
- Ensure policies that guarantee equal access to education and elimination of gender disparities in education, including vocational training, science and technology and completion of basic education for girls, especially for those living in rural and deprived areas, and opportunities for continuing education at all levels for all women and girls;
- Support the implementation of plans and programmes of action to ensure quality education and improved enrolment retention rates for boys and girls and the elimination of gender discrimination as well as gender stereotypes in educational curricula and education material, as well as in the process of education;
- Accelerate action and strengthen political commitment to close the gender gap in primary and secondary education by 2005 and to ensure free compulsory and universal primary education for both girls and boys by 2015 as advocated by several global conferences and eliminate policies which have been proven to worsen and perpetuate the gap;
- Develop gender sensitive curricula from kindergarten to elementary schools to vocational training and universities in order to address gender stereotyping as one of the root causes of segregation in working life;

- Design and implement policies that promote and protect women's enjoyment of all human rights and fundamental freedoms and create an environment that does not tolerate violations of the rights of women and girls;
- Create and maintain, a non-discriminatory, as well as a gender sensitive legal environment by reviewing legislation with the view to striving to remove discriminatory provisions as soon as possible, preferably by 2005, and eliminating legislative gaps that leave women and girls without protection of their rights and without effective recourse against gender-based discrimination;
- Ratify the Convention on the Elimination of All Forms of Discrimination against Women, limit the extent of any reservations to it and withdraw reservations which are contrary to the object and purpose of the Convention or otherwise incompatible with international treaty law;
- Consider signing and ratifying the Optional Protocol to the Convention on the Elimination of All Forms of Discrimination against Women;
- Develop, review and implement laws, procedures to prohibit and eliminate all forms of discrimination against women and girls;
- Take measures, including programmes and policies, to ensure that maternity, motherhood, parenting and the role of women in procreation are not used as a basis for discrimination nor restrict the full participation of women in society;
- Ensure that national legislative and administrative reform processes, including those linked to land reform, decentralization and reorientation of the economy to promote women's rights, particularly those of rural women and women living in poverty, and take measures to promote and implement those rights through women's equal access to and control over economic resources, including land, property rights, right to inheritance, credit and traditional saving schemes, such as women's banks and cooperatives;
- Mainstream a gender perspective into national immigration and asylum policies, regulations and practices, as appropriate, in order to promote and protect the rights of all women, including the consideration of steps to recognize gender-related persecution and violence when assessing grounds for granting refugee status and asylum;
- Take all appropriate measures to eliminate discrimination and violence against women and girls by any person, organization or enterprise;
- Take necessary measures for the private sector and for educational establishments to facilitate and strengthen compliance with non-discriminatory legislation;
- As a matter of priority, review and revise, where appropriate, legislation, with

a view to introducing effective legislation including on violence against women, and take other necessary measures to ensure all women and girls are protected against all forms of physical, psychological, and sexual violence, and are provided recourse to justice;

- Treat all forms of violence against women and girls of all ages as a criminal offence punishable by law including violence based on all forms of discrimination;
- Establish legislation and/or strengthen appropriate mechanisms to handle criminal matters relating to all forms of domestic violence, including marital rape and sexual abuse of women and girls, and ensure that such cases are brought to justice swiftly;
- Develop, adopt and fully implement laws and other measures as appropriate, such as policies and educational programmes, to eradicate harmful customary or traditional practices including female genital mutilation, early and forced marriage, and so-called honour crimes that are violations of the human rights of women and girls, obstacles to the full enjoyment by women of their human rights and fundamental freedoms and to intensify efforts, in cooperation with local women's groups, to raise collective and individual awareness on how these harmful traditional or customary practices violate women's human rights;
- Continue to undertake research to develop a better understanding of the root causes of all forms of violence against women in order to design programmes and take measures towards eliminating these forms of violence;
- Take measures to address through policies and programmes, racism and racially motivated violence against women and girls;
- Take concrete steps, as a priority and with their full voluntary participation, to address the impact of violence on indigenous women, in order to implement appropriate, effective programmes and services to eliminate all forms of violence;
- Promote women's and girls' mental well being, integrate mental health services into primary health-care systems, develop gender-sensitive supportive programmes and train health workers to recognize gender-based violence and care for girls and women of all ages who have experienced any form of violence;
- Adopt and promote a holistic approach to respond to all forms of violence and abuse against girls and women of all ages, including girls and women with disabilities, as well as vulnerable and marginalized women and girls in order to address their diverse needs including education, provision of appropriate

health care and services and basic social services;

- Approve and promote a holistic approach to combat violence against women during all their life cycle and circumstances;
- Take appropriate measures to address the root factors, including external factors, that encourage trafficking in women and girls for prostitution and other forms of commercialized sex, forced marriages and forced labour in order to eliminate trafficking in women, including by strengthening existing legislation with a view to providing better protection of the rights of women and girls and to punishing the perpetrators, through both criminal and civil measures;
- Devise, enforce, and strengthen effective measures to combat and eliminate all forms of trafficking in women and girls through a comprehensive anti-trafficking strategy consisting of, *inter alia*, legislative measures, prevention campaigns, exchange of information, assistance and protection for and reintegration of the victims and prosecution of all the offenders involved, including intermediaries;
- Consider preventing, within the leading framework and in accordance with national policies, victims of trafficking, particularly women and girls, from being prosecuted for their illegal entry or residence, taking into account that they are victims of exploitation;
- Consider setting up or strengthening a national coordinating mechanism, for example, a national rapporteur or an inter-agency body, with participation of the civil society including NGOs, to encourage the exchange of information and to report on data, root causes, factors and trends in violence against women, in particular trafficking;
- Provide protection and support to women and their respective families and develop and strengthen policies to support family security;
- Consider adopting, where appropriate, national legislation consistent with the Convention on Biological Diversity to protect the knowledge, innovations and practices of women in indigenous and local communities relating to traditional medicines, biodiversity and indigenous technologies;
- Adapt environmental and agricultural policies and mechanisms, when necessary, to incorporate a gender perspective, and in cooperation with civil society, support farmers, particularly women farmers and those living in rural areas, with education and training programmes;
- Adopt policies and implement measures to address, on a prioritized basis, the gender aspects of emerging and continued health challenges, such as malaria, tuberculosis, HIV/AIDS and other diseases having a disproportionate impact

on women's health, including those resulting in the highest mortality and morbidity rates;

- Ensure that the reduction of maternal morbidity and mortality is a health sector priority and that women have ready access to essential obstetric care, well-equipped and adequately staffed maternal health-care services, skilled attendance at delivery, emergency obstetric care, effective referral and transport to higher levels of care when necessary, post-partum care and family planning in order to, *inter alia,* promote safe motherhood, and give priority attention to measures to prevent, detect and treat breast, cervical and ovarian cancer and osteoporosis, and sexually transmitted infections, including HIV/AIDS;
- Take measures to meet the unmet needs in good quality family planning services and in contraception, namely regarding the existing gap in services, supplies and use;
- Collect and disseminate up-dated and reliable data on women's health, including mortality and morbidity of women, and conduct further research regarding how social and economic factors affect the health of girls and women of all ages as well as research about the provision of health care services to girls and women and the patterns of their use of such services and the value of disease prevention and health promotion programmes for women;
- Ensure universal and equal access for women and men throughout the life-cycle, to social services related to health care, including education, clean water and safe sanitation, nutrition, food security and health education programmes;
- Ensure the provision of safe working conditions for health care workers;
- Adopt, enact, review and revise, where necessary or appropriate, and implement health legislation, policies and programmes in consultation with women's organizations and other actors of civil society, and allocate the necessary budgetary resources to ensure the highest attainable standard of physical and mental health, so that all women have full and equal access to comprehensive, high quality and affordable health care, information, education and services throughout their life cycle; to reflect the new demands for service and care by women and girls as a result of the HIV/AIDS pandemic and new knowledge about women's needs for specific mental and occupation health programmes and for the ageing process; to protect and promote human rights by ensuring that all health services and workers conform to ethical, professional and gender-sensitive standards in the delivery

of women's health services, including by establishing or strengthening, as appropriate, regulatory and enforcement mechanisms;

- Eliminate discrimination against all women and girls in access to health information, education, and health care and health services;
- Design, and implement programmes to encourage and enable men to adopt safe and responsible sexual and reproductive behaviour, and to effectively use methods to prevent unwanted pregnancies and sexually transmitted infections, including HIV/AIDS;
- Take all appropriate measures to eliminate harmful, medically unnecessary or coercive medical interventions as well as inappropriate medication and overmedication of women and ensure that all women are properly informed of their options, including likely benefits and potential side effects, by properly trained personnel;
- Adopt measures to ensure non-discrimination against and respect for the privacy of those living with HIV/AIDS and sexually transmitted infections, including women and young people, so that they are not denied the information needed to prevent further transmission of HIV/AIDS and sexually transmitted infections and are able to access treatment and care services without fear of stigmatization, discrimination or violence.

Prevention of unwanted pregnancies must always be given the highest priority and every attempt should be made to eliminate the need for abortion. Women who have unwanted pregnancies should have ready access to reliable information and compassionate counselling. Any measures or changes related to abortion within the health system can only be determined at the national or local level according to the national legislative process. In circumstances where abortion is not against the law, such abortion should be safe. In all cases, women should have access to quality services for the management of complications arising from abortion. Post-abortion counselling, education and family-planning services should be offered promptly, which will also help to avoid repeat abortions", consider reviewing laws containing punitive measures against women who have undergone illegal abortions:

- Promote and improve comprehensive gender-specific tobacco prevention and control strategies for all women, particularly adolescent girls and pregnant women, which would include, *inter alia*, education, prevention and cessation programmes and services, and the reduction of people's exposure to environmental tobacco smoke and support the development of the World Health Organization's Framework Convention on Tobacco Control;
- Promote or improve information programmes and measures including

treatment for the elimination of the increasing substance abuse among women and adolescent girls, including information campaigns about the risks to health and other consequences and its impact on families;

- Mainstream a gender perspective into key macro economic and social development policies and national development programmes;
- Incorporate a gender perspective into the design, development, adoption and execution of all budgetary processes, as appropriate, in order to promote equitable, effective and appropriate resource allocation and establish adequate budgetary allocations to support gender equality and development programmes which enhance women's empowerment and develop the necessary analytical and methodological tools and mechanisms for monitoring and evaluation;
- Increase as appropriate and effectively utilize financial and other resources in the social sector, particularly in education and health, to achieve gender equality and women's empowerment as a central strategy for addressing development and poverty eradication;
- Strive to reduce the disproportionate presence of women living in poverty particularly rural women by implementing national poverty eradication programmes with a focus on a gender perspective and the empowerment of women, including short and long-term goals;
- Undertake socio-economic policies that promote sustainable development and support and ensure poverty eradication programmes, especially for women, by inter alia , providing skills training, equal access to and control over resources, finance, credit, including micro-credit, information, technology, and equal access to markets to benefit women of all ages, in particular those living in poverty and marginalized women, including rural women, indigenous women, and female headed households;
- Create and ensure equal access to social protection systems, taking into account the specific needs of all women living in poverty, demographic changes and changes in society, to provide safeguards against the uncertainties and changes in conditions of work associated with globalization and strive to ensure that new, flexible and emerging forms of work are adequately covered by social protection;
- Facilitate employment for women through *inter alia* promotion of adequate social protection, simplification of administrative procedures, removal of fiscal obstacles, where appropriate, and other measures, such as access to risk capital, credit schemes, micro credit and other funding, facilitating the establishment of micro enterprises and small and medium enterprises;

- Establish or reinforce existing institutional mechanisms at all levels to work with national machineries to strengthen societal support for gender equality, in cooperation with civil society, particularly women's NGOs ;
- Take action at the highest levels for the continued advancement of women particularly by strengthening national machineries to mainstream the gender perspective to accelerate the empowerment of women in all areas and ensure commitment to gender equality policies;
- Provide national machineries with the necessary human and financial resources, including through exploring innovative funding schemes so that gender mainstreaming is integrated in all policies, programmes and projects;
- Consider establishing effective commissions or other institutions to promote equal opportunities;
- Strengthen efforts to fully implement national action plans developed for the implementation of the Beijing Platform for Action and, when necessary, adjust or develop national plans for the future;
- Ensure that the design of all government information policies and strategies is gender-sensitive;
- Provide national statistical offices with institutional and financial support in order to collect, compile and disseminate data disaggregated by sex, age, and other factors as appropriate, in formats that are accessible to the public and to policy-makers for *inter alia* gender-based analysis, monitoring and impact assessment, and support new work to develop statistics and indicators, especially in areas where information is particularly lacking;
- Develop national capacity to undertake policy-oriented and gender-related research and impact studies by universities and national research/training institutes to enable gender-specific knowledge-based policy-making.

5.1.2 Actions to be taken by Governments, Private Sector, Non-governmental Organizations and other Actors of Civil Society

- Encourage the creation of training and legal literacy programmes, which build and support the capacities of women's organizations to advocate for women's and girls' human rights and fundamental freedoms;
- Encourage collaboration and, where appropriate, among various levels of Governments, NGOs, grass-roots organizations , traditional and community leaders for the promotion and protection of all human rights and fundamental freedoms of women and girls and the dignity and worth of the human person and equal rights for women and men;
- Adopt a holistic approach to women's physical and mental health throughout the life cycle, take further measures to redesign health information, services

and training for health workers in order to make them gender-sensitive, promote gender balance at all levels of the health care system, and reflect women's perspective and right to privacy, confidentiality, voluntary and informed consent;

- Reinforce efforts to ensure universal access to high quality primary health care, throughout the life cycle, including sexual and reproductive health care, not later than 2015;
- Review and revise national policies, programmes and legislation to implement the "Key actions for the further implementation of the Programme of Action of the International Conference on Population and Development" adopted by the twenty-first special session of the General Assembly, paying particular attention to achieving the specific benchmarks to reduce maternal mortality, to increase the proportion of births assisted by skilled attendants, to provide the widest achievable range of safe and effective family planning and contraceptive methods and reduce young people's risk of HIV/AIDS;
- Strengthen measures to improve the nutritional status of all girls and women, recognizing the effects of severe and moderate malnutrition, the life-long implications of nutrition and the link between mother and child health, by promoting and enhancing support for programmes to reduce malnutrition, such as school meal programmes mother-child-nutrition programmes and micro-nutrient supplementation, giving special attention to bridging the gender gap in nutrition;
- Review, with the full participation of women, and monitor the impact of health sector reform initiatives on women's health and their enjoyment of human rights, in particular with regard to rural and urban health service delivery to women living in poverty, and ensure that reforms secure full and equal access to available, affordable and high quality health care and services for all women, taking into account the diverse needs of women;
- Design and implement programmes with the full involvement of adolescents as appropriate, to provide them with education, information and appropriate, specific, user-friendly and accessible services without discrimination to address effectively their reproductive and sexual health needs taking into account their right to privacy, confidentiality, respect and informed consent and the responsibilities, rights and duties of parents and legal guardians to provide in a manner consistent with the evolving capacities of the child appropriate direction and guidance in the exercise by the child of the rights recognized in the Convention on the Rights of the Child and in conformity with CEDAW and ensuring that in all actions concerning children, the best

interests of the child are a primary consideration. These programmes should, *inter alia,* build adolescent girls' self esteem and help them take responsibility for their own lives; promote gender equality and responsible sexual behaviour; raise awareness about, prevent and treat sexually transmitted infections, including HIV/AIDS and sexual violence and abuse; counsel adolescents on avoiding unwanted and early pregnancies;

- Design and implement programmes to provide social services and support to pregnant adolescents and adolescent mothers, in particular to enable them to continue and complete their education;
- Give particular attention to developing and improving access to improved and new technologies and to safe and affordable drugs and treatments to meet women's health needs, including, *inter ali*a, cardio/pulmonary diseases, hypertension, osteoporosis, breast-, cervical-and ovarian cancer and family planning and contraceptive methods, for both women and men;
- Develop and use frameworks, guidelines and other practical tools and indicators to accelerate gender mainstreaming, including gender-based research, analytical tools and methodologies, training, case studies, statistics and information;
- Provide equal opportunities and favourable conditions for women of all ages and backgrounds on equal terms with men by encouraging their entry into politics and their participation at all levels;
- Encourage the nomination of more women candidates, including, *inter ali*a, through political parties, quotas or measurable goals, or other appropriate means for election to parliaments and other legislative structures, to increase their share and contribution in the formulation of public policy;
- Promote and protect the rights of women workers and take action to remove structural and legal barriers as well as stereotypical attitudes to gender equality at work, addressing *inter alia*: gender bias in recruitment; working conditions; occupational segregation and harassment; discrimination in social protection benefits; women's occupational health and safety; unequal career opportunities and inadequate sharing, by men, of family responsibilities;
- Promote programmes to enable women and men to reconcile their work and family responsibilities, and to encourage men to share equally with women household and childcare responsibilities;
- Develop or strengthen policies and programmes to support the multiple roles of women in contributing to the welfare of the family in its various forms, which acknowledge the social significance of maternity and motherhood, parenting, the role of parents and legal guardians in the upbringing of children

and caring for other family members. Such policies and programmes should also promote shared responsibility of parents, women and men and society as a whole in this regard;

- Design, implement and promote family friendly policies and services, including affordable, accessible and quality care services for children and other dependents, parental and other leave schemes, campaigns to sensitize public opinion and other relevant actors on equal sharing of employment and family responsibilities between women and men;
- Develop policies and programmes to enhance the employability of women and their access to quality jobs, through improving access to formal, non formal and vocational training, life long learning and retraining, long-distance education, including in information and communications technology and entrepreneurial skills, particularly in developing countries, to support women's empowerment in the different stages of their lives;
- Take action to increase women's participation and to bring about a balanced representation of women and men in all sectors and occupations in the labour market, among others by encouraging the creation or expansion of institutional networks to support the career development and promotion of women;
- Develop and/or strengthen programmes and policies to support women entrepreneurs, including those engaged in new enterprises, through access to information, training, including vocational training, new technologies, networks, credit and financial services;
- Initiate positive steps to promote equal pay for equal work or work of equal value and to diminish differentials in incomes between women and men;
- Encourage and support the education of girls in science, mathematics, new technologies including information technologies, and technical subjects and encourage women, including through career advising to seek employment in high growth and high wage sectors and jobs;
- Analyze and respond, as necessary, to the major reasons why men and women may be affected differently by the process of job creation and retrenchment associated with economic transition and structural transformation of the economy, including globalization.

5.2 Actions to be Taken at the International Level by the United Nations System, International and Regional Organizations

- Assist Governments, at their request, to build institutional capacity and develop national action plans, or further implement existing action plans, for the implementation of the Platform for Action;

- Support non-governmental organizations, especially women's organizations, to build their capacity to advocate for, implement, assess, and follow up the Platform for Action;
- Strengthen or establish where appropriate, national collaborative and regular reporting mechanisms , with the participation of NGOs, especially women's organizations, to monitor progress on the implementation of national policies, programmes and benchmarks for achieving gender equality;
- Allocate sufficient resources to regional and national programmes to implement the Platform for Action in its twelve critical areas;
- Assist Governments in countries with economies in transition to further develop and implement plans and programmes aimed at economic and political empowerment of women;
- Encourage the Economic and Social Council to request the Regional Commissions within their respective mandates and resources, to build up a data base to be updated regularly, in which all programmes and projects carried out in their respective regions by agencies or organizations of the United Nations system are listed, to facilitate their dissemination, as well as the evaluation of their impact on the empowerment of women through the implementation of the Platform for Action;
- Continue to implement and evaluate and follow up the mandated work of the UN agencies, drawing on the full range of expertise available within the UN system, as well as ECOSOC Agreed Conclusions and other programmes and initiatives to mainstream a gender perspective into all policies, programmes and planning of the UN system, including through the integrated and coordinated follow-up to all major UN conferences and summits, as well as to ensure the allocation of sufficient resources and maintenance of gender units and focal points to achieve this end;
- Support national efforts, particularly in developing countries, for enlarged access to new information technology as part of the efforts to develop collaborative research, training and information dissemination, including through the Gender Awareness Internet Networking System (GAINS) being developed by the International Research and Training Institute for the Advancement of Women (INSTRAW), while at the same time supporting traditional methods of information dissemination, research and training;
- Ensure that all UN personnel and officials at headquarters and in the field, especially in field operations, receive training in order to mainstream a gender perspective in their work, including gender impact analysis, and ensure appropriate follow-up to such training;

- Support the Commission on the Status of Women, within its mandate, in assessing and advancing the implementation of the Beijing Platform for Action and its follow-up;
- Assist governments, upon their request, to incorporate a gender perspective as a key dimension of development into national development planning;
- Assist States Parties, upon their request, in building capacity to implement the Convention on the Elimination of All Forms of Discrimination against Women, and in this regard encourages States Parties to pay attention to the concluding comments as well as the general recommendations of the Committee;
- Assist Governments, upon request, in developing gender-sensitive strategies for the delivery of assistance and, where appropriate, responses to humanitarian crises resulting from armed conflict and natural disasters;
- Invite the United Nations High Commissioner for Refugees, other relevant United Nations agencies, within their respective mandates, and other relevant humanitarian organizations as well as Governments to continue to provide adequate support to countries hosting large numbers of refugees and those with displaced persons, in their efforts to provide protection and assistance, paying particular attention to the needs of refugee and other displaced women and children;
- Ensure and support the full participation of women at all levels of decision-making and implementation in development activities and peace processes, including conflict prevention and resolution, post-conflict reconstruction, peace-making, peace-keeping and peace-building and in this regard, support the involvement of women's organizations, community based organizations and NGOs;
- Encourage the involvement of women in decision-making at all levels and achieve gender balance in the appointment of women and men, with full respect for the principle of equitable geographical distribution, including as special envoys and special representatives and to pursue good offices on behalf of the Secretary-General, inter alia in matters relating to peace-keeping, peace-building, and in operational activities, including resident coordinators;
- Take further effective measures to remove the obstacles for the realization of the right of peoples to self-determination, in particular peoples living under colonial and foreign occupation, that continue to adversely affect their economic and social development;
- Support activities aimed at the elimination of all forms of violence against

women and girls, including providing support for the activities of women's networks and organizations within the United Nations system;

- Consider launching an international "zero tolerance" campaign on violence against women;
- Encourage implementation of measures designed to achieve the goal of 50/50 gender balance in all posts including at the professional level and above, in particular at the higher levels in their secretariats including in peacekeeping missions and peace negotiations and in all activities and report thereon as appropriate, and enhancing management accountability mechanisms;
- Take measures, with the full participation of women, to create, at all levels, an enabling environment conducive to the achievement and maintenance of world peace, for democracy and peaceful settlement of disputes with the full respect for the principles of sovereignty, territorial integrity and political independence of states and non-intervention in matters which are essentially within the jurisdiction of any state, in accordance with the Charter of the United Nations and international law, as well as, the promotion and protection of all human rights, including the right to development, and fundamental freedoms.

5.3 Actions to be Taken at the National and International Level by Governments, Regional and International Organizations, Including the United Nations System and International Financial Institutions

- Take steps with a view to the avoidance of, and refrain from any unilateral measure, not in accordance with international law and the Charter of the United Nations, that impedes the full achievement of economic and social development by the population of the affected countries, in particular women and children, that hinders their well-being and that creates obstacles to the full enjoyment of their human rights, including the right of everyone to a standard of living adequate for their health and well-being and their right to food, medical care and the necessary social services. Ensure that food and medicine are not used as tools for political pressure;
- Take urgent and effective measures in accordance with international law with a view to alleviating the negative impact of economic sanctions on women and children;
- Create an enabling environment as well as design and implement policies that promote and protect the enjoyment of all human rights - civil, cultural, economic, political and social rights, including the right to development - and fundamental freedoms, as part of the efforts to achieve gender equality, development and peace;

- Continue to review, modify and implement macroeconomic and social policies and programmes, including *inter alia* , through an analysis from a gender perspective of those related to structural adjustment, external debt problems, in order to ensure women's equal access to resources and universal access to basic social services;
- Promote international cooperation to support regional and national efforts in the development and use of gender-related analysis and statistics by, *inter alia*, providing national statistical offices, upon their request, with institutional and financial support in order to enable them to respond to requests for data disaggregated by sex and age for use by national governments in the formulation of gender-sensitive statistical indicators for monitoring and policy and programme impact assessments, as well as to undertake regular strategic surveys;
- Assist countries, upon their request, in developing methods for, and compiling statistics on the contributions of women and men to society and the economy, and the socio-economic situation of women and men, in particular in relation to poverty, and paid and unpaid work in all sectors;
- Regularly compile and publish crime statistics and map trends in law enforcement concerning violations of the rights of women and girls to increase awareness in order to develop more effective policies;
- Develop with the full participation of all countries an international consensus on indicators and ways to measure violence against women and consider establishing a readily accessible database on statistics, legislation, training models, good practices, lessons learned and other resources with regard to all forms of violence against women, including women migrant workers;
- In partnership, as appropriate, with relevant institutions promote, improve, systemize and fund the collection of data disaggregated by sex, age and other appropriate factors, on health and access to health services, including comprehensive information on the impact of HIV/AIDS on women, throughout the life-cycle;
- Eliminate gender biases in bio-medical, clinical and social research, including by conducting voluntary clinical trials involving women, with due regard for their human rights and in strict conformity with internationally accepted legal, ethical, medical, safety, and scientific standards and gather, analyze and make available to appropriate institutions and to end-users, gender-specific information about dosage, side-effects and effectiveness of drugs, including contraceptives and methods that protect against sexually transmitted infections;

- Develop and support the capacity of universities, national research and training institutes and other relevant research institutes to undertake gender related and policy oriented research in order to inform policy makers and to promote full implementation of the Platform for Action and its follow-up;
- Develop a South-South cooperation programme with a view to assisting in the capacity building of national machineries on women through, among others, the sharing of expertise, experiences and knowledge of national machineries on women's empowerment, gender issues and gender mainstreaming methodologies and approaches on the 12 critical areas of the Platform for Action;
- Support Governments in their efforts to institute action-oriented programmes and measures to accelerate the full implementation of the Platform for Action, with time-bound targets and/or measurable goals and evaluation methods, including gender impact assessments, with full participation of women for measuring and analysing progress;
- Undertake appropriate data collection and research on indigenous women, with their full participation, in order to foster accessible, culturally and linguistically appropriate policies, programmes and services;
- Continue research on all current trends that may be creating new gender disparities in order to provide a basis for policy action;
- Take measures to develop and implement gender sensitive programmes aimed at stimulating women's entrepreneurship and private initiative and assist women-owned business to participate in and benefit from, *inter alia*, international trade, technological innovation and investment;
- Respect, promote and realize the principles contained in the ILO Declaration on Fundamental Principles and Rights at Work and its follow-up and strongly consider ratification and full implementation of ILO Conventions which are particularly relevant to ensure women's rights at work;
- Encourage the strengthening of existing and emerging micro-credit institutions and their capacity, including through the support of international financial institutions, so that credit and related services for self-employment and income generating activities may be made available to an increasing number of people living in poverty, in particular women and to further develop, where appropriate, other micro-finance instruments;
- Reaffirm commitment to gender-sensitive development and support women's role in sustainable and ecologically sound consumption and production patterns and approaches to natural resource management;
- Adopt measures to ensure that the work of rural women, who continue to play

a vital role in providing food security and nutrition, and are engaged in agricultural production, and enterprises related to farming, fishing and resource management, and home-based work, especially in the informal sector, is recognized and valued in order to enhance their economic security, their access to and control over resources and credit schemes, services and benefits, and their empowerment;

- Encourage and implement curriculum changes in training for public officials to make them fully gender-sensitive;
- Develop policies and implement programmes including education programmes, particularly for men and boys, on changing stereotypical attitudes and behaviours concerning gender roles and responsibilities to promote gender equality and positive attitudes and behaviours;
- Strengthen and promote programmes to support the participation of young women in youth organizations and encourage dialogue among youth between and among developed and developing countries;
- Support national efforts to promote formal and non-formal education and mentoring programmes for women and girls, in order to enable them to acquire knowledge, develop self-esteem and skills in leadership, advocacy and conflict resolution;
- Undertake comprehensive actions to provide skills training for women and girls at all levels, in order to eradicate poverty, in particular the feminization of poverty, through national and international efforts;
- Strengthen gender-awareness campaigns and gender equality training among women and men, girls and boys to eliminate the persistence of harmful stereotypes;
- With the full voluntary participation of indigenous women, develop and implement educational and training programmes that respect their history, culture, spirituality, languages and aspirations and ensure their access to all levels of formal and non-formal education, including higher education;
- Continue to support and strengthen national, regional and international adult literacy programmes with international cooperation in order to achieve a 50 percent improvement in levels of adult literacy by 2015, especially for women, and equitable access to basic and continuing education for all adults;
- Continue to examine the decline in enrolment rates and the increase in the drop-out rates of girls and boys at the primary and secondary education levels in some countries, and, with international cooperation, design appropriate national programmes to eliminate the root causes and support lifelong learning for women and girls, with a view to ensuring achievement of

relevant international targets on education set by the relevant international conferences;

- Ensure equal opportunities for women and girls in cultural, recreational and sports activities, as well as in participation in athletics and physical activities at national, regional and international levels, such as access, training, competition, remuneration and prizes;
- Design and implement policies and programmes, to fully address specific needs of women and girls with disabilities, to ensure their equal access to education at all levels, including technical and vocational training and adequate rehabilitation programmes, to health care and services and employment opportunities, to protect and promote their human rights and, where appropriate, eliminate existing inequalities between women and men with disabilities;
- Develop and maintain consultative processes and mechanisms, in partnership with women's organizations including NGOs and community groups, to ensure that all women, with attention to those who face particular barriers to their participation in public life, are fully involved in and informed about decisions which impact their lives;
- Apply and support positive measures to give all women, particularly indigenous women, equal access to capacity-building and training programmes to enhance their participation in decision-making in all fields and at all levels;
- Increase cooperation, policy responses, effective implementation of national legislation and other protective and preventive measures aimed at the elimination of violence against women and girls, especially all forms of commercial sexual exploitation, as well as economic exploitation, including inter alia, trafficking in women and children, female infanticide, crimes committed in the name of honour, crimes committed in the name of passion, racially motivated crimes, abduction and sale of children, dowry related violence and deaths, acid attacks and harmful traditional or customary practices such as FGM, early and forced marriages;
- Increase awareness and knowledge of the Rome Statute of the ICC which affirms that rape, sexual slavery, enforced prostitution, forced pregnancy, enforced sterilization and other forms of sexual violence constitute war crimes and, in defined circumstances, crimes against humanity, with the aim of preventing such crimes from occurring and take measures to support prosecution of all persons responsible for such crimes and provide avenues for redress to victims; also increase awareness of the extent to which such

crimes are used as a weapon of war;

- Provide support to NGOs, in collaboration with the UN system, *inter alia* through regional and international cooperation, including women's organizations, and community groups in addressing all forms of violence against women and girls, including for programmes to combat race and ethnic-based violence against women and girls;
- Prosecute the perpetrators of all forms of violence against women and girls and sentence them appropriately and introduce actions aimed at helping and motivating perpetrators to break the cycle of violence and take measures to provide avenues for redress to victims;
- Provide gender sensitive training to all actors, as appropriate, in peacekeeping missions in dealing with victims of violence, particularly women and girls, including sexual violence;
- Provide gender sensitive training to all actors, including police, prosecutors and the judiciary in dealing with victims of violence, particularly women and girls, including sexual violence;
- Encourage and support public campaigns, as appropriate, to enhance public awareness of the unacceptability and social costs of violence against women and undertake prevention activities to promote healthy and balanced relationships based on gender equality;
- Intensify cooperation between states of origin, transit and destination to prevent, suppress and punish trafficking in persons, especially women and children;
- Support the ongoing negotiations on the draft protocol to prevent, suppress and punish trafficking in persons, especially women and children which supplements the UN Convention against Transnational Organized Crime;
- As appropriate, pursue and support national, regional and international strategies to reduce the risk to women and girls, including those who are refugees and displaced, as well as women migrant workers, of becoming victims of trafficking; strengthen national legislation by further defining the crime of trafficking in all its elements and by reinforcing the punishment accordingly; enact social and economic policies and programmes, as well as information and awareness raising initiatives, to prevent and combat trafficking in persons, especially women and children; prosecute perpetrators of trafficking; provide measures to support, assist and protect trafficked persons in countries of origin and destination; and facilitate their return to and support their reintegration in countries of origin;
- Improve knowledge and awareness of the remedies available for violations of

women's human rights;

- Promote and protect the human rights of all migrant women and implement policies to address the specific needs of documented migrant women and, where necessary, tackle the existing inequalities between men and women migrants to ensure gender equality;
- Promote respect for the right of women and men to the freedom of thought, conscience and religion. Recognize the central role that religion, spirituality and belief play in the lives of millions of women and men;
- Encourage co-operation between governmental authorities, parliamentarians and other relevant authorities and women's organizations including NGOs, as appropriate, in ensuring that legislation is non-discriminatory;
- Encourage, through the media and other means, a high awareness of harmful effects of certain traditional or customary practices affecting the health of women, some of which increase their vulnerability to HIV/AIDS and other sexually transmitted infections and intensify efforts to eliminate such practices;
- Take necessary measures to protect individuals, groups and organs of society engaged in promoting and protecting women's human rights;
- Encourage States parties to continue to include a gender perspective in their reports to the treaty bodies; also encourage these bodies to continue to take into account a gender perspective in the implementation of their mandates, taking into account the need to avoid unnecessary duplication and overlapping of their work; further encourage human rights mechanisms to continue to take into account a gender perspective in their work;
- Take measures to enable all older women to be actively engaged in all aspects of life, as well as assume a variety of roles in communities, public life and decision-making, and develop and implement policies and programmes to ensure their full enjoyment of human rights and quality of life, as well as to address their needs, with a view to contribute to the realization of a society for all ages;
- Support innovative programmes to empower older women to increase their contribution to and benefit from development and efforts to combat poverty;
- Promote comprehensive human rights education programmes, inter alia in cooperation, where appropriate, with education and human rights institutions, the relevant actors of civil society, in particular NGOs and the media networks, to ensure widespread dissemination of information on human rights instruments, in particular those on human rights of women and girls;
- Take measures, through inter alia, supporting and strengthening existing

mechanisms entrusted with prosecuting perpetrators of violations of human rights of women, to eliminate impunity;

- Take measures to eliminate violations of international law and the United Nations Charter. Many of these violations have a negative impact on the promotion and protection of human rights of women;
- Address the root causes of armed conflict in a comprehensive and durable manner as well as the differences in the impact of armed conflict on women and men and take them into account in relevant policies and programmes, in order to, *inter alia*, enhance the protection of civilians, particularly women and children;
- Consider signing and ratifying the Rome Statute of the International Criminal Court;
- Ensure release of hostages, particularly women and children, including those subsequently imprisoned, in armed conflict;
- Develop and support policies and programmes for the protection of children, especially girls, in hostilities, in order to prohibit their forced recruitment and use by all actors, and to promote and/or strengthen mechanisms for their rehabilitation and reintegration, taking into account the specific experiences and needs of girls;
- Improve and strengthen the capacity of women affected by situations of armed conflict including women refugees and displaced women by inter alia, involving them in the design and management of humanitarian activities so that they benefit from these activities on an equal basis with men;
- Seek to ensure the full and equal participation of women in the promotion of peace, in particular, through the full implementation of the Declaration and Programme of Action on a culture of peace;
- Provide support to and empower women who play an important role within their families as stabilizing factors in conflict and post-conflict situations;
- Strengthen efforts towards general and complete disarmament under strict and effective international control, based on the priorities established by the United Nations in the field of disarmament, so that released resources could be used for, inter alia, social and economic programmes which benefit women and girls;
- Explore new ways of generating new public and private financial resources, *inter alia*, through the appropriate reduction of excessive military expenditures and the arms trade and investment for arms production and acquisition, including global military expenditures, taking into consideration national security requirements, so as to permit the possible allocation of

additional funds for social and economic development, *inter alia* for the advancement of women;

- Take measures to ensure the protection of refugees, especially women and girls, and their access to and the provision of gender sensitive appropriate basic social services, including education and health;
- Cooperate and work with private sector partners and media networks at national and international levels to promote equal access for women and men as producers and consumers, particularly in the area of information and communications technologies, including through encouraging the media and the information industry consistent with freedom of expression to adopt, or develop further codes of conduct, professional guidelines and other self-regulatory guidelines to remove gender stereotypes and promote balanced portrayals of women and men;
- Develop programmes that support women's ability to create, access and promote networking, in particular through the use of new information and communications technology, including through the establishment and support of programmes to build the capacity of women's NGOs in this regard;
- Capitalize on the new information technologies, including the Internet, to improve the global sharing of information, research, strengths, lessons learned from women's experiences, including "Herstories" related to achieving gender equality, development and peace, and study other roles that these technologies can play towards that goal;
- Take effective measures to address the challenges of globalization, including through the enhanced and effective participation of developing countries in the international economic policy decision-making process, in order to *inter alia* , guarantee the equal participation of women, in particular those from developing countries, in the process of macro-economic decision making;
- Take measures with the full and effective participation of women to ensure new approaches to international development cooperation, based on stability, growth and equity with the enhanced and effective participation and the integration of developing countries in the globalizing world economy, geared towards poverty eradication and the reduction of gender-based inequality within the overall framework of achieving people centred sustainable development;
- Design and strengthen poverty eradication strategies with the full and effective participation of women that reduce the feminization of poverty and enhance the capacity of women and empower them to meet the negative social and economic impacts of globalization;

- Intensify efforts to implement poverty eradication programmes and evaluate, with the participation of women, the extent to which these programmes have an impact on the empowerment of women living in poverty, in terms of access to quality training and education as well as health care, employment, basic social services, inheritance, and access to and control over land, housing, income, micro-credit and other financial instruments and services, and introduce improvements to such programmes in the light of the above assessment;
- Recognizing the mutually reinforcing links between gender equality and poverty eradication, elaborate and implement, where appropriate, in consultation with civil society, comprehensive gender sensitive poverty eradication strategies addressing social, structural and macro-economic issues;
- Encourage the establishment, in partnership with private financial institutions where appropriate of "lending windows" and other accessible financial services with simplified procedures that are specifically designed to meet the savings, credit and insurance needs of all women;
- Undertake comprehensive actions to provide and support quality skills training for women and girls at all levels, on the basis of strategies developed with their full and effective participation, to achieve agreed targets to eradicate poverty, in particular the feminization of poverty, through national, regional and international efforts. National efforts need to be complemented by intensified regional and international cooperation in order to tackle the risks, overcome the challenges and ensure that opportunities created by globalization benefit women, particularly in developing countries;
- Establish, with the full and effective participation of women and in consultation with civil society, particularly NGOs, in a timely manner, social development funds, where appropriate, to alleviate the negative effects on women associated with structural adjustment programmes and trade liberalization and the disproportionate burden borne by women living in poverty;
- Identify and implement development-oriented and durable solutions which integrate a gender perspective to external debt and debt-servicing problems of developing countries, including least-developed countries, *inter alia* , through debt relief, including the option of ODA debt cancellation, in order to help them to finance programmes and projects targeted at development, including the advancement of women;
- Support the Cologne initiative for the reduction of debt, particularly the

speedy implementation of the enhanced Heavily Indebted Poor Countries Debt Initiative, ensure the provision of adequate funds for its implementation, and the provision that funds saved should be used to support anti-poverty programmes that address gender dimensions;

- Promote and accelerate the implementation of the 20/20 initiative that integrates a gender perspective to fully benefit all, particularly women and girls;
- Call for continued international cooperation including the reaffirmation to strive to fulfil the yet to be attained internationally agreed target of 0.7 percent of the gross national product of developed countries for overall official development assistance as soon as possible, thereby increasing the flow of resources for gender equality, development and peace;
- Facilitate the transfer to developing countries and countries with economies in transition of appropriate technology, particularly new and modern technology and encourage efforts by the international community to eliminate restrictions to such transfers, as an effective means of complementing national efforts for further acceleration in achieving the goals of gender equality, development and peace;
- Recommend to the Preparatory Committee for the Millennium Assembly to make an effort within the context of gender mainstreaming in the UN system, to integrate a gender perspective in all activities and documents related to the Millennium Assembly and Summit, including in the consideration of poverty eradication;
- Create and strengthen an enabling environment, in accordance with national laws, to support the capacity of women's NGOs to mobilize resources to ensure sustainability of their development activities;
- Encourage the establishment and strengthening of multi-stakeholder partnerships/cooperation at all levels among international and inter-governmental organizations, with relevant actors of civil society including NGOs, private sector and trade unions, and women's organizations and other NGOs, communications and media systems in support of the goals of the Fourth World Conference on Women;
- Encourage partnerships and cooperation among governments, international organizations, in particular international financial institutions, and multilateral organizations, the private sector institutions and civil society including NGOs, especially women's and community-based organizations to support poverty eradication initiatives focused on women and girls;
- Support the work of NGOs and community based organizations in helping

disadvantaged women, in particular rural women, in having access to financial institutions in establishing businesses and other sustainable means of livelihood;

- Recognize the crucial role of and support women and women's NGOs and CBOs in the implementation of Agenda 21, by integrating a gender perspective in the formulation, design and implementation of sustainable environmental and resource management mechanisms, programmes and infrastructure;
- Promote gender-sensitivity and social responsibility of the private sector, inter alia through management of work time, and dissemination of gender-sensitive information and advocacy campaigns;
- Promote programmes for healthy active ageing that stress the independence, equality, participation, and security of older women and undertake gender-specific research and programmes to address their needs;
- As a matter of priority, especially in those countries most affected, and in partnership with NGOs, wherever possible, intensify education, services and community based mobilization strategies to protect women of all ages from HIV and other sexually transmitted infections, including through the development of safe, affordable, effective and easily accessible female-controlled methods, including methods such as microbicides and female condoms that protect against sexually transmitted infections and HIV/AIDS; voluntary and confidential HIV testing and counselling, and the promotion of responsible sexual behaviour, including abstinence and condom use; development of vaccines, simple low-cost diagnosis and single dose treatments for sexually transmitted infections;
- Provide access to adequate and affordable treatment, monitoring and care for all people, especially women and girls, infected with sexually transmitted diseases or living with life threatening diseases, including HIV/AIDS and associated opportunistic infections, such as tuberculosis. Provide other services, including adequate housing and social protection, including during pregnancy and breastfeeding; assist boys and girls orphaned as a result of the HIV/AIDS pandemic; and provide gender sensitive support systems for women and other family members who are involved in caring for persons affected by serious health conditions, including HIV/AIDS;
- Take effective and expeditious measures to mobilize international and national public opinion concerning the effects of different dimensions of the world drug problems on women and girls and ensure that appropriate resources are provided to this end;

Encourage partnerships between Governments and NGOs in the implementation of commitments made at the Fourth World Conference on Women and at other United Nations World Conferences and Summits in order to promote gender equality, development and peace in the twenty-first century.

Appendix 2

Edited Extracts from India's Eleventh Five Year Plan (2007-12) on Women Welfare and Development

---

Introduction

Women are significant contributors to the growing economy and children are assets of the future. Almost fifty per cent of our population today comprises of women while 42 percent is under the age of 18. For growth to be truly inclusive, we have to ensure their protection, well-being, development, empowerment and participation.

India has committed to meeting the Millennium Development Goals and is a signatory to many international conventions, including Convention for Elimination of all forms of Discrimination against Women and the Convention on the Rights of the Child. Yet, at the start of the Eleventh Five Year Plan, women and children continue to be victims of violence, neglect and injustice. The Eleventh Plan will address these problems by looking at gender as a cross-cutting theme. It will recognize women's agency and the need for women's empowerment. At the same time it will ensure the survival, protection and all round development of children of all ages, communities and economic groups.

Approach to the Eleventh Five Year Plan

The vision of the Eleventh Five Year Plan is to end the multifaceted exclusions and discriminations faced by women and children; to ensure that every woman and child in the country is able to develop to her/his full potential and share the benefits of economic growth and prosperity. Success will depend on our ability to adopt a participatory approach that empowers women and children and makes them partners in their own development. The roadmap for this has already been laid in the National Policy on Women 2001 and the National Plan of Action for Children 2005.

The Eleventh Plan recognizes that women and children are not homogenous categories; they belong to diverse castes, classes, communities, economic groups, and are located within a range of geographic and development zones. Consequently, some groups are more vulnerable than others. Mapping and addressing the specific deprivations that arise from these multiple locations is essential for the success of planned interventions. Thus apart from the general programme interventions, special targeted interventions, catering to the differential needs of these groups will be undertaken during the Eleventh Plan.

In the Eleventh Plan, for the first time, women are recognised not just as equal citizens but as agents of economic and social growth. The approach to gender equity is based on the recognition that interventions in favour of women must be multi-pronged and they must (i) provide women with basic entitlements (ii) address the reality of globalization and its impact on women by prioritizing economic empowerment (iii) ensure an environment free from all forms of violence against women–physical, economic, social, psychological, and (iv) ensure the participation and adequate representation of women at the highest policy levels, particularly in Parliament and Assemblies (v) strengthen existing institutional mechanisms and create new ones for gender mainstreaming and effective policy implementation.

The child development approach in the Eleventh Plan is to ensure that children do not lose their childhood because of work, disease and despair. It is based on the understanding that the rights of all children, including those who do not face adverse circumstances, must be protected everywhere and at all times so that they do not fall out of the social security net. Successful integration of survival, development, protection and participation policies are important for the overall well being of the child. The essence of the Eleventh Plan strategy for Women Agency and Child Rights is below.

Essence of the Approach

- Recognition of the right of every woman and child to develop to her/his full potential.
- Recognition of the differential needs of different groups of women and children.
- Need for inter-sectoral convergence as well as focused women and child specific measures through Ministry of Women and Child Development.
- Partnership with civil society to create permanent institutional mechanisms that incorporate the experiences, capacities and knowledge of voluntary organizations and women's groups in the process of development planning.

Monitorable Targets for the Eleventh Plan

The Eleventh Plan lays down six monitorable targets.

- Raise the sex ratio for age group 0-6 from 927 in 2001 to 935 by 2011-12 and to 950 by 2016-17.
- Ensure that at least 33 percent of the direct and indirect beneficiaries of all

government schemes are women and girl children.

- Reduce infant mortality rate (IMR) from 57 to 28 and maternal mortality ratio (MMR) from 3.01 to 1 per 1000 live births.
- Reduce malnutrition among children of age group 0-3 to half its present level.
- Reduce anaemia among women and girls by 50 percent by the end of the Eleventh Plan.
- Reduce dropout rate for primary and secondary schooling by 10 percent for both girls as well as boys.

Status of Women: A Brief Overview

Due to the untiring efforts of the women's movement, the country amended and enacted women-related legislations during the Tenth Plan. The Married Women's Property Act (1874), the Hindu Succession Act (1956) were amended and the Protection of Women from Domestic Violence Act, (2005) was passed. The Union Budget 2005-06, for the first time, included a separate statement highlighting the gender sensitivities of the budgetary allocation under 10 demands for grants. Gender Budgeting Cells were set up in 52 Central Ministries/Departments to review public expenditure, collect gender disaggregated data and conduct gender based impact analysis.

Under WCP, efforts were made to ensure that not less than 30 percent of funds/benefits under various schemes of all Ministries/Departments were earmarked for women. The performance however has been far from satisfactory. The Mid Term Appraisal of Tenth Plan revealed that while 42.37 percent of the gross budgetary support (GBS) to the Department of Education flowed to women under WCP, only 5 percent of the GBS of Ministry of Labour (against 33.5 percent in the Ninth Plan) went to women in the first three years of the Tenth Plan. Several Ministries and/or Departments which had earlier reported on the WCP in their sectoral budgets stopped doing so. Within the Ministry of WCD, the financial allocation for women specific schemes during the Tenth Plan was ₹ 1,246 crore. As a result of this modest allocation of resources and ineffective implementation of existing schemes, we have fallen far short of our Tenth Plan targets.

Schemes (Major) for Women during Tenth Plan

- **Swayamsidha**—Implemented in 650 in selected blocks. Target: 16,000 SHGs; Achievement: 1767.
- **Support to Training and Employment Programme for Women (STEP)**—Target: provide training to 2.5 lakh;. Achievement: 2.31 lakh.

- **Swawlamban Scheme**—Target: 5 lakh; Achievement: 2.32 lakh.
- **Hostels for Working Women**—Target: construct 125 hostels benefiting 12,500 women; Achievement: 111 hostels were constructed during the Plan benefiting 6976 women.
- **Swadhar**—To provide shelter, food, clothing and care to the women living in difficult circumstances. No specific target; Achievement: 21464 women benefited.

Demography

Female population of the country rose marginally from 48.1 percent of the total population in 1991 to 48.3 percent of the total population in 2001, an increase of 89.4 million. At 23.08 percent, the growth rate of female population for the 1991-2001 decade was slightly higher than the male population decennial growth rate of 22.26 percent. This is because life expectancy at birth for women has been rising steadily from 58.6 years in 1987-91 to 66.91 years in 2001-06; it is higher than the male life expectancy of 63.87 years. Demographic imbalances between men and women, however, continue to exist, even worsen, in certain regions.

While the overall sex ratio improved slightly from 927 in 1991 to 933 in 2001, the Child Sex Ratio (0-6 years) plummeted from 945 to 927. At 880, the sex ratio at birth for 2003-05 was even lower.

During the decade 1991-2001, 70 districts in 16 States and Union Territories recorded more than a 50 points decline in sex ratio. Fatehgarh Sahib District in Punjab registered the lowest sex ratio at 754. What is truly worrying is the dip in child sex ratio in economically prosperous states like Punjab (793), Delhi (865), Haryana (820) and Gujarat (878). This negates the popular belief that female foeticide stems from illiteracy and poverty and will cease with economic growth. The Census of 2001 and Sachar Committee report (2006) also reveal that the sex ratio varies across communities and social groups. At 950, child sex ratio for Muslims is much higher than Hindus (925).

Health and Family Welfare

Discrimination against women and girls impinges upon their right to health and manifests itself in the form of worsening health and nutrition indices. Thus, India continues to grapple with unacceptably high MMR, IMR and increasing rates of anaemia, malnutrition, HIV/AIDS among women. According to NFHS 3, incidence of anaemia has risen from 49.7 percent to 57.9 percent in pregnant women and from 51.8 percent to 56.2 percent in ever married women within a period of seven years (1998-99 to 2005-06). This has raised anaemia among children by 5 percentage points (to 79.2 percent) and is also partially responsible for the high MMR. Maternal mortality has a direct correlation with lack of accessibility to health care facilities. Paucity of resources and age old discriminatory practices deny large number of women access to good nutrition and care before, during and after child birth, thus increasing their mortality. Only 22 percent of mothers consume IFA tablets for 90 days or more, and less than half of them receive 3 ante natal care visits. As many as 51.7 percent births take place without assistance from any health personnel. Practices such as female foeticide, also affect women's health, as they are forced to go through multiple pregnancies and abortions. As a result, although MMR has fallen from 398 in 1998 to 301 in 2001-2003 (SRS), we are far from meeting the Tenth plan target of reducing MMR to 200 per 100000 live births. States like Uttar Pradesh (707), Uttaranchal (517), Assam (409) and Madhya Pradesh (498) have very high MMRs.

While the mean age of marriage of women has increased from 15.5 years in 1961 to 19.5 in 1997, 44.5 percent of women are still married off by the age of 18. Certain states such as Jharkhand (61.2 percent), Bihar (60.3 percent) and Rajasthan (57.1 percent) have a much higher percentage of underage marriage among girls. Among other things, this results in early pregnancies and takes its toll on the health of the woman as well as the child.

Women also disproportionately lack access to health services. Inaccessibility of health centres and poverty prevent them from getting timely medical aid. Absence of toilets and drinking water adversely impacts their health. NFHS 3 data reveals that only 27.9 percent households in rural areas and 70 percent in urban areas have access to piped water. Further, only 25.9 percent households in rural areas have access to toilets.

Inadequacies of clean cooking fuels adversely impacts women and children's work burden, health and nutrition. Till date, 92 percent of rural domestic energy comes from unprocessed biofuels (firewood, crop waste, cattle dung), and 85 percent of rural cooking fuel is gathered from forests, village commons and fields. Women and girls spend a great deal of time gathering fuel, adversely affecting their productivity and education. Use of firewood and inferior fuels such as weeds or crop wastes leads to smoke-related ailments including respiratory diseases, cancer and cataracts resulting in blindness.

Then there are the sexually transmitted diseases. NACO estimates that 1 in 3 persons living with HIV in India is a woman. An NCAER survey shows that women account for more than 70 percent of the caregivers, 21 percent of who are themselves HIV positive. Disowned by family and disinherited from property, they are unable to access drugs to prevent mother-to-child-transmission. Nearly 60 percent of HIV-positive widows are less than 30 years of age and live with their natal families; 91 percent of them receive no financial support from their marital homes. Thus not only are women more vulnerable to getting infected, but when they are found positive they face much greater discrimination than their male counterparts.

Education

The growth rate for female literacy in the last decade has been 3 percent higher than the growth rate for male literacy resulting in a decline in the absolute numbers of illiterate women - from 200.7 million in 1991 to 190 million in 2001. Gender differential in education, however, continues to be high at 21.7 percent. This can be attributed to a number of factors- lack of access to schools, lack of toilets and drinking water, parents feeling insecure about sending girl children, poor quality of education in government schools and high fees charged by the private ones. Also with increasing feminization of agriculture, the pressure of looking after younger siblings, collecting cooking fuel, water and maintaining the household, all fall upon the girl child, putting a stop to her education and development.

Work and Employment

Entrenched patriarchal norms and customs mean that women's work goes unnoticed and is unpaid for. The double burden of work placed on her (unrecognized household work and low pay in recognized work) coupled with social norms that prevent her from getting the requisite educational and technical skills result in a low female work participation rate, either real or statistical. Female workforce participation rate in India was 28 percent (2004) as compared to other developing nations like Sri Lanka (30 percent), Bangladesh (37 percent) and South Africa (38 percent).

A sectoral breakdown of women workers reveals that 32.9 percent are cultivators, 38.9 percent agricultural laborers (as against 20.9 percent men) and 6.5 percent workers in the household industry. Much of the increase in employment among women has been in the form of self-employment; 48 percent of urban and 64 percent of rural women workers describe themselves as "self-employed". The Tenth Plan has, however, seen a welcome increase in the share of regular employment among female workers in urban India.

As in the case of education, women's employment characterisation differs across communities. The Sachar Committee Report shows that work participation rate among Muslim women is 25 percent, and as low as 18 percent in urban areas.

A larger proportion (73 percent) of Muslim women are self-employed compared to 55 percent Hindu women. A much smaller proportion of SC/ST women are self-employed; 45 percent of SC/ST women are casual workers compared to around 20 percent Muslim and 15 percent of upper caste Hindu women.

Another worrying fact is that despite a slight increase in employment, the average earning for rural women has declined between 1999-2000 and 2004-05. This decline is more pronounced among poorer women i.e. illiterate women and women who have dropped out of primary, secondary or higher secondary. The average wage for men has, on the other hand, shown an increase across all categories, leading to a widening of the wage disparity ratio (ratio of female wage/male wage) from 0.89 in 1999-00 to 0.59 in 2004-05 for rural and 0.83 in 1999-00 and 0.75 in 2004-05 in urban areas, for all categories.

Unorganized Sector

On an average, unorganized sector workers earn one-fourth the wage of organized sector workers, often doing similar jobs. It is estimated that 118 million workers or 97 percent of the female work force are involved in the unorganized sector. Agriculture is the main employer of women informal workers. 75 percent of the total female work force and 85 percent of rural women are employed in agriculture as wage workers or workers on own/contracted household farms. As men migrate to non-farm jobs; there has been an increasing feminization of agriculture. But even as the face of the farmer becomes increasingly female, few women have direct access to agricultural land affecting their ability to optimize agricultural productivity.

The non-agriculture segment of the informal sector engages 27 million workers or 23 percent of the female work force. It estimated that more than half the 31 million construction workers in India (90 percent of them informal) are women. The seasonality of work and the lack of alternate avenues lead to exploitation and ensure that these women remain the poorest and most vulnerable.

Home-based Workers

Due to lack of qualifications and training, absence of childcare support, loss of formal employment, social and cultural constraints and absence of alternatives, around 57 percent of working women are home-based workers. As home based work is sometimes the only alternative for the poorest communities, it inevitably involves children, especially girls.

Services Sector

The number of women in the services sector has increased. According to

NSSO data, in 2000, 12 percent of the female work force was employed in the tertiary sector. Women, however, remain underrepresented in higher level and higher paid jobs. The biggest single increase after apparels, has been among those employed in private households. More than 3 million women or over 12 per cent of all women workers in urban India work as domestic servants. These women are poorly paid and often are forced to work under harsh conditions. It is also important to note that nearly 60 percent of the women from the organized sector are employed in community, social and personnel services.

Government Sector

Women's representation in government sector has improved from 11 percent in 1981 to 18.5 percent in 2004. At the grassroots level, women are playing a more active role in Panchayati Raj bodies and their representation in Panchayats has gone up from 33.5 percent in 1995 to 37.8 percent in 2005. Women's presence in Parliament has, however, only increased slightly; from 6.1 percent in 1989 to 9.1 percent in 2004. The issue of reservation of seats for women in Parliament remains unresolved. In 2004, only 6 Ministers of State and one Cabinet Minister were women.

Violence against Women

Despite improving education levels and consistent economic growth, every form of violence against women including female foeticide, rape, abduction, trafficking, dowry death, domestic violence and witch-hunting, has been increasing. We have 10 million missing girls in India and this number is rising. Dowry deaths rose from 6822 in 2002 to 7026 in 2004. In 2005, highest number of dowry deaths were registered in Uttar Pradesh, followed by Bihar and Madhya Pradesh. NFHS 3 shows that more than half of all Indian women believe that husbands can beat wives if they have an appropriate reason and 37 percent admit to being victims of spousal violence. Data from NCRB reveals little or no change in crime trends in rape and molestation. In 84-89 percent of the rape cases in the years 2002-04, the victim knew the offenders. In nine per cent cases, the offender was the father, family member or close relative, highlighting the prevalence of incestuous and child sexual abuse. Abduction and trafficking for sexual and other exploitations accounted for 19.4 percent and 7.2 percent cases registered in 2005. Campaigns and stricter laws notwithstanding, 8.3 percent of registered cases in 2005 were dowry deaths, a fall of 0.3 percent from 2004.

Despite the high incidence of VAW, reporting is rare and conviction rates for reported cases, abysmally low; conviction rate for cruelty by husband was 19.2 percent, for dowry 25.5 percent and for trafficking of girls just 6.3 percent. For other forms of abuse like rape, kidnapping etc., the conviction rates usually range from 18 percent to 35 percent.

Challenges in the Eleventh Plan

The challenges for gender equity and the roadmap for the Eleventh Five Year Plan can be clubbed under a five fold agenda.

1. Ensuring Economic Empowerment.
2. Engineering Social Empowerment.
3. Enabling Political Empowerment.
4. Effective Implementation of Women Related Legislations.
5. Creating institutional mechanisms for gender mainstreaming and strengthening delivery mechanisms.

Ensuring Economic Empowerment

Employment of Women in the Unorganized Sector: The Eleventh Plan recognizes that women in the unorganized sector need social security covering issues of leave, wages, work conditions, pension, housing, child care, health benefits, maternity benefits, safety and occupational health, and complaints committee for sexual harassment. While it is difficult to tackle some of these issues immediately due to the nature of unorganized enterprises, steps will be taken to ensure safety, childcare facilities, toilets etc for women. The Plan will ensure increased availability of micro-credit to women in the unorganized sector.

Women in Agriculture: The challenge in the Eleventh Plan is to improve the availability of agricultural inputs, credit, marketing facilities, technology and skill training for the increasing number of women farmers. Resource pooling and group investment, financial and infrastructural support will be provided. Women in Agriculture will be on the top of the Eleventh Plan agenda and a two-pronged strategy will be adopted: (a) Ensuring effective and independent land rights for women and (b) Strengthening women's agricultural capacities.

A specific scheme will be devised by Ministry of Women and Child Development for identifying and helping women in states where agrarian crisis has ravaged families. Women's vulnerabilities resulting from farmer suicides due to crop failure and inability to pay loans will be addressed.

Land: Land rights not only empower women economically but strengthen their ability to challenge social and political inequities. The Eleventh Plan will carry out a range of initiatives to enhance women's land access. It will ensure direct transfers to them through land reforms, anti-poverty programmes and resettlement schemes. It will include individual or group titles to women in all government land transfers, credit support to poor women to purchase or lease land, records and legal support for women's inheritance rights, incentives and subsidies on women owned land. The group approach to women's ownership of land and productive assets will be explored and appropriate linkages will be made with the SHG movement. In case of displacement, a gender sensitive rehabilitation policy that includes equitable allocation of land to women will be devised. The Eleventh Plan will also ensure the rights of poor, landless and tribal women over forest land, commons and other resources.

Impact of Globalisation and Eleventh Plan Strategy

Liberalization has led to a paradigm shift in the country's economy. We have moved towards technology dominated sectors. While this has provided increased opportunities, it has also posed challenges. Many traditional livelihoods which have high employment potential like handlooms and other home based non-agro enterprises which are women dominated, have become unviable. Wage differentials, job vulnerability and unpaid work burden for women has increased, while their social safety nets have been eroded. Unequal access for women to schooling, land, credit facilities, alternate employment, skill training and technology has led to the crowding of women in the lowly paid jobs of most sectors. The

Eleventh Plan will examine the impact of globalization on women, especially poor women including gender differentials in wage rates, exploitation of women in the unorganized sector, lack of skill training, technology and marketing support etc. While seeking to provide relief to deprived and women dominated sectors i.e. agriculture, small enterprises, the Plan will also work towards mainstreaming women in new and emerging areas of the economy through necessary skill training, vocational training and technology education. It will work towards a social security policy that mitigates the negative impact of globalization on women.

Women in the Services Sector

The challenge in the Eleventh Plan is to promote women's participation, especially in areas where there is a poor gender ratio. This will entail special tax incentives for women headed enterprises, women employees, firms employing more women and women entrepreneurial ventures. The Plan will encourage private public partnerships and corporate social responsibility programs for women's training, capacity building and empowerment.

In view of the large number of women employed as domestic workers, the plan will make attempts to organize them and frame regulations with respect to hours of work, holidays etc for them. Cases of brutality and abuse will be registered immediately and legal support will be provided to the domestic workers to prevent their exploitation.

Skill Development

Globalization has put a premium on skills and higher levels of education, which are often out of reach of women in the unorganized sector. A key issue in the Eleventh Plan is to enable these women to secure higher level and better paid jobs through vocational training and skill development. Women need technology support, credit facilities and marketing support to take up entrepreneurial activities in new and emerging trades. At the same time, women's traditional skills such as knowledge of herbal plants, weaving, food processing or providing 'care' will be recognized and marketed.

Making Employment and NREGA Gender Responsive

Currently, most of the works included under NREGA require strenuous physical labour and women are sometimes effectively "disqualified". The Eleventh Plan will ensure that wage works conducive to women and their skills are also included under NREGA.

It will guarantee that if they demand, women will be provided employment opportunities under NREGA. It will also ensure that the Minimum Wages Act, 1948 and Equal Remuneration Act, 1976 are implemented by all states and that their implementation is monitored by the Ministry of Labour and Employment. It will encourage higher representation of women among Labour Officers. Besides ensuring equal pay for work, it will also ensure that no work is defined as "man's" work and hence denied to women.

Access to Resources and Economic Assets

International evidence shows that women's access to land or homestead is positively linked to the family's food security, child survival, health, education, and children's exposure to domestic violence. Women with land and house are also at lower risk from spousal violence, have greater bargaining power in the labour market and are better able to protect themselves and their children from destitution if the father dies from ill health, natural disaster or HIV/AIDS. Indirectly, it also reduces maternal mortality both by enhancing women's nutrition and medical support and reducing the risk of domestic violence during pregnancy. These synergies and interlinkages are what make asset creation in women's hands a critical part of the Eleventh Plan agenda for women's economic empowerment.

Amenities for Urban Poor Women

The Eleventh Plan recognises slum dwellers, most of whom are employed in the informal sector, as important contributors to cities' economy. Even though relocation of slums may sometimes be inevitable, appropriate measures need to be taken to ensure that the slum dwellers, especially women, do not lose access to livelihood opportunities and basic amenities. Today, almost 30-40 percent of India's urban population lives in slums. Over 62 percent of this population does not have access to sanitation services and 25 percent does not have access to water (World Bank, 2007). Since it is generally women who fetch water, they spend much of their time and energy at water pumps, in water queues or walking to other colonies. The Asian Development Bank (2007) estimates that India's housing shortage is as high as 40 million units, suggesting that more than 200 million people are living in chronically poor housing conditions or on the pavements. In the absence of toilets, poor women are forced to defecate in public places such as railway tracks, parks, open spaces or even public pavements. Not only do they feel shamed by this, but it is a serious health and security hazard as they can only use these public spaces in the dark. Thus provision of clean drinking water, toilets and sanitation in urban slums will be an important challenge for ensuring gender justice in the Eleventh Plan.

Homes and Homesteads for Poor Women

Home ownership not only provides shelter but also serves as collateral in credit markets and increases social status and security in the event of natural or man-made disasters. As more than half the women workers in the unorganized, non-agricultural sector work from their own homes, a home is a productive and wealth-generating asset for millions of low-income women. There is well documented evidence to show that in both the urban and rural context, women's ownership of housing offers a vital form of security against poverty and enhances associated economic and social status. There are three main sources of access to land: family, state and market. The challenge in the Eleventh Plan is to tap all these three sources. With the amendment of the Hindu Succession Act we have already taken the first step towards enhancing women's claims through inheritance. This should be strengthened by enacting gender-equal laws, adopting vigilance in recording women's claims, increasing legal awareness, and providing legal aid. All housing provided by the government during the Eleventh Plan should either be half in the name of the woman in the household or in the single name of the woman. Single women, widows and women in difficult circumstances will be given priority. Finally, the Eleventh Plan agenda will strive to support women's access via banks by developing a system of reaching housing finance at reasonable rates to poor women. This will require provision of subsidised credit, changes in land tenure policies and in norms for mortgages and housing loans.

Ensuring Food Security

During the Eleventh Plan attempts will be made to strengthen the PDS system and revise BPL census norms to ensure that women in vulnerable situations, particularly widows, single women, internally displaced women and women in conflict situations, are covered.

The agrarian crisis is taking a heavy toll on women, with farmer suicides leaving women behind to take care of family and indebtedness. The Eleventh Plan will have a comprehensive package of inputs from various sectors like agriculture, rural development, KVIC, Ministry of Women and Child Development, along with micro-credit facilities and capacity building inputs for women from affected families.

Self-Help Groups (SHGs)

While strengthening SHG initiatives, policies and schemes in the Eleventh Plan will simultaneously increase women's awareness, bargaining power, literacy, health, vocational and entrepreneurial skills. It will prioritize training, capacity building inputs and the creation of backward/forward linkages, which are essential to generate sustainable livelihood opportunities. Given the scale of the phenomenon, there is a need to review the SHG interventions and the ground level realities to determine how SHGs may better serve the interests of poor women, and suggest changes required in overall SHG policy frameworks. The Eleventh Plan recognizes the importance of this issue and proposes a High Level Committee to conduct a review of SHG related policies and programmes.

Engineering Social Empowerment

Health: Healthcare access remains low for many women, especially the poor and marginalized who suffer from multiple exclusions and stigmatized groups such as sex workers and women with alternative sexualities. The Plan recognizes the gender dimension of health problems and seeks to address issues of women's survival and health through a life cycle approach. Making ordinary women partners in their own healthcare is an underpinning of Women's Health in the Eleventh Plan.

The Eleventh Plan agenda is to move beyond the traditional focus on family planning and reproductive health, to adopt a holistic perspective on women's health. For this, allocation towards health is being stepped up.

The high rates of MMR and IMR, poor pre natal and post natal care, combined with the low proportion of institutional deliveries is a grave cause of concern. Empowering adolescent girls through information about health, sexuality, and increased awareness to negotiate rights with families, future partners and in the workplace is equally important. The challenge is to create an enabling environment with information, services and health programmes for women to exercise their rights and choices.

The effect on women of HIV/AIDS is a critical area. There is an increase of mother to child transmission of HIV and pediatric HIV cases. The Eleventh Plan will commit resources to move towards a multisectoral, decentralized, gender sensitive community based health service of which HIV/AIDS prevention and treatment is an integral part. It will prioritize information dissemination on a mass scale for prevention and treatment of HIV/AIDS. Resources will have to be made available to address the socioeconomic problems faced by HIV positive women, including access to ARV treatment, medical services, child care, and livelihood security. Enacting legislation which protects HIV positive women against discrimination in education, livelihood opportunities, workplace, medical treatment and community will be the gender equity agenda for the Eleventh Plan.

Many other factors affect the health of women. For instance women's risk of mortality from indoor air pollution resulting from use of unprocessed fuels is estimated to be 50 percent higher than of men. While over time, community investment in low cost clean fuel such as biogas will be encouraged, in the interim, firewood needs to be made available. Provision of clean drinking water and sanitation facilities are also important for good health. Inter sectoral convergence to ensure the health and well being of women in this regard is a major challenge before the Eleventh Plan.

Curbing Increasing Violence against Women (VAW)

During the Eleventh plan period, the justice delivery mechanism as well as the legislative environment under the Protection of Women from Domestic Violence Act, 2005 will be strengthened. VAW will be articulated as a Public Health issue and training will be provided to medical personnel at all levels from PHCs to premier health facilities. It will be included in medical education because the medical and health establishments are often the first point of contact for women in a crisis situation.

Training and sensitization of health personnel will include recognizing and dealing with injuries resulting from VAW and providing psychological support. Multiple forms of sexual violence against women in conflict zones and in communal or sectarian violence, where they are specifically targeted as embodiments of community honour are cause for great concern. In the Eleventh Plan period, a National Task Force on Violence Against Women in Zones of Conflict will be set up in NCW with adequate budgetary allocations to make it effective in monitoring VAW in conflict zones and facilitating relief and access to justice for affected women.

Mental Health has long been a neglected and invisibilized area. NFHS-3 shows disturbing evidence that women have internalized domestic violence leading to intense mental illness.

Education

The challenge in the Eleventh Plan is to retain girls in school and to bridge gender disparities in educational access, specifically for SC, ST, Tribal and Muslim communities through allocation of greater resources and more context-specific programming. This calls for strategies to increase the number of women and girls from these socially disadvantaged communities in professional, technical and higher education and in posts of teachers.

Ensuring Equality for Muslim Women: A Big Challenge

Even today, 59 percent Muslim women have not attended school and 60 percent are married by the age of 17. Overall, Muslims have a literacy rate of 59.1 percent, 5.7 percentage points lower than the national average. While in Haryana, one-fifth of Muslim women are literate, the figure is about one third in Bihar and Uttar Pradesh. In 15 States, the literacy level among Muslim women is less than 50 percent. Muslims register the lowest work participation rate of 31.3 percent, and just about 14 percent of Muslim women are registered as workers. Even in Kerala and Tamil Nadu, which have high literacy rates among all communities, including Muslims, the work participation rate of Muslims is 14 percentage points lower than that of Hindus.

Ensuring that Muslim women get access to education, health and livelihoods, not just at par with Muslim men but with female and male counterparts from other religions will be a critical challenge for the Eleventh Plan.

The Eleventh Plan will make concerted efforts to examine why young girls, especially those belonging to particular socioeconomic and cultural groups are unable to access education despite the SSA. Through provision of crèches, scholarships and adequate infrastructure especially toilets in schools, it will facilitate enrolment and retention of girls in the education system.

Women and Media

Much of television programming propagates patriarchal values and portrays women roles in detrimental ways. As the nodal agency for the empowerment of women, one of the important tasks for the Ministry of Women and Child Development during the Eleventh Plan will be to curtail the harmful effects of television on women's lives through a gender-informed media policy. It will harness this powerful medium to promote the message of gender equity through positive programming and information dissemination on laws and schemes. For this, Ministry might engage in a professional public-private partnership with media experts with gender specialization. In order to operationalize an aggressive and professional multi-media strategy, there may be a need to set up a separate media unit within the Ministry of Women and Child Development, with the participation of professional media consultants and women's media groups.

Reaching Marginalized and Vulnerable Women

Intersections between gender and other social and economic variables reinforce vulnerability of more than one type and result in double and triple discrimination amongst women belonging to particular groups. Sectoral planning often fails to capture this. Our ability to recognize these intersections and address the specific deprivations will be the real test of the Eleventh Plan agenda of inclusive growth.

Zero Tolerance for Discrimination against SC/ST Women

It is critical that the Ministries of WCD, Social Justice and Empowerment, and HRD join hands to enforce penalties for blatant violations of the Constitution and the Scheduled Caste and Scheduled Tribes (Prevention of Atrocities) Act, 1989. Crimes of caste-based discrimination, untouchability, devadasi/jogini and manual scavenging will be strictly punished according to law. Institutions like National Commission for Women, National Human Rights Commission, SC/ST Commission, Safai Karmacharis Commission will be urged to take up SC/ST women's issues as priority. Implementation of the Scheduled Caste Sub Plan (SCSP) and Tribal Sub Plan (TSP) will be maximized by earmarking of the funds in proportion to the SC/ST population under all schemes of the various line Departments. Distinct provisions for SC women will be made in the planning of programmes, allocation of finances and in distribution of reservation facilities in education and employment.

An important agenda for the Eleventh Plan is to ensure that the rights of tribal women over community land and forest produce are recognized and established. The economic base of tribal and other villages will be strengthened to prevent migration. The Plan also purports to encourage, document and popularize tribal women's knowledge of indigenous, traditional healing practices. It will try to include voices of tribal women in both national and state level planning forums that deal with women's issues.

Minority Women

Minority women are typically engaged in home-based, subcontracted work with lowest levels of earnings. The Sachar Committee Report has pointed out the absence of adequate social and physical infrastructure and civic amenities in Muslim dominated habitations and the multiple discriminations faced by Muslim women. To fulfil its agenda for inclusive growth, the Eleventh Plan will ensure that Muslim localities are provided with universal benefits of primary and elementary schools, water, sanitation, electricity, public health facilities (PHCs), anganwadis, ration shops, roads, transport facilities, access to government development schemes and facilities such as BPL cards and widow pensions. Education will be made accessible for Muslim girls, by locating educational institutions near Muslim areas establishing some girls schools; and increasing scholarships for Muslim girls. The challenge is to make technical and higher education opportunities available to Minority women and to link them to employment. Access to low interest credit, markets, technical training, leadership training and skill development for Muslim female home-based workers and entrepreneurs will be ensured. Representation of religious minorities in public employment will be increased and Minority women will be provided access to institutional and policy level decision-making.

In view of the double discrimination faced by Muslim women, the Prime Minister's 15-point programme for the minorities is a critical statement of intent. To further this agenda of inclusive growth, Ministry of Women and Child Development will work on a pilot scheme for 'Minority Women' to empower them and place them in the forefront of making the government system at the grassroots responsive to the needs of the minority community. Such a scheme will provide critical learning and benchmarks to launch more ambitious programmes for minority women in subsequent plans. In addition to this, targeted development of SC, ST and minority women will be made a stated part of implementation strategies of all WCD programmes/schemes and of the Sarva Shiksha Abhiyan. It will be made a mandatory part of their parameters of review and monitoring guidelines.

Leadership Development of Minority Women: A Proposed Pilot Scheme

To tackle the double discrimination faced by Muslim women, the MWCD will formulate and implement a pilot scheme for *'Leadership Development for Life, Livelihood, and Civic Empowerment of Minority Women'*. This scheme will reach out to minority women and provide them with support, leadership training and skill development so that they can move out of the confines of home and community and assume leadership roles in accessing services, skills and opportunities which will improve their lives and livelihoods. The scheme will give them training, inputs, information, and the confidence to interact with the government system, banks and intermediaries at all levels. Implementation of the scheme through NGOs in the initial phase will also encourage the NGO sector to take up work with this neglected community. Initially the pilot scheme can be launched in 5 states with large minority populations. It is expected that this scheme will reach 35,000 to 50,000 women directly and hundreds of thousands indirectly.

Internally Displaced Women

Internal displacement due to social strife and upheaval affects men and women differently. Adult and adolescent males are separated from families and the number of female-headed households increases. Even when families remain together, trauma and stress of displacement destroys the family unit and incidence of domestic violence, abuse goes up; internally displaced women are at greater risk of gender-based violence including physical and sexual attacks. They suffer psychological and physical trauma. The Eleventh Plan is committed to mitigating the negative impact on women of displacement due to natural or man-made calamities, incidents of communal violence or social upheaval and development projects. It will formulate gender sensitive relief and rehabilitation policies; women will have joint rights to any land or assets that are part of rehabilitation packages.

Hope for Single Women

Tagore's poem "Ekla Chalo Re", which exuded confidence in self, truth and dignity, finds echo in the ideals of the "Ekal Nari Shakti Sangathan"- Association of Strong Single Women established in January 2000 in Rajasthan. This grassroots mass membership organization has widows, separated, abandoned and abused women as its members. In the last seven years, the Sangathan has sought to address every day issues of these women. It has altered the destiny of many, fighting injustice, red-tapism and parochial mindsets. By mid-2007, Ekal Nari had 21,325 members in 26 of the 32 districts of Rajasthan.

This Organization is a mass movement. These Ekal women have achieved the impossible-from closing down liquor shops and revolting against age-old practices to increasing pensions and assistance for widows. The group has also introduced pension for low income, separated women. Using both satyagraha and open defiance as strategy the Sangathan has ensured employment to women who were facing manipulation and threats. Today the movement has spread to Himachal Pradesh, Jharkhand and Gujarat.

Women with Disability

Women with disabilities are considered a financial burden and social liability by their families; denied opportunities of mobility and access to education; viewed as asexual, helpless and dependant; taken advantage of and abused; denied aspirations for marriage and motherhood; and are isolated and neglected with no hope of a normal life. Although a rights-based approach today defines the disability rights movement, the specific concerns of women with disabilities have to be adequately reflected in the planning process. RCH programmes will pay attention to reproductive health needs of women with disabilities. Violation of their reproductive rights through forced sterilization, contraception and abortion especially in institutions will be dealt with severely. In the Eleventh Plan, women with disabilities will be specifically included in gender equity programmes, both as beneficiaries and as project workers. The Eleventh Plan sensitization programs of government departments, police, health care personnel will include sensitization to the needs of women with disabilities. Laws will be strictly enforced in cases of discrimination.

Women Affected by Disasters

Disasters, both natural and man-made, have the worst impact on women. Their lower social status results in various kinds of exclusions from rehabilitation and relief benefits. This posits a serious challenge to the Eleventh Plan goal of gender equity and gender justice. To overcome this, disaster management policies in the Eleventh Plan will ensure representation of women in relief committees. Resource allocations will be made for sensitization of government, aid workers, armed forces and all personnel involved in relief work. Social equity audits will be conducted. The Plan will promote the collection and use of gender-disaggregated data to inform relief and rehabilitation policies. It will also examine and review the Relief Code and Disaster Management Bill to ensure gender mainstreaming.

In addition to the categories of vulnerable and marginalized women discussed above, the Eleventh Plan will also have to pay special attention to other categories including migrant women, urban poor women and single women to fulfil its commitment of equality and gender justice.

To tackle the problem of child marriage, the Eleventh Plan will call for compulsory registration of marriages and verification of age at the time of marriage.

Enabling Political Empowerment

Panchayati Raj Institutions (PRIs): Notable constitutional, legislative and policy reforms, and continued administrative decentralization have demonstrated the government's commitment to increase women's grassroots political participation. Although only one-third of seats were reserved for women by the 73rd and 74th constitutional amendments, the actual representation is higher at all levels. Women's increased political participation has yielded a range of positive results, not only for women, but also for their families and communities.

Central issues in development such as health, nutrition, family income and education are finding their way to the top of the agenda for action. Women's participation brings about more inclusive governance and effective community-cantered development. Yet in many places, especially in states like UP, Bihar and Rajasthan, women continue to serve as proxies. The challenge for the Eleventh Plan is to ensure that women panchayat members are empowered to take their own decisions.

The Eleventh Plan will undertake the following measures to accelerate the process of women's political empowerment and participation in PRIs:

- The no-confidence clause is often used to remove women sarpanches. State governments will be advised to ensure that women sarpanchs cannot be removed for at least a year and a half by a no-confidence motion. If a no-confidence vote is passed, the replacing incumbent should also be a woman from the same social group as the earlier incumbent;
- States should revisit the two-child norm laws which prevent those who have more than two children from holding office. This law has been repealed across some states because it was found to be used against women and it disproportionately impacted poor, SC, ST, Muslim and Tribals. More tragically, the norm led to increasing female foeticide;
- Increase resource allocation for capacity building of all PRI members (male and female) in diverse areas pertaining to gender sensitization and women's rights, as well as in the political skill-building of women members of PRIs;
- Greater effort to include poor and other excluded women on State Planning Boards and Commissions;
- Funds for time-series evaluations of the impact of women on PRIs, and on enabling policy conditions and contextual factors for women's political participation;
- Accelerate the State Governments' process of devolution and decentralization

of powers, so that PRIs are not handicapped in carrying out their mandated duties.

Effective Implementation of Women Related Legislations

During the Tenth Plan period, some important legislations have been passed and amended. For example, besides the Hindu Succession (Amendment) Act 2005 and Protection of Women from Domestic Violence Act 2005 (PWDVA) mentioned earlier, the Dowry Prohibition Act was reviewed. A very active civil society has been relentlessly campaigning on these issues. Their experiences and recommendations will be taken on board to ascertain that the rights of every woman are enshrined in laws.

Under the Eleventh Plan budgetary allocations will be made for publicity and for creating the required infrastructure for effective implementation of these legislations. Ministry of Women and Child Development will appoint Protection Officers and setup district level cells to be responsible for monitoring and implementation of PWDVA and other Acts under its charge.

Panchayat Women: Ground Realities

Till some time back, Kanjiguzhy village panchayat in Allepey district of Kerala was a backward area of the district. Today it has an annual turnover of over ₹ 10 crore, thanks to an active Panchayat Samiti headed by a dynamic woman pradhan Jalaja Chandra. Ask her about the number of families in her area, number of SHGs, employment statistics, net profit, amount spent on different development works and she answers confidently. It is not difficult to see why this village has prospered. Kotli Village in Fatehgarh Sahib district of Punjab is headed by Paramjeet Kaur who has managed to convince her villagers to let their girl children live. So in a district that made headlines for having the worst child sex ratio in the country, Kotli now boasts of a positive sex ratio. While these and many such women have clearly demonstrated what political empowerment of women can achieve, in many parts of the country woman panchayat members are yet to get their due.

In Bhimra village of Barmer district of Rajasthan, the sarpanch is a woman. She never opens her mouth; it is always the husband who speaks. The fate of her ghoonghat clad counterpart in a Kol village in Eastern UP is no different. Here the Pradhanpati makes all decisions. In Bihar, power rests with the MPs and SPs –Mukhiyapatis and Pradhanpatis. In Ongna village of Udaipur district (Rajasthan), the women panchayat members rue the day they were elected. "We have no powers; we are never allowed to attend meetings. When villagers come and ask us why we haven't done anything, what do we say?" they question.

Ministry of WCD will also try and ensure the enactment of other legislations that benefit women. The Government is already contemplating the unorganized sector bill to provide social security to unorganized sector workers; schemes for life and health insurance have already been introduced. These should be implemented with a special emphasis on safeguarding the interests of women. The Dowry Prohibition Act (DPA) will be reviewed to clarify existing provisions relating to the definition of the dowry and penalties for guilty parties. Implementation of PWDVA with DPA will be linked to enable PWDVA protection officers to take action under the DPA. The Eleventh Plan will also have provisions for sensitization of medical professionals on recording of evidence in cases of dowry deaths, training and capacity building of law enforcement functionaries and awareness generation about problems of dowry. Efforts will be made to ensure effective monitoring and enforcement of PC and PNDT Act through Central and State Supervisory Boards and adequate allocation of funds. Public awareness and community mobilization will be generated along with training the authorities to deal with the issue of sex determination and sex selective abortions.

The Ministry of Women and Child Development will ensure the enactment of the Bill to prevent sexual harassment at the workplace. The Prevention of Immoral Trafficking Act is already being reviewed to ensure that women in prostitution are not victimised further. In addition to this, the Eleventh Plan will strengthen interregional networks to check forced migration and trafficking. Special police officers will be appointed to promote community level vigilance to reduce trafficking. There will be special training modules on trafficking for police, judiciary, and other government personnel. More rehabilitation homes will be established.

To tackle the conflict-related VAW, the Eleventh Plan will ensure the inclusion of provisions of sexual violence in the draft law on the prevention of communal violence. It will look into setting up Special Courts to deal with cases of VAW in conflict situations, including those involving security personnel. It will encourage women's involvement in peace keeping, community dialogues and conflict resolution. There will be special measures for compensation, financial assistance, and support to widows and female headed households in conflict areas.

The Eleventh Plan will foster women's access to legal services through a range of measures. Women will be exempted from paying fees to fight cases of human rights violations. Funds for legal assistance will be provided to poor women seeking legal redress. Legal awareness programmes will be carried out in all States in collaboration with NGOs working at the grassroots level. Legal Aid

Cells consisting of committed and gender sensitive lawyers will be set up at the Panchayat level to provide information and support to rural women, especially poor women. Lok Adalats will be organized to encourage alternate dispute settlement mechanisms for efficacious settlement of cases. The Plan will also work towards increasing the percentage of women in police and judicial services. Training on use of gender specific laws will be provided to all Members and Authorities involved in providing legal services. Concept of Jan Sunwaiye will be adopted to listen to people's voices.

Creating Institutional Mechanisms for Gender Mainstreaming and Strengthening Delivery Mechanisms

In the Eleventh Plan, institutional mechanisms will carry forward the process of gender mainstreaming and will be strengthened. National Commission for Women (NCW) and State Commissions for Women will be strengthened to enable them to effectively play their role as the nodal agencies for the protection of rights of women. Towards this end, efforts will be made in the Eleventh Plan to suitably amend the NCW Act to give the Commission more powers. The states likewise, will be urged to review the powers of their Women's Commissions. In addition to this, more functional and financial autonomy and a statutory base will have to be ensured for these organisations to strengthen their legal status. This will not only ensure that these bodies remain non-partisan, it will also increase their credibility. A mechanism will be created to periodically report to the National Development Council the progress on Women's Plans with respect to the National Policy for Empowerment of Women. Action Plans for Women's Empowerment at national and state levels will be drawn up in consultation with all sectoral agencies and civil society including women's groups, lawyers, activists, women's study centres etc. Cross cutting issues such as unpaid work, land and asset entitlements, skill development and vocational training, child care, occupational health, wages, violence against women will be mainstreamed. Parivarik Mahila Lok Adalats will be organized, which will supplement the efforts of District Legal Service Authority (DLSA). Resource Centres for women will be set up at national and state levels and linked with Women's Study Centres.

Gender budgeting and Gender outcome assessment will be encouraged in all Ministries/Departments at Central and State levels. Gender Budgeting helps assess the gender differential impact of the budget and takes forward the translation of gender commitments to budgetary allocations. During the Eleventh Plan efforts will continue to create gender budgeting cells in all ministries and departments. Data from these cells will be collated on a regular basis and made available in the public domain.

Gender outcome assessment of fund flows has been made a mandatory part of the outcome budget prepared by every ministry/department as part of their budget documents. In 2005-06, this exercise covered 10 Departments and the total magnitude of the Gender Budget (i.e. women specific allocations) was recorded at 4.8 percent of total Union Government expenditure. In 2006-07, 24 Departments of the Union Government were included and the magnitude of the Gender Budget was 3.8 percent of total budget estimates. It was found that schemes, which do not have a 100 percent women's component also found a mention as women specific schemes. The Eleventh Plan will therefore ensure that each Ministry/Department of both Centre and State should put in place a systematic and comprehensive monitoring and auditing mechanism for outcome assessment. In addition, the Ministry of WCD, Ministry of Finance and Planning Commission will facilitate national level gender outcome assessments through spatial mapping of gender gaps and resource gaps. They will undertake gender audits of public expenditure, programmes, and policies and ensure the collection of standardized, gender disaggregated data (including data disaggregated for SC/ST and Minority women) at national, state and district levels.

In the Eleventh Plan period, the existing system of gender based planning will be extended to other Ministries and Departments and not confined only to those, which have historically been perceived as "women-related". Ministries and Departments such as Education, Health and Family Welfare, Agriculture, Rural Development, Labour, Tribal Affairs, Social Justice and Empowerment which have the potential to exceed the 30 percent WCP requirement will be encouraged to administer more women related programmes. During the Eleventh Plan, efforts will be made to extend the concept of gender based plan component to PRIs and to the 29 subjects transferred to them under the 73rd Constitutional Amendment. Recognizing that some women suffer greater deprivation and discrimination than others, the Eleventh Plan will refine the norms of WCP to prioritize the most vulnerable as beneficiaries, particularly SC, ST women, Muslim women, single women, differently-abled and HIV positive women, among others.

The Eleventh Plan period will also seek to engender all national policies and programmes right from their inception and formulation stages. The Ministry of Women and Child Development is the nodal Ministry for gender budgeting and the coordination mechanism for Gender Budgeting will ensure that all policies including fiscal and monetary policies, agricultural policies, non-farm sector, information and technology policies, public policy on migration, health insurance schemes, disaster management policies, media policy, and the legal regime among others are relevant from a gender perspective and are thoroughly examined. It will ensure that all legislations before they are presented to Parliament for enactment are cleared by the Parliamentary Committee on Women's Empowerment.

The Eleventh Plan is committed to ensuring the participation of women in governance through the smooth passage of the much-delayed Women's Reservation Bill. There will be simultaneous training and inputs for women in the PRIs to enable them to influence gender sensitive local planning and implementation. Gender disaggregated data on the participation of women, especially SC/ST and minority women, in Parliament, state legislative assemblies, Council of Ministers, premier services, and in the overall government sector will be collected and made available in the public domain. The Plan will also make pro-active efforts to provide competitive exam training and prioritize recruitment of women to All India Services especially IAS, IFS and IPS.

The Ministry of Women and Child Development will take the lead in creating and maintaining a comprehensive gender-disaggregated data base, for quantitative and qualitative data. The purpose would be (i) to base new initiatives on facts and figures, (ii) assess the gender impact of programmes and (iii) assess the level of women's participation in planning and implementing programmes.

Eleventh Plan Schemes

Swayamsiddha, an integrated scheme for women's empowerment through Self-help Groups (SHGs) will be the major scheme to be implemented by the Ministry of WCD in the Eleventh Plan. Swayamsidha Phase-II will be launched as a countrywide programme with larger coverage in states lagging behind in women development indices. The lessons learnt from Swayamsiddha Part 1 and Swashakti, especially regarding capacity building of poor women through Self-help Groups, promoting thrift and credit activities amongst the women themselves, emphasising on participatory approach towards poverty alleviation, and addressing common problems and issues through the SHGs, will be incorporated in the universalized Swayamsidha.

Support to Training and Employment Programme (STEP), a scheme for skill training of women, will be revamped during the Eleventh plan based on evaluation results (under way) and will be integrated with Swayamsidha to ensure adequate outlay for country wide implementation as a Centrally Sponsored Scheme. The Rashtriya Mahila Kosh will also be integrated with STEP and Swayamsidha for credit linkages, but will be reviewed in the Eleventh Plan period before considering any further expansion.

A separate Women Empowerment and Livelihood Project assisted by IFAD will be implemented during the Eleventh Plan in four districts of U.P and two districts of Bihar.

Various social empowerment schemes for women will be implemented during the Eleventh Plan. Condensed Courses of Education will be run to facilitate skill development and vocational training of adult girls and women who could not join mainstream education system or were forced to dropout from formal schools. This will improve their social and economic status by making them employable. The Ministry will use mass media to run an Awareness Generation Project on issues relating to the status, rights and problems of women. Through this project it will also try to ensure a balanced portrayal of women in newspapers, media channels, serials, films etc.

The most important programme for women to be run by the Ministry of WCD during the Eleventh Plan will be the provision of maternity benefits. The ICDS scheme will have a component of conditional maternity benefits under which pregnant and lactating mothers will be entitled to cash incentives for 3 months before birth and 3 months after the birth of the child. This will encourage and enable mothers to avoid physically stressful activities, meet medical and nutrition supplementation expenses during the last trimester and spend time with the child after birth. The benefits under the scheme will be conditional to the mother being registered with the Anganwadi, having regular health check up and immunization.

Ministry of WCD will continue to run its schemes offering support services. Under a revised Working Women's Hostel scheme, financial assistance will be provided to NGOs, co-operative bodies and other agencies for construction/renting of buildings for hostels to provide safe and affordable accommodations to working women. The scheme of Swadhar Homes for destitute women and women in difficult circumstance will continue, albeit with modifications. A women's helpline foundation will also be set up. Under the Short-stay Home scheme, suitable accommodation with basic amenities and services like counselling, legal aid, medical facilities, vocational training and rehabilitation will be provided for women and girls who are victims of marital conflict, crime or homelessness.

The Central Social Welfare Board (CSWB) will continue financing NGOs for implementation of various women and child related schemes. But during the Plan, all the existing schemes of the CSWB will be reviewed and restructured in the light of current requirements. If necessary, some of them will also be merged with schemes of WCD.

National and State Machineries

Relief and Rehabilitation of Rape victims: The Hon'ble Supreme Court in

Delhi Domestic Working Women's Forum vs. Union of India and others writ petition (CRL) No. 362/93 had directed the National Commission for Women to evolve a "scheme so as to wipe out the tears of unfortunate victims of rape." It observed that given the Directive principles contained in the Article 38(1) of the Constitution, it was necessary to set up a Criminal Injuries Compensation Board. Besides the mental anguish, rape victims frequently incur substantial financial loss and in some cases are too traumatized to continue in employment.

The Court further directed that compensation for victims shall be awarded by the Court on conviction of the offender and by the Criminal Injuries Compensation Board irrespective of whether or not a conviction has taken place. The Board shall take into account pain, suffering and shock as well as loss of earnings due to pregnancy and the expenses of child birth if this occurs as a result of rape. Accordingly, NCW has drafted a scheme titled "Relief and Rehabilitation of Rape Victims". This scheme will be initiated in the Eleventh Plan as "Scheme for Relief and Rehabilitation of Victims of Sexual Assault". For this, the Eleventh Plan will allocate sufficient resources to sensitize law enforcement agencies, medical establishments etc. It will ensure immediate online filing of FIR and recording of the victim's statement by female police officers. It will set up more forensic labs and DNA testing centres in various districts and provide special care for minor rape victims. It will also ensure the safety of rape victims to testify in courts and appoint a specially designated Judge in the District Court to deal with rape cases. These schemes along with the measures suggested above will ensure that when we enter the 12th Plan, women are no longer seen as "Victims," but as agents of socio-economic growth and development for the country.

Bibliography

Bibliography

Ahluwalia, M.S (1978), 'Rural Poverty and Agricultural Performance in India', *Journal of Development Studies*, Volume 14 (3), April.

Biradar, R.R. (2005), 'Incidence of Poverty Among Social Groups in Rural India: Why Do SCs/STs Experience Greater Incidence of Poverty', Paper Presented at the Foundation-Day Seminar, National Institute for Rural Development (NIRD), Hyderabad, held during November 9-10, 2005.

Chadha, G.K. and Alakh N. Shanna (eds.) (1997), '*Growth, Employment and Poverty: Change and Continuity in Rural India,* Vikas Publishing House Pvt. Ltd., New Delhi.

Deaton, A. and Jean Dreze (2002), 'Poverty and Inequality in India: A Re-examination', *Economic and Political Weekly*, September 7.

Dreze, J and Srinivasan, P.V. (1997), 'Widowhood and Poverty in Rural India: Some Inferences from Household Survey Data", *Journal of Development Economics*, 54 (2) 217-34.

Dreze, Jean and A. Sen (2002): *India: Development and Participation*, Oxford University Press.

Dreze, Jean and Amartya Sen (1995), *Indian Economic Development and Social Opportunity,* Oxford University Press, New Delhi.

Dutta, B. and B. Ramaswami (2001), 'Targeting and Efficiency in the Public Distribution System,' *Economic and Political Weekly*, Volume 36, May.

Fan, Shenggen, Peter B.R. Hazell and Sukhadeo Thorat (2000), 'Government Spending, Growth and Poverty in Rural India', *American Journal of Agricultural Economics*, 82(4), 1038-51.

Fisher, Thomas, Sriram. M.S (2000), *Beyond Micro-credit: Putting Development Back into Micro-finance*, Vistaar Publications, 2000.

Government of India, Ministry of Women and Child Development, *Annual Report* (various years).

——Ministry of Social Justice and Empowerment, *Annual Report* (various years).

——Ministry of Rural Development, *Annual Report* (various years).

——Ministry of Panchayati Raj, *Annual Report* (various years).

——*Economic Survey* (various years).

——Ministry of Finance, *Budget Papers (various years).*

——Ministry of Law, Justice, and Company Affairs, *Constitution of India.*

——Ministry of Environment and Forests, *Annual Report* (various years).

——Planning Commission, Plan Documents from First Five Year Plan (1951-56) to Approach Paper to Twelfth Five Year Plan (2012-17).

Greening. H, Bikki. Randhwa (1999), 'A Framework for Regulating Microfinance Institutions', Published by the World Bank.

Hirway, Indira (1986), '*Wage Employment Programmes in Rural Development,* Oxford and IBH Publishing Co. Pvt. Ltd., New Delhi.

Joshi, Sandeep (2000), *Panchayat Raj Institutions and Poverty Alleviation,* Rawat Publications, Jaipur.

Klaauw, B.V. and Limin Wang (2004), *Child Mortality in Rural India,* World Bank, Washington, D.C.

Minhas. B.S., L.R. Jain and S.D. Tendulkar (1991), 'Declining Incidence of Poverty in the 1980s: Evidence vs. Artefacts', *Economic and Political Weekly,* Volume 26, July 6-13.

Narasimhan, Sankuntala (1999), *Empowering Women: An Alternative Strategy from Rural India*, Sage Publications, New Delhi.

P.K. Bardhan (1973), 'On the Incidence of Poverty in Rural Areas', *Economic and Political Weekly*, February.

Panchmukhi V.R. and Brahamananda (1987), *Development Process of the Indian Economy,* Bombay: Himalaya Publishing House.

Patnaik, Prabhat (2005), 'On the Need for Providing Employment Guarantee', *Economic and Political Weekly,* January.

Purushothaman, Sangeetha (1998), *The Empowerment of Women in India: Grassroots Women's Networks and State*, Sage Publications, New Delhi.

Radhakrishna, R., K. Hanumantha Rao, C. Ravi, B. Sambi Reddy (2004), 'Chronic Poverty and Malnutrition in 1990s, *Economic and Political Weekly,* 10 July.

Rajasekhar, D. (2000), 'Non-government Organizations (NGOs) in India: Opportunities and Challenges', *Journal of Rural Development*, Volume 19, No. 2.

Ravallion, Martin (2000), 'What is Needed for a More Pro-Poor Growth Process in India', *Economic and Political Weekly*, Volume 35, March 25-31.

Ray, R. (2000), 'Poverty, Household Size and Child Welfare in India', *Economic and Political Weekly*, September 23.

S. Subramanian (2011), 'Inclusive Development" and the Quintile Income Statistic', *Economic and Political Weekly,* Volume 46, January 22.

S.M. Hashemi (2000), 'Micro Credit in Rural Development; Beyond Safety Netting to Poverty Alleviation', CIRDAP Report (July).

Saurabhj Sinha (1998), 'Micro Credit: Impact, Training and Sustainability', Institute of Development Studies (IDS), Volume 29, No. 4, October, University Sussex, U.K.

Shetty, S.L. (2003), *Credit Flows to Rural Poor*, mimeo, EPW Research Foundation, Mumbai.

Stern, Nicholas H. (2001), *Building a Climate for Investment, Growth and Poverty Reduction in India*, 16th Exim Bank Commencement Day Annual Lecture, Mumbai.

Thorat, Sukhadeo (2004), '*Persistence of Poverty: Why do Scheduled Castes and Scheduled Tribes Stay Chronically Poor?*' Working Paper for Centre for Chronic Poverty, London.

Vijay Mahajan (2005), 'Micro Finance to Livelihood Finance', *Economic and Political Weekly*, Volume. XL, No.41.

Viswanath, Vanita (1993), *NGOs and Women's Development in Rural South India: A Comparative Analysis*, Vistaar Publications, New Delhi.

Websites

Ministry of Women and Child Development
Ministry of Social Justice and Empowerment
Ministry of Rural Development
Ministry of Panchayati Raj
Ministry of Rural Development
Ministry of Environment and Forests
Planning Commission
National Bank for Agriculture and Rural Development

Index

Index